I'll Tell You What!

I'll Tell You What!

Robbie Savage

Constable • London

CONSTABLE

First published in Great Britain in 2015 by Constable

A CIP catalogue record for this book
is available from the British Library.

ISBN 978-1-47212-316-9 (hardback)

Typeset in Bembo by Hewer Text UK Ltd, Edinburgh
Printed and bound in Great Britain by Clays Ltd

Papers used by Constable are from well-managed
forests and other responsible sources

MIX
Paper from
responsible sources
FSC® C104740

Constable
An imprint of
Little, Brown Book Group
Carmelite House
50 Victoria Embankment
London EC4Y 0DZ

An Hachette UK Company
www.hachette.co.uk

www.littlebrown.co.uk

I'd like to dedicate this book to my late father, Colin, who was both my mentor and my inspiration. Love you, Dad.

Dear Rob,

Just a note to say what I find difficult to say in words to your face. I have been a lucky man. As well as having been lucky enough to have found a woman like your mum, I have been the luckiest man in the world to have had two boys like you and Jonathan. You now have an opportunity that millions of other young men would give their right arm for. Please don't waste it. You have a God-given gift, so use it, and remember, HARD WORK SUPPLIES ITS OWN REWARD. Take my advice, and remember to be very wary of the workmates that forever moan about everything under the sun. You usually find that the ones that moan are the ones that don't like hard work. It goes without saying that, no matter what problems you have when you're in Manchester, no matter how big or small, your family – Mum, Jonathan and me – are always here to help. We will all miss you, but most of all Mum. She will miss you like hell, so try to ring home as often as possible. Finally, never stop believing in yourself. We know you are the best, so believe that your-self. There is a great deal of difference between self-confi-dence and being a bighead. Fortunately, being a bighead has never been a problem with you, so be CONFIDENT. I love you lots, the best of luck, and work hard,

Dad

Acknowledgements

As you'll find out from reading this book, retiring from being a professional footballer can be a very difficult experience and since hanging up my boots in 2011 I've been lucky enough to work with some fantastic people at some brilliant organizations.

William Hill and the *Daily Mirror* both began employing me long before I retired as a footballer and I'm proud to say that my relationship with both companies is as strong now as it's ever been. At William Hill, I would like to thank Lee Phelps, Mike Grenham and James Henderson and former CEO Ralph Topping, who all have been tremendous, and at the *Daily Mirror* the extremely talented Lloyd Embley and Mike Walters. All six are so easy to work with and over the years we've done some fantastic work together. Thanks, guys!

Working on *Match of the Day* was obviously a dream come true for me but when it comes to my work with the BBC it's *606* that makes me most proud. I've been there right from the start of its latest incarnation and over the years we've enjoyed hundreds of debates, a few raised voices and millions of laughs. I would like to thank everyone I've worked with at the corporation, but especially Mark Cole, Danny Cohen and Jonathan Wall.

Next I would like to pay tribute to Grant Best and the team at BT Sport, not only for showing a tremendous amount of faith in me but for also giving me the chance to try something new with *Fletch & Sav* and become part of their Champions League team. It's a pleasure to be involved with such a positive and forward-thinking organization. My thanks and best wishes to everyone there.

Writing this book has been a great laugh and I'm very proud of what you're about to read. I would like to say thanks to James Hogg who helped me write the book, Howard Watson, and to Andreas Campomar, Claire Chesser and everyone at the publishers, Little, Brown.

The two people who have to put up with me on an almost daily basis are my agent, Jake Mallen at New Era Global Sports Management, and my old mate at BreatheSport, Luke Sutton. It can't be an easy job but come on, lads, it's got to be rewarding!

One person I can't thank enough is the amazing Mr Darren Fletcher, who has been my broadcasting partner for the past five years. He doesn't seem at all embarrassed by the fact that I have to carry him week-in, week-out, and I can only admire him for that. Seriously though, working with Fletch is a privilege as not only is he a brilliant broadcaster but he's also a fantastic bloke. Thanks for everything, buddy.

Forgive me for name-checking these guys one last time, but Danny Cohen, Jonathan Wall, James Henderson, Ralph Topping, Lloyd Embley and Grant Best have all put a tremendous amount of faith in me and as somebody who has often had to try that little bit harder it means the world. I'll always be grateful.

Contents

Introduction

One phrase you'll see quite a lot in this book is 'Love me or loathe me' or words to that effect. It seems I divide opinion like Moses divided the Red Sea and I'm sure the majority of people reading this book will hold one of two opinions about me: either I'm okay or I'm a bit of a so-and-so. There's rarely any middle ground when it comes to opinions of yours truly but then that's me all over. If I have colours they're nailed to the mast – big time!

The purpose of this book, though, is simple: to entertain, and possibly even inform, through a mutual love of football. I've been attached to the game for well over thirty years now and along the way I've met a lot of interesting people. It's fair to say that I haven't always bonded with all of them, but at least they can say that they've met me.

I've also played with and against some pretty awesome players along the way, not to mention some pretty bad ones, and I've had a pretty similar experience with managers, I suppose – some good and some less so. The fact is that I've probably had one of the most varied careers in football but I can only really say that now I've spent a few years working in the media. That's a very different side of the coin and has given me many new experiences but, as you already know, I'm as contentious in this life as I ever was in my previous one. And do you know what? I love every single second.

You would probably be forgiven for believing that you're about to read *The Life and Times of a Lucky Man*, but that couldn't be further from the truth. Some of you will be thrilled to learn that within these pages you'll find at least one near-death experience, some severe embarrassments, a badly burned hooter and even a short but nevertheless passionate affair with a mop. You see, it's not all cava and Worthington Cup finals.

Intrigued?

I hope so.

Managers

I've played for a lot of managers over the years, both domestic and international, and between them they probably cover it all.

When it comes to who I got on best with, I honestly don't know if I could choose one over the other. Martin O'Neill would have to be up there, along with Nigel Clough; but then I also got on really well with Steve Bruce, Mark Hughes, Micky Adams and Peter Taylor. Peter Taylor is a lovely bloke and he got on with pretty much everybody when he managed Leicester, and there was never that barrier there like there is with some managers. I could probably ring up Peter now and arrange to go for a beer with him. We'd talk football all night and have a right laugh. He's just a lovely bloke, not to mention a great coach. Could I do the same with Martin O'Neill? Yes, I could. There'd be a different dynamic though. Martin's the kind of person you'd just enjoy listening to and learning from. When he was at Leicester he was the catalyst for why I did as well as I did in my career and so I owe him a lot. With Martin there was a line though, a line that you didn't cross, and he also had an air of authority about him that came straight out of the Brian Clough School of Football Management. It won't surprise you to know that I crossed that line on more than one occasion, and each time I got put firmly back in my place.

I'll give you an example. We were on the team coach once on our way to Sunderland and I was sitting opposite Martin. He was telling a story at the time (he was always telling stories) and as he spoke I pretended to fall asleep. I gave it the full works, snoring, dribbling – the lot. Then all of a sudden he stopped, mid-sentence. Even though I had my eyes closed I knew he was looking at me. I also knew he was angry. I could feel it. What he did next still embarrasses me to this day. The previous week we'd played against Manchester United and I'd had a pretty torrid time, giving away a goal. After the match I'd cried like a baby and this was about to come back and haunt me. As I opened my eyes Martin looked at me and pretended to cry, just like I'd done the week before. I could feel myself going red as everyone began laughing. After that he didn't speak to me for about a week. I'd crossed the line and that was what I got in return. He could manipulate your emotions at the drop of a hat. It's the same with most managers. Just when you think you're getting close to them and having a laugh – BAM! You're back in your place. And in my opinion that's the way it should be.

I often get asked which managers I'd liked to have played for and, believe it or not, Neil Warnock would probably be up there. I couldn't stand him when I was a player but I have got to know him since and he's a very clever man – football through and through. He was also very passionate and animated as a manager, which is one of the reasons why he got on people's nerves. Who does that remind you of?

Another would have to be José Mourinho for the simple reason that if you work hard he rewards you. I think he would have loved a player like me in his team. Honestly, I do! My work rate was phenomenal when I was in my prime and I think I would have complemented some of the more skilful players. I heard José talking about the young midfielder Ruben Loftus-Cheek after Chelsea's game against Sydney FC on their tour at the end of the 2014/15 season, and he was critical of the lad's work rate. He said that it doesn't matter who you are, hard work is the key, and I think he's absolutely right.

Mark Hughes was a strange manager to play under for two reasons. First off, he was a mate of mine. He'd taken over from Bobby Gould as the Wales boss in 1999 and by then I'd already known him for ten years. He was scoring buckets of goals at Manchester United while I was there as an apprentice and we'd also played together a few times for Wales. For the first three months after he took over I called him Sparky. His assistant had to have a word with me one day and ask me to call him Gaffer. The second reason is that he was, and still is, a big hero of mine, and that has always affected my behaviour around him. Even when I meet him now I get embarrassed. He lives not far away from me and a couple of weeks ago I asked him if he fancied a game of golf.

'Sure, just knock on the door,' he said.

But I thought, 'I can't just knock on Mark Hughes's door. He's Mark Hughes!'

It's ridiculous really, but I just can't do it.

5

Today I wouldn't be a manager for a million pounds a week. No way. I mean, look at Nigel Clough. In year one he saved Sheffield United from relegation and got them to an FA Cup semi-final. Not bad, eh? Then the following year he gets them into the semi-finals of the League Cup, not to mention the playoffs, and then they sack him! Nigel Adkins takes his place and that's it: you're out, mate. It's not Nigel Adkins's fault, of course, but when you see a good honest manager like Nigel Clough get treated so diabolically, why on earth would you ever want to put yourself in that position? No thanks.

I considered doing my coaching badges at one point, but when I sat down and thought about what it takes to be a good football manager I realized that coaching badges don't come into it. That might sound a bit controversial to some but for me being a manager is all about managing people. The clue's in the name. Let the coaches do the coaching and let them take the badges. The manager has to man-manage the players, and that is one hell of a task. Believe me, I know. I've been tempted to go for loads of jobs over the years but I've always been put off by the fact that in order to even apply for them you need to have your badges. That's madness. Coaches coach and managers manage, end of story. What does it take to be a good coach though? Well for me, if you can take a training session with a group of highly paid individuals who get bored after five minutes, and keep them interested and leave them wanting more, that makes you a good coach – in the Premier League at least. I could never do it. I'm far too shy, believe it or not.

I used to love training when I was in the Premier League but I absolutely hated it when I was a schoolboy. A lot of people assume that because the standard is higher the training must be more intense, but it's the opposite. I played under Dario Gradi at Crewe as a schoolboy and I used to dread training. It was very regimented and very stop-start. Everyone seemed to be very serious, too. But when I look back on it now I can appreciate that we were learning the game and that it was all for the good. By the time I got to Leicester it was just a case of keeping fit, refining your game and concentrating on what you were good at. It was all fun and five-a-sides. Training was a pleasure, not a chore.

I used to look at Mark Hughes when he was managing Wales. Eddie Niedzwiecki and Mark Bowen used to do the coaching and Sparky would manage the players and make all the final decisions. Martin O'Neill was the same and so was Brian Clough. Fergie, too. He had people alongside him like Brian Kidd and Archie Knox, who are fantastic coaches. That's why a manager has backroom staff, so that he can get on with what he's being paid to do. In the army, if a general picks up a gun and starts showing the lads how to shoot, who's going to plan the battle? Who's going to delegate? Who's going to make sure you don't lose the war? It helps if he's actually been there in the thick of it, I suppose, but for me the main job of a manager is to hold everything together and have an overview. He's the top of the pile, the boss, the gaffer. I think I've made my point.

Even though I've said I wouldn't want to do the job, I think I would make an excellent man manager. I also appreciate the value of a good coach because, at the end of the day, you're only as good as the people around you. But why *do* managers have to take their badges? Surely if you're an ex-professional the experience you've gained as a player should see you through. I've played at every level, the lower leagues and the Premier League, and I've been coached by some of the best. I may not be qualified as a coach, but I know quite a bit about it. All footballers do. But coaching is not what being a manager is about, so why demand the badge upfront? Why not allow new managers to take the badges if and when they get the job?

I suppose I could bite the bullet and take them, but perhaps I'm just a bit lazy. What's the point of spending months sitting in a classroom studying for something that will have little or no bearing on what you're applying for? It would be like training to be a hairdresser and then applying to be a mechanic. If you want to prepare managers for the job, send them on a man-management course, because believe me not all of them are up to that side of the job. I know!

I can't believe I seem to be talking myself into wanting to become manager. It's ridiculous! If somebody called me up and said, 'Robbie, I want you to come and manage my club. You'll have some cracking coaches working under you and it'll be your job to man-manage the players, know the opposition, work out formations and make all the big decisions', then I would probably have a go at it. I'll tell you what: I would give it absolutely everything, just like I did when I was a player.

If you're going to be a good manager you've got to be able to motivate people. That's half the game when it comes to man management, and once again I've experienced the good, the bad and the absolutely diabolical. I'm not going slag off the ones who were rubbish at it, but I will tell you about one of the more unusual examples of how to get the best out of a player. I think they call it reverse psychology. Once again it involves Martin O'Neill.

It was 18 September 1999 and my team Leicester City had just drawn 2–2 with the mighty Liverpool. I'd played out of my skin that day and although I wasn't handed the man-of-the-match award, I had been the best player on the pitch – easily. Later on that evening I switched on *Match of the Day*, sat back with my wife Sarah and told her that she should prepare herself for a treat. Sure enough the match was shown and I was just as good as I thought I was. Better, even!

'Brilliant,' I thought. 'I wonder if the manager will mention me in the post-match interview.' In fact, he talked about me straight away.

'Well Martin,' said the reporter, 'you must have been delighted with the performance of Robbie Savage.'

'Yes,' he replied. 'But Robbie lacks just one thing – ability.'

I went so red you could have fried an egg on my face. I thought I'd been our best player – *the* best player!

On the following Monday Martin ordered me into his office.

'Did you watch *Match of the Day*?'

'Yes, I did,'

'Do you play every week?'

'Yes, I do.'

'As a manager, I look for a lot of things. Ability is not every-thing. What's better: having all the ability in the world with no heart and desire, or having no ability but all the heart and desire?'

'The second one, Gaffer.'

'Right. And you're playing every week. Now get out.'

I'd gone from feeling totally dejected after playing out of my skin to feeling like I was king of the world, and all after being insulted in front of millions of people. If that's not reverse psychology, I don't know what is.

I miss the camaraderie and I miss the banter that you get in a dressing room, so that's another reason why, yes, if the right offer did come along with the right team, I would probably have a go at it. First of all, I would make sure I had the right people around me. John Hartson and Craig Bellamy spring to mind. They've both done their badges and have experience coming out of their ears. They're also totally passionate about football. We would be like the Welsh Mafia. After that I'd get all the players together and I'd tell them that it doesn't matter if you're on ten grand or a hundred grand a week, you all start on the same level. That's the way to do it. Give everyone a fair chance. I would have to be a shirt-and-tie manager, of course, with a nice scarf around my neck. Like Roberto Mancini, just much better looking. What I would strive for most though in the early days of being a manager would be to try and make the players *want* to play for me. After that I'd be able to get to work on those flaming badges!

Kids' Teams and
Football Academies

There's only one part of kids' football I don't like and that's the parents or at least some of them. Back in my day mums and dads were supportive when they came to watch their kids play, and although you sometimes got the odd idiot mouthing off from the touchline, things rarely went beyond that. These days it's different. In fact, it's diabolical.

Some of the things I've seen and heard would make your teeth itch: parents threatening to punch referees; kids cowering in fear of their fathers when they make a mistake. It's horrible to watch and it's wrong. But, believe me, it's everywhere. What's the problem then? In my opinion it's greed. It's as simple as that. Some parents have got it into their heads that if their kid makes it as a professional footballer they'll all be set for life. That's probably true, but what are the chances of it actually happening? About the same as they are of winning the National Lottery. So what happens when the majority of these kids don't make it? And they won't, I'm afraid. They're going to feel like they've let their parents down. How can you put a young kid through that? I realize that taking children to football training and matches takes a lot of time, money and dedication from the parents, but you can't put kids under that kind of pressure. It's not fair.

What *really* gets on my nerves with these kinds of pushy parents is that they take all of the enjoyment out of the game. I see it all the time. A lot of kids look worried when they play football these days and that's just ridiculous. Football at that age should be all about enjoyment. If they've got talent, fine, nurture it. But do it at a pace that's right for them. Don't shout at them and intimidate them – encourage them! It's a game of football, for heaven's sake. If I had a pound for every child I'd seen crying after they've been bawled out by a parent at a football match I would be able to buy a new car. The look of fear on some of these kids' faces! It makes me scared for them. These aren't just lone parents, though. You often get small gangs of them. And the way they go for the referees and linesmen is disgraceful. They're just hooligans. It has got so bad that a while ago the FA had to introduce something called the Respect Programme, which tells parents and carers how to behave on the touchline. Parents need to be told how to behave on the touchline? That really is ridiculous. What's the world coming to when the governing body of a sport has to waste time, money and resources informing the *parents* that it's wrong to swear at referees? I think it's a massive problem.

A while ago I was watching my little boy play and almost got into a ruck with some of these idiots. The linesman was a young lad, only a kid, and he called an offside decision that they didn't agree with. Some of the language they used against this lad was disgusting, and in front of the kids too, not to mention the other parents. In the end I had to stick up for this linesman and so they all started on me. Water off a duck's back, mate! I've had entire stadiums calling me all kinds, so dealing with a group of foul-mouthed pushy parents was a doddle. It makes you sick though, doesn't it? I think the FA even considered banning parents from the touchline at one point. Isn't that always the way – a few idiots spoiling it for the rest?

I know us old timers always say, 'It was a lot better in our day', but the fact of the matter is that it was, even if you still got the odd idiot. My dad was the manager of the kids' team I played for and one day he got slapped round the face by an irate woman because he didn't play her son. You can't win.

I was lucky. Not because my dad was the manager, but because from a very young age I was attached to professional clubs, the first one being Crewe Alexandra. In those days the only distractions you had to put up with were the instructions shouted at you by the coaches. They could get a bit over-excited sometimes but they never swore at you or tried to belittle you. Not that my dad ever did anything like that. He was like the majority of parents out there – vocal but supportive.

Okay, that's the pushy parents sorted. Now for the players.

I first joined Manchester United as a schoolboy in 1988 and then, in 1990 when I was sixteen, I signed as an apprentice. That was like a boot camp, except that in between all the jobs, discipline, lessons and so on, you were doing something you really loved – and we all loved playing football. It was a great life. Back then, believe me, the chores we had to do and the discipline were just as important to our development as the training was.

So what did we have to do, then? Well, after we'd finished training we had to wait to be dismissed by Eric Harrison, who was the man in charge of the youth set-up. I'm pleased to say that he always was and still is a really good friend of mine. Eric, a Yorkshireman hailing from Halifax, was a real disciplinarian and you never went anywhere unless he said so. Once he'd dismissed us we all got on with our chores. 'Right lads, off you go,' he would shout. 'And make sure you do a good job!'

First up for me was cleaning Mark Hughes's and Bryan Robson's boots, which was actually a dream come true for a young football fanatic. I used to sit there and think, 'Mark Hughes and Bryan Robson have just been playing in these. Mark Hughes and Bryan Robson!' The boots would usually be in a right state, but not half as bad as the toilets, which was my second job of the day. Actually, I should change that to jobbie! That's right, Robbie Savage started life as a toilet cleaner. I should have been given protective clothing to wear because some of those loos were unbelievable.

These days when a young player turns up with a Louis Vuitton washbag they think they've made it!

Once we'd finished our chores Eric would then do an inspection, and if our work wasn't up to scratch we would have to start again. 'Robbie, look at that toilet bowl, it's a disgrace! Start again, lad.' While you were doing that all the other lads would have to stand in position and wait. We were a team, you see, and the sense of responsibility that comes with being part of a team was drilled into us at every opportunity – as were manners and respect. They were obligatory at Manchester United and if you ever spoke out-of-hand to Eric or any of the other members of staff you would be for it. Not that we ever did. We were all too scared of being thrown out. It was a privilege being at Manchester United and that fact wasn't lost on any of us. Things were even stricter with the first-team players. We only ever spoke to them if they spoke to us first, and if you ever had to go into their dressing room, which we did to collect the boots we had to clean, you always knocked first. These people were like gods to us.

So that work ethic, that discipline and respect, was it a bad thing? Was it a waste of time? Well, somebody obviously thought it was because I'm telling you now that it doesn't exist as much anymore – or at least certainly not in the Premier League. I was paid £29.50 a week when I started as an apprentice at Manchester United and I got an extra tenner for the bus fares. These days you've got teenagers driving Ferraris and earning fifty grand a week. Don't get me wrong, I've got no problem with that, but just because you're getting paid a lot of money doesn't mean you have to act like an idiot. Why ditch the manners? What's wrong with having respect for people? If anything, being wealthy should make you even more respectful, but it very rarely works out like that. I could give you dozens of examples of people letting money go to their heads, and not just in football. These days, apprentices and young pros have people cleaning *their* boots and cleaning *their* toilets for them. They're more concerned with wearing diamond earrings than they are about practising good manners.

It sounds like I'm having a pop at these lads but I'm not. You see, I don't think it's all their fault: it's the people at the top. Think about it. If a little kid behaves badly the first place you look to is the parents, because either they have picked up whatever it is they're doing from their parents or their parents have refused to tell them not to do it. I know one or two kids like that, we all do, but as much as they get on my nerves I keep reminding myself that they're not actually the problem – the parents are.

And that's exactly what's happening at football clubs. As opposed to teaching these lads respect, discipline and manners, they surround them with yes-men who do everything for them. How can you create a team ethic on those terms? The answer is that you can't. These days it's every man for himself: who can buy the biggest car or the most expensive ring. I would be interested to find out if the same thing's happened in other sports like rugby or cricket. I have a feeling it probably has, but to a far lesser extent.

In return for getting paid tens of thousands of pounds a week these lads should be taught the value of money and the value of their privileged position. Sure, the clubs provide them with advisers who tell them about pensions and investments, but at the end of the day they're just yes-men like the rest. I remember when I played in the Premier League. We had all kinds of people advising us. Put your money here, put it there. But that was just the senior team rather than the kids. I don't mean any disrespect to these financial guys – they're just doing their jobs – but they're only a small part of what these young footballers need. They don't teach them values. Why can't you make them clean their own boots or even a urinal or two? What are they going to do, go on strike? Well, if they do it's because the club has failed them. It's all about education. If the likes of Dario Gradi at Crewe and Eric Harrison at United hadn't taught me the game I would never have made it as a professional footballer. You can't expect these lads to behave like model professionals instinctively. Give them the tools and then see what happens.

When I joined Manchester United there was a hierarchy. There were apprentices, junior pros and then seniors. It's pretty much the same today, of course, except that instead of junior pros earning £400 a week and the seniors £8,000, which is about what it was in the early 1990s, the junior pros all earn around £20,000 a week and the seniors around £100,000. Why try? You're already a millionaire several times over. Don't get me wrong, we all wanted to earn good money when we were at Manchester United, but it was never going to happen overnight. You had to behave in a certain way and you had to prove yourself year after year after year, and you only became a millionaire if you were good enough. If market forces say you have to pay every player a fortune, fine, I've got no problem with that. But what's wrong with teaching them a bit of discipline? Would it really be that bad?

Okay, let's just say that as a sport we've moved on from making these lads clean the boots of the senior players. Why not make them clean the cars instead? Or, as opposed to making them clean the toilets, get them to help out in the kitchens or something. Anything! Just try and give them some responsibility off the pitch. Teach them to appreciate the value of what they've got. In terms of the people involved, the only difference between the Class of '92 at Manchester United and the players of 2015 is that everybody now earns a lot of money. So what? They're still human beings and they still have a love of football, although I would argue that it's not as great as ours was. Back then it was *all* about football. Nothing else mattered and certainly not money. I can't see any advantage whatsoever in doing away with things like chores and discipline. It helps to create a strong team ethic, and God knows there are enough football teams that are lacking in that department.

If there's somebody out there who thinks there's an advantage in not instilling these kinds of values into the young players of today, let me know. Maybe you think it's a cultural thing: 'People don't have to say please and thank-you anymore. It's outdated.' That may be your opinion but you'll never convince me that it's the right way to behave or that it's improved the game. Not in a million years. Teams in the lower leagues still concentrate of respect and discipline, thank heavens, but the Premier League clubs, and even some of the Championship clubs, need to get this sorted out. It's not good for the game's reputation.

What are we creating as role models? Spoiled young men who don't know how to behave?

How Should
Footballers Behave?

A lot of people will take one look at this chapter title and think, 'Hang on, Robbie Savage talking about how players should behave? Is he's having a laugh?' Footballers don't come much more controversial than me – on the pitch at least (I was well behaved off it) – and there'll be a lot of people out there who think that I was anything but the model professional. Well, it might surprise you to learn that I actually think I was a good professional – most of the time.

Was I perfect? Of course I wasn't. Nobody was. Did I do things I'm embarrassed about? Yes I did, but I don't regret many of them. Life's too short. I think the only incident I possibly do regret was when I got Justin Edinburgh sent off. I went in for a challenge, which I believe was fair, but he didn't like it. Stupidly, he swung his arm at me and I knew that under most circumstances that would be a straight red. Going down and claiming he'd caught me was just an insurance policy. His hand did brush against my hair though, which in my book should be against the law! That was definitely the heat of the moment. It was Wembley, the 1999 Worthington Cup Final, and for most of us it was the biggest game of our careers. I received death threats after that, and all because of a game of football. That's just madness.

What is cheating in football? Is it diving? What if somebody clearly kicks a ball over the touchline but still appeals for a throw-in? Surely that's just as bad. It's still blatant cheating. If that is the case then every exaggeration should be treated the same. You can't pick and choose.

I believe that as a professional footballer you should do whatever it takes to win a game. Rightly or wrongly that was always my mindset as a player, and it still is now. We've seen the best players do it and we've seen the worst players do it, and that's one of the reasons why I've got no problem with it. Look at Cristiano Ronaldo at the 2006 World Cup. He was more than instrumental in getting Wayne Rooney sent off and he wasn't even involved in the incident. And remember the wink afterwards? He was saying, 'There you are lads, job done. Rooney's off and now we're going to win', and they did. The whole of England went absolutely berserk and Ronaldo received almost as many death threats as me. Welcome to my world, Cristiano! The thing is that Wayne Rooney admitted afterwards that he would have done exactly the same thing. He also said that before he got sent off he'd been telling the referee that Ronaldo was diving and that he should give him a yellow card. Players speak to the referee a lot, and that isn't always highlighted. It's all part and parcel of the game. Everybody wants to win.

Look at Stuart Broad. In 2013 when he refused to walk after getting a nick against Australia at Trent Bridge during the Ashes there was absolute uproar. Remember how the Aussies reacted? Oh yeah, Australians would never indulge in gamesmanship, would they? Broad was officially the most hated man in Australia after that and Darren Lehmann, the Australian coach, even branded him a cheat, although to be fair he did apologize. As far as I'm concerned, it was the Australians who came out worse from the whole affair, and not just because of the ridiculous overreaction. It was the Australians themselves who had taught Broad not to walk. He played out there in Australia a lot in his teens and so he was partly a product of their game.

I'm not sure if it was a team philosophy, but Broad's mentality was definitely 'win at any cost' and I'm with him on that 100 per cent. Seriously, once you're in that zone nothing else matters. Nothing!

On *606* I get dads calling in saying, 'What does that show my kids?' Well, I'm not being funny but at nine or ten years old it's not a professional sport, and that's the point – these days, sport is a business. You can whinge all you like about the lack of sportsmanship in a game, but when livelihoods are at stake that goes out of the window. Good sportsmanship's not going to feed your family.

Here's an example. If you're playing for a team who have to win to avoid relegation and the ball comes over and ends up going in off your arm, are you honestly going to stop and shout, 'Ref, it went in off my arm. No goal'? Of course you're not. Imagine the consequences, especially if you're in danger of leaving the Premier League. Wages would get halved, players would have to leave and staff might be made redundant. And that's to say nothing about the knock-on effect it would have on the town or city. There would be fewer visiting fans, which would mean less money coming into the area. And what about morale in the town? More miserable faces would mean less productivity. The consequences are never ending. Now, you could argue that by not owning up to the handball you would still be consigning another team to that very same fate, but at the end of day it's not them who pay your wages.

There are so many footballers out there who say, 'Oh, I'd never do anything like that', but I'm not having it. Nearly every footballer has indulged in a bit of gamesmanship, whether it's grassing up a player to the ref and ultimately trying to get that player booked or sent off, or waving your arm for a throw-in when you know full well that the ball's come off your knee. Everybody does it. Think about it for a minute. How many examples of gamesmanship did you see the last time you watched a match? Did somebody dive? Possibly. Did somebody pretend to be injured to waste a few seconds? More than likely. What about players waving their arms trying to claim a corner when they knew full well the ball had come off their own striker? Definitely! A variation of that old chestnut probably happens every other minute during a game.

A lot of fans are also under the illusion that gamesmanship didn't exist back in the good old days. They think that it was all handshakes and 'Well done, old chap.' Well, that's rubbish. I admit it probably wasn't as widespread as it is these days, but back then the coverage was minimal. Today you've got cameras everywhere – thousands, if you count the spectators' mobile phones. We just see it happening more.

This brings me on to how footballers should behave off the pitch. Some of them really do think that they're invisible, although I think more and more are beginning to realize that they're not. Social media, like anything, has its advantages and its disadvantages, and from a footballer's point of view one of the disadvantages is that not only are you likely to get photographed or filmed if you're doing something stupid, but within seconds it can be broadcast to quite literally billions of people. It's quite frightening when you think about it. You've got to be on your guard because these days there's no hiding place.

Some people say that if sportspeople are going to do stupid things they should make sure they do it in private, but I'd actually go further than that. For me if you want to get plastered, smoke cigarettes or inhale laughing gas out of a balloon, do it when you retire. If you play till your mid-thirties you'll probably have fifty-odd years to do all that. If you start playing at seventeen and finish at thirty-five, that's eighteen years of behaving sensibly. Is it really too much to ask? Okay, sometimes you might have the odd blip, but if you try and get it into your head that doing these sorts of things before you retire is wrong, you'll be far less likely to do them. Providing you don't stay within the media once you retire nobody will give a monkey's.

Education can help to a certain extent but that's going to take time. At the end of the day, self-control has to come from the player. It has to be their decision. If you tell a young footballer with loads of money not to go out, they're not going to take a blind bit of notice of you. That in itself is wrong but that's the culture these days and you can't change it overnight. The younger players just don't understand the word 'no'. It's not part of their vocabulary. But if you try and advise them that living correctly is the right thing to do and also tell them why that is, you might actually get somewhere. These lads aren't stupid. They've just been left to their own devices far too much. If it was up to me I'd send in some top ex-players to speak to them. People like Gary Lineker and Alan Shearer. They're two of the best strikers England's ever had and they always behaved immaculately off the pitch. It's a pity they've let themselves go as much as they have, but that's life. Only joking, lads!

If it was up to me you would get one chance and if you messed up a second time you would be out because, in my opinion, being a professional footballer is a privilege. I can go and watch a team play in the park on a Sunday and I might see a player and I think, 'Hey, he's good.' But even so, how many levels below the Premier League will he be? There are only 800-odd players registered with Premier League clubs. Eight hundred! That might sound like a lot but when you consider how many players there are in the Championship and the two other leagues, not to mention the Conference and all the amateur divisions – well, let's just say he would have a very long way to go to be the best of the best. So to be included in that list of 800 Premier League players should be nothing less than an honour.

I certainly feel privileged to have played there. Never in a million years did I think I would get anywhere near that division. Even when I signed for Manchester United as a schoolboy I knew that the chances of me making it as a professional, let alone as a Premier League player, were tiny – thousands to one. What I achieved and what I have now means more to me than to a lot of other Premier League players for the simple reason that I had to work harder to get it. Remember what Martin O'Neill said? 'Robbie lacks just one thing – ability.' Well, I'm the first to admit that he was right. My success was based on four things: a little bit of ability (you've got to have some), clean living (generally), a bit of personality and a tremendous amount of hard work. I knew that I was punching above my weight as a player but instead of just dropping into the lower leagues or dropping out of the game like a lot of players did, I worked hard, looked after myself, played to my strengths and turned myself into one of the most written-about players the Premier League has ever had. Okay, some of the headlines weren't that complimentary, but you all remember me. Not bad for a Manchester United reject with no ability. People sometimes accuse me of being bitter at being released by Manchester United, but how can I be bitter? I played 350 games over eleven seasons in one of the best leagues in the world, and I achieved that partly by staying out of trouble.

It sounds like I'm just bragging here but I'm not. What I'm trying to get across is the value and the enormity of being part of something so big. When I walked out on to the pitch at Filbert Street or St Andrew's, Ewood Park, Old Trafford, Anfield or Highbury, there weren't just a few thousand people watching in the stands, and there weren't just a few million more watching on TV at home. There were tens of millions of people watching these games all over the world. The Premier League is bigger than Hollywood with regards to how much money it generates and how many people it attracts. That's a fact.

So, yes, it does annoy me when I see footballers with all the ability in the world acting like they don't give a damn. They're an insult to the game, they're an insult to the fans and they're an insult to all the players who actually try hard but don't have that kind of ability. I'll tell you what, if I'd had even half the natural ability that some of these boys have then I might have been able to play in the Champions League. I wouldn't have wasted it. I'd have nurtured it, treasured it, and would have used it to my advantage. I'm not going to mention players by name because it would take up too much paper, but I'll tell you what, lads, in fifteen years' time when you're at the end of your career all you're going to have to show for it, if you're not careful, is a whole heap of regret, and that would be a massive shame. Don't waste it and don't let yourselves down.

Ronaldo v. Messi –
Real v. Barça

Who's the best – Cristiano Ronaldo or Lionel Messi? This seems to be one of the biggest questions in football at the moment. It's certainly one of the most talked about. As far as I'm concerned it's obviously a far more relevant one than the old Pelé v. Maradona discussion, for the simple reason that those two played in different eras, not to mention different countries and competitions. They were both unbelievable players, of course, but I think you'll find that the majority of people who favour Diego Maradona, and I'm one of them, haven't seen much footage of Pelé. I don't remember seeing a lot of Santos games on TV, do you? Go on, admit it. With Messi v. Ronaldo there are no such excuses. Everything's there for everyone to see, the footage, the stats, the lot. And, best of all, they're playing in the same league and for two of the best teams in Europe – if not the world. No, this one's the real deal, and if you ask me it's going to keep us talking for decades.

On 1 June 2015 I took part in an online chat for BreatheSport with Gary Lineker, Ian Wright and Phil Neville. It was a review of the 2014/15 football season and the Ronaldo v. Messi question was one of the first ones we were asked. Funnily enough, it's probably the one that caused the most disagreement but that's because it's such a hot topic and has been for years.

Gary Lineker suggested that Messi was on a different planet to Ronaldo, but I disagreed. It's more even than that. For me, Messi is the better player, in that he's a better dribbler and a better goal scorer, but Ronaldo is two-footed and is great in the air. You see, it's not easy. I used to think Ronaldo was the better player, but now it's Messi. They're definitely good for each other, though, in that they drive each other on. There's no doubt about that. If either was out on their own I don't think they would have nearly as much ambition.

I played against Ronaldo a few times and back in 2009 he was accused by some (although not by me) of spitting at me. This happened at Pride Park when I was playing for Derby. I got the better of him in a tussle, he fell to his knees and then he spat, but as far as I was concerned it wasn't aimed at me. That's not what the papers said, but then from a certain angle it probably did look like he had. This time around the camera was telling porkies.

He was an amazing player then and he is now, but I still think Messi's the second-best player who ever lived behind Maradona. By the time he retires I might believe he's the best because, if you ignore the 2013/14 season when he was struggling with injury, he's just been getting better and better, and he's only twenty-seven, whereas Ronaldo's an old man of thirty. In the

2014/15 season, Messi was ridiculous. Look at the way he enabled Luis Suárez and Neymar to play, and then look at Ronaldo, Gareth Bale and Karim Benzema. There's a totally different chemistry there. One works perfectly, almost like you know what's going to happen, whereas the other's much more unpredictable. Those three Barça lads are on exactly the same wavelength and it's fantastic to watch.

People often say, 'But Messi hasn't done it at international level like Maradona', and I used to be one of them. But when you look at it now all the best players in the world play in the Champions League. It's an argument in itself but in my opinion the Champions League is better than the World Cup, certainly in terms of quality.

Put it this way, if Barcelona played Germany in a one-off match who would win? I think Barcelona would beat them, and not just because the team plays together week-in, week-out. That would definitely give them an advantage but even if it wasn't the case I still think Barça would beat them because they have better players. And I think Real Madrid would beat them, too.

Saying that, the reason I still think that Maradona is the best is because of all those international goals he scored. They're engrained on my mind, especially the two he scored against Belgium in 1986. If you haven't seen them in a while go and YouTube them now. They're absolutely astonishing and have got to be two of the best goals ever scored at the World Cup. But then you look at the goal Messi scored in the final of the Copa del Rey against Athletic Bilbao. That was something else and for me it is one of the greatest goals ever scored – anywhere!

So you see, by the time Messi retires I might be saying something different. By the time I finish writing this chapter I might be saying something different!

I wish I had seen Pelé play more because when you look at his record it's ridiculous. He scored 619 goals in 638 appearances for Santos and 77 goals in 92 appearances for Brazil. You don't get much more prolific than that. But it's not just a numbers game, is it? When we were taking part in that online review, Phil Neville, who prefers Ronaldo, argued that he'd scored more goals in La Liga than Messi during that season, and straight away Gary Lineker said, 'Yes, but he doesn't fill you with joy like Messi does, and that's what it's all about.' Would you agree with that? I would. Then again, when Gary and Ian Wright say that Ronaldo isn't on the same planet as Messi, in my opinion that's not true.

I would love to know what the dressing room is like at Real Madrid. Gareth Bale, who I think is an unbelievable player, went in there under the banner of being the most expensive footballer ever, and that won't have done him any favours. Imagine if you're Ronaldo. You've won the Ballon d'Or three times, you're scoring fifty or sixty goals a season and you've even got shops outside the stadium selling nothing but merchandise with your name on it. You are Real Madrid! And then, all of a sudden, in comes this new lad who is supposed to be the new you. I wonder if it had an effect. These players are all big personalities and there'll be some big egos in that dressing room.

I used to love watching Gareth Bale in full flight when he played for Spurs. That hat-trick he scored against Inter Milan – three fantastic goals and all taken from exactly the same spot

– was unbelievable. It's just a pity he hasn't been able to recapture that form at Real. His first season was fantastic, but his second not so much. Some argue that Ronaldo could do more to help Bale, but it's not that simple. He's got his reputation to think of, not to mention his scoring record. The last thing he wants is a younger version of himself ripping up the turf at the Bernabéu and knocking in fifty goals a season. I think the old *Galácticos* nickname sums up Real Madrid's problems as it basically means 'a team of superstars'.

Football can be a team game but it can also be a very individual game. If you can make the most talented footballers in the world play like a team you're home and dry. Barcelona have managed it. The personalities and the egos must still be there, but somehow they managed to keep them at bay – or at least make them work for the good of the team. It's different with international football because you all have one thing in common – your country – and that drives you to perform well as a team. It's a pity Real can't get it together as consistently as Barcelona because if their front three could gel on an ongoing basis like Barcelona's have, God knows what might happen.

Billionaire Owners,
Money and Commitment

In the 1994/95 season, Jack Walker at Blackburn Rovers became the first chairman to buy a Premier League title. He wasn't a billionaire – there weren't many around back then – but he can't have been that far off. He brought in players like Alan Shearer and Chris Sutton, lived the dream and won the league, although just the once.

It kind of became a bit of a trend after that – rich businessmen spending millions on teams trying to buy success – but they were no match for the Manchester Uniteds and Arsenals of this world. Those two clubs had a bit of money behind them too, but they also had fantastic youth systems, and that's why they dominated the Premier League for the first eleven years and between them won ten FA Cups between 1993 and 2005. If anyone was going to challenge those two teams seriously for a sustained period without waiting years to develop a youth system like the one I was attached to, you would need to have some serious money. A lot more than a few hundred million. Step forward Roman Abramovich, who I believe has been great for the Premier League.

When he turned up in London he didn't just turn Chelsea and the Premier League on its head, but football in general. Sure, he swaps and changes managers a bit, but he wants success and likes good football, and that's great. He loves it! What I can't stand is when a billionaire owner comes in and doesn't love the football club. He might have bought it as an ego boost or a hobby, or as a present for his son or his pal or whatever. Either way it's wrong. I know that the Premier League vets potential owners about money, but how about vetting them for commitment and ambition?

Roman Abramovich just sits in the background and gets on with it, as do the majority of the owners, and that's the way it should be. It's the ones who don't care and the idiotic eccentrics who get on my nerves the most – people who try to change a club's identity. That's absolutely unforgivable. Owners come and go, and that will never change. Even Abramovich will probably sell up one day. But the club will always be bigger than its owner and that's the first thing these people should be told when they're looking to buy a club. It doesn't matter how rich they are: the fans were there before they were and will still be there when they depart.

As a player I don't think you really care who owns the club you're at, but if you see a billionaire owner take over and if you're liked at the club you must be thinking, 'Eh, if I carry on doing well I could be in for more money.' And why not? On the other hand you might be thinking, 'Hang on, what if he brings in a load of better players? I could be out.' On the whole, though, I don't think you take a great deal of notice.

People often ask me which club I would buy if I was a billionaire, and I keep telling them I already am! Most of it goes on grooming, though. I mean, you can't look this good on the cheap.

My first choice would obviously have to be Wrexham, which is my home-town club, but with a population of just 60,000 we would only be able to achieve so much. There are so many sleeping giants out there – Leeds, Sheffield Wednesday and Newcastle spring to mind – but if we're talking about pure potential, and if I ever did have a few billion in the bank, I think I would probably have to buy West Ham. Just think about it. They're going to have a new stadium soon with a capacity of over 54,000. That's only a few thousand less than the Emirates. They've already got a massive fan base at the club – passionate old-school fans – and they also have a great history. Everything's in place really. It just needs money. And because the club's in London they're also going to attract more players. That may be sad, but I'm afraid it's true.

I think the only way that money ever becomes a problem in the dressing room is when a new owner takes over or when a team gets promoted to the Premier League. When either of those takes place everything usually changes quite fast, and that's never good. You see, if you've been playing week-in, week-out, for ten or fifteen grand a week and then suddenly a load of new players come in who are earning fifty grand a week, you're going to have problems. From the moment you find out how much they're all getting you'll start comparing yourself to them, both in training and during a game, and unless they really live up their billing and the price tag, you're going to start to resent them, big time. Whatever people say, footballers do talk, and within a few weeks of joining a club you can find out what everybody else is earning to within a few grand. A player might tell you himself if he wants to wind you up or you might read about their salary in the newspapers. Whatever you might think about the press, they're never that far off when it comes to things like that.

You can't have everybody on the same wage. Life's just not like that. If I was earning ten grand a week at a club and Messi or Ronaldo came in earning three hundred grand a week I honestly would not mind, providing they were putting in a full shift. As long as they did that I would be fine. In fact, it would be a pleasure to play alongside them. But if I thought that they were just warming the bench week-in, week-out, and I was playing out of my skin for a thirtieth of what they were earning, I would be absolutely furious, and so, I hope, would the club. It does happen, though. And that's when money can cause massive havoc in a dressing room.

Staying on the financial subject, a lot of people think that players' wages are becoming excessive these days but I think that's absolute rubbish. I can understand why they might think that to a certain extent, but at the end of the day it's all relative. Wayne Rooney's the one who usually gets it in the neck, not that I think that it bothers him very much. England's all-time leading goal scorer, as Wayne recently became, earns around £300,000 a week, which is over £15 million a year. Sure, that's a lot of money, but it's nowhere near as much as some of the Formula One drivers earn or some of the basketball or American football players. Wayne almost seems poor in comparison. According to *Forbes Magazine*, he was only the forty-third highest paid athlete of 2014. But what's the most popular sport in the world? Is it Formula One? No chance. Is it American football? You're having a laugh, aren't you? No, it's football, and like him or loathe him, Wayne Rooney is one of the biggest names in the game. And the sums are all relative. In 2014 Manchester United raised income of over £433 million and a lot of that money would have been generated by Wayne Rooney. Why shouldn't he get his fair share?

People might not like the amount of money that's going into the game but they might as well try and get used to it because, mark my words, it's never going to change. There are loads of positives that come from having so much money going into football. Granted, there are also one or two negatives, but at the end of the day nothing's perfect. Look at what the Premier League is doing with all that new TV money. Of the £5.1 billion it will earn between the 2016/17 and 2018/19 seasons, over £1 billion of that will be invested into grass-roots facilities, youth coaching, payments to the lower leagues and improving disabled access. How can you not consider that to be a good thing? It's amazing!

So can you honestly blame a player for getting paid a lot of money? Well, of course you can't. Don't be ridiculous. I mean, what is he going to say? 'I think your offer of £300,000 a week is far too much. Could you go and blunt your pencil and come back with something worse?' It's all about market forces. House prices go up because people have more money, and it's exactly the same with football clubs and players. They work out what that player is worth to them, both on the pitch and off it, and then they make them an offer. That's how it works.

But then you'll get people who say, 'Yes, but he wasn't trying. How can he earn so much money and play like that?' I've never heard as much nonsense in my life. The vast majority of footballers try when they're on that pitch – fact. The odd one or two might look a bit lazy from time to time, but the majority of footballers when they cross that white line – regardless of what they're getting paid – will try. If you don't put in the effort you're going to get found out pretty quickly. First, the fans are going to get frustrated, then the manager will get frustrated, and before you know it you'll get subbed. It's as simple as that. There's no hiding place once you're on the field and that whistle goes. Fans believe that they pay your wages, and whether that's via a season ticket, a football shirt, a pint of lager or a subscription to BT Sport or Sky, they really do. Believe it or not all the football players and ex-football players that I know are all aware of that fact – and they respect it.

You would think that with the amount of money flying around the Premier League everything would be rosy, but the problems that the Premier League faces today have nothing to do with cash. If anything, they are more to do with the weather. Seriously. You see, for some reason a lot of players just don't want to play here. Big-money marquee signings were common-place up until a few years ago, but over the past few years we haven't seen that many. All the record signings are going elsewhere. Maybe the tide will turn again, but who were the last really big-name players to come into the Premier League? Alexis Sánchez to Arsenal? Ángel Di María to Manchester United? I can't think of many who I would consider to be genuinely world-class players. These days, you've also got quite a few like Di María who soon decided to leave the Premier League, and that never happened before. Look at David de Gea. Manchester United may have helped him become a star goalkeeper, but it wasn't long until he started thinking about going home and playing in La Liga again.

There's still plenty of money being spent, and there are more billionaires buying up Premier League clubs than ever before, but it seems that most of the *real* superstars are either staying in or choosing to play in La Liga. The Premier League might still be the most watched football league in the world in terms of TV audiences, but the clubs need to think of ways in which they can get some of the big boys back. Seriously, where have all the superstars gone? The Zolas, the Vieiras, the Keanes and the Di Canios. The Bergkamps and the Ginolas. The Klinsmanns, Overmars and Beckhams. I miss not talking about the very, very best, and for many years the Premier League had the best. Could it honestly be the weather? That's been shocking these past few years and I must admit that it gets me down from time to time. Where would you rather ply your trade, especially if you were used to good weather, Manchester or Madrid? It's a no-brainer really.

The Premier League doesn't have a monopoly on billionaires

like it did a few years ago and so what can it offer a player from Argentina, Spain, Portugal or Brazil that La Liga, Serie A or even Ligue 1 can't? That's a difficult one, but knowing the Premier League like I do, it'll already be on the agenda.

The Premier League in Europe

Despite the lack of marquee signings, when it comes to
breadth of talent the Premier League is probably still up
there with La Liga all-told, and is still miles ahead of Serie A,
the Bundesliga and France's Ligue 1. Don't get me wrong, there
are some fantastic players in those other leagues – plenty of
talent – but not consistently throughout the division like there
is in La Liga and the Premier League. So the questions you have
to ask are, 'Why are Premier League clubs failing in Europe?'
and 'Is it a long or short-term problem?'

There's nothing wrong with the Premier League brand, so
what's up then? Is it a case of style over substance? Is too much
effort being put into building 'Brand Premier League' to the
detriment of the football? I don't think so for the simple reason
that those people in charge of the brand have very little to do
with the football side of things; in fact, it's because they do such
a good job with the brand that the clubs are able to meet massive
transfer fees and pay players so much money. The really big
names, such as Messi and Ronaldo, might be missing which is a

shame, but pound for pound the Premier League probably has more talent per capita than any other league in the world.

What about the old winter-break argument?

Managers of the top clubs have been going on about this for donkey's years and you can see their point, especially as the majority of the other European countries have a winter break. This means that by the time the Champions League trophy has been polished and is ready to hand over, the Premier League boys have been at it for two weeks longer than the rest. Would it solve the Premier League's European problems? Not all together, but it would certainly put the Premier League back on a more even playing field. I've spoken to a number of players who've played abroad and they all said it makes a difference so why not?

Here's another plausible reason – tactics.

I certainly don't think you can play four–four–two in the Champions League again because if you play with a flat four across the middle and three of them don't run back you've got no chance, especially against quality opposition. I think that's one of the reasons Manchester City struggled last time round but they seem to have addressed that now in the Premier League, at least. Let's see if they can transfer that to the Champions League.

How about competition?

Surely it's no coincidence that the Premier League's dominance of the Champions League coincided with it having all the money in the game or at least most of it. These days, we no longer have a monopoly on Russian oligarchs and mega-rich men from the Middle East. Look at Paris Saint-Germain. Their starting line-up in last year's Champions League was one of the most expensive ever in the competition – second only to Real Madrid, I think. Bearing in mind the rest of the clubs in the competition, well, that's some serious cash. Also, just look at La Liga. A few years ago it was a two-team league with only Barcelona and Real Madrid being able to challenge for the big stuff in Europe but that's no longer the case. Look at Atlético Madrid – a very strong team with a great manager, a new stadium and a healthy bank balance. To their credit Atlético have also been very clever in cashing in on their assets and then replacing them. Players like Fernando Torres and Diego Costa spring to mind.

There was an all-German final featuring Bayern against Borussia Dortmund in 2013, but the Bundesliga is as it was, really, with just Bayern Munich regularly challenging in Europe. Have you noticed that Serie A teams are starting to pull back some ground, though? As a league they've spent over 400 million euros in the off-season so are really getting back in among them. I'm not saying that the likes of Chelsea and Arsenal have become complacent. I just think that the other leagues have caught up.

One other argument that keeps getting raised is that the football played in the Premier League is no longer defensive enough. Once again, I think there's some substance here. We certainly have some very good defenders but do we have any great defensive partnerships, à la Rio Ferdinand and Nemanja Vidić, John Terry and Ricardo Carvalho or Jamie Carragher and Sami Hyppiä, at the moment? I don't think so. Why is that? Could it just be that the media is not really discussing them? I doubt it. They would soon latch on to an effective Premier League defensive partnership and start talking about it if one existed.

Maybe that's one for the managers to answer. It's something else that really could be having an effect, especially when you look the record of some of those great defensive duos in the Champions League. One display that springs to mind is when Ferdinand and Vidić helped Manchester United keep two clean sheets against an unbelievable Barcelona side in the 2008 Champions League semi-finals. Given who they were playing against, that has to be one of the greatest defensive achievements ever.

There we are then, more theories and arguments than you can shake a stick at.

Let's also get things into perspective a bit, shall we? Okay, so 2012/13 and 2014/15 were bad years for the Premier League in Europe. Fair enough. How about 2013/14? Well, Manchester United made the last eight and Chelsea made it to the semi-finals, eventually losing to an absolutely blistering Atlético Madrid team. Not the success we would have wanted, of course, but it was hardly a disaster. Trying to make out it was a disaster is an insult to the rest of the teams, so if that's what we think then perhaps we are becoming complacent and maybe a tad arrogant.

My own theory encapsulates all of the above. Success in football, like in any sport, rotates — it goes in cycles. People change, styles change, financial situations change and so does your luck. I don't think there'll be many people out there who believe the dip in the Champions League form of Premier League teams is due to just one of the above or, indeed, any other single theory. How can it be? You mark my words, it might not happen immediately but things will start to level out sooner or later.

Manchester United are going through a transitional period at the moment and to a certain extent you could say the same about Liverpool. Both have spent big in order to regain ground so it'll be interesting to see what happens. They'll come good, though, given time. And do you honestly think that the Professor and the Special One haven't spent weeks on end thinking about what's gone wrong and how they can put it right? Of course they have. Believe me, there'll be more internal meetings going on regarding the Champions League at those clubs than there will be about anything else.

You see, once you weigh everything up, the current poor form of the Premier League in Europe is not really that extraordinary, is it?

Superstitions

As a player I used to have one of the strangest superstitions known to man, but football is full of superstitious people, and I mean full, and the rituals you hear about go from the bizarre to the ridiculous. I've heard some absolute crackers in my time, from the chairman of Real Madrid burying a clove of garlic under the centre circle to stop a curse in the Copa del Rey to the French national team having to listen to Gloria Gaynor's hit 'I Will Survive' before every match.

Alan Rough, the former Scottish international goalkeeper, was one of the most prolific of players in terms of superstitions. Not only did he refuse to shave before every game but he always carried a thistle-shaped keyring with him on to the pitch, not to mention a tennis ball. A tennis ball?! If that wasn't enough, he apparently always insisted on having the No. 13 peg in the dressing room and would always wear his old No. 11 shirt from his days as a winger underneath his strip. Last of all, and this is my favourite bit, he would try and blow his nose as often as possible during a match.

Even the absolute greats have form here. Pelé once gave away one of his playing shirts to a fan and when he started suffering a dip in form he became convinced it was because he wasn't wearing the shirt. He then persuaded a friend to try and track down the shirt and, after it was eventually presented back to him, Pelé started scoring goals again. It wasn't the shirt Pelé thought it was, though. His mate hadn't been able to find that particular one and so had simply handed him the one he'd worn most recently.

It gets worse, though.

Raymond Domenech, the former France national manager, apparently used to pick his team according to horoscopes! I even read that some of the players who played under him claim that he dropped them because the stars were not aligned properly – or something like that. I also read the other day that Barry Fry, who was manager at my old club Birmingham City in the mid-1990s, used to believe that there was a curse at St Andrew's and that it could only be removed by weeing on the corner flags. I don't think it worked.

This curse had apparently been around a long time though because about ten years previous to that Ron Saunders used to order his players to paint the soles of their football boots red in order to rid the club of the very same curse. That's amazing! I have to say I never noticed anything while I was there.

My favourite ritual belongs to the great Johan Cruyff, who, just before an Ajax game began, would slap his keeper Gert Bals in the stomach before spitting his chewing gum into the opposition's half. Apparently, when Ajax lost the European Cup to

AC Milan in 1969, it was because Cruyff had forgotten his chewing gum. Ridiculous! My pal Roberto Mancini, who is now the manager at Inter Milan, is extremely particular about salt pots. I used to have lunch with him quite a bit and if he ever asked me for the salt I had to push the pot across the table as opposed to passing it, otherwise he would go spare.

Talking of salt, a former president of the Italian club, AC Pisa, used to believe that sprinkling some on the pitch prior to a match would bring the team no end of good luck, and the bigger the game, the more salt required. The most he ever dumped on the pitch was a reported 26 kilograms, but apparently they still lost the match.

A lot of people ask why players don't stop their rituals once they realize they're not actually that lucky, but I'm afraid that's not how it works.

One of Hibernian's current strikers, Farid El Alagui, apparently had a 'lucky' £1 coin, which he found on the pitch during a pre-match warm-up while playing for Falkirk FC. He took it with him everywhere after that and just before a match would hand the coin carefully to one of the coaching staff. When he eventually arrived at Hibs in 2014 he won the first game, lost the next two and was then out injured for six months. He'd have been better off spending it on a lottery ticket.

Nevertheless, my own superstition has to be one of the strangest of all time. It all started at Leicester City with something called the Thursday Night Club, which basically consisted of me, my wife and some friends of ours, and every Thursday night we would go out and have a meal and some wine at an

Italian restaurant. The first time we had one of these meals I drank an absolute skinful, which, for somebody who had hardly ever touched alcohol before, was potentially quite dangerous. I was with my friends and I wanted to impress. You know what it's like, though. 'Go on, have another!' You just go with the flow. Forty-eight hours later, as opposed to leaving the pitch feeling like death warmed up, I won the man-of-the-match award. Honestly, I played out of my skin. Back in the dressing room it was all pats on the back and stuff. I was the toast of the club.

The next week I did the same: got hammered, played a blinder and was the man of the match. 'I'm on to a good thing here,' I thought, 'guaranteed success! The more I drink the better I play.'

This was getting daft as I was now sure that having a big drink before a match was making a difference. I honestly believed it.

After a while the sessions with the Thursday Night Club didn't seem like enough, which is when I started smuggling a bottle of wine or two into my overnight bag. Then, once I got to my hotel room, I'd open one up and have a few glasses. I say 'smuggling' because if anyone at the club had found out I would have got into massive trouble. Back then, you weren't supposed to touch a drop the night before a game. These days they're stricter still – I'm pretty sure players get tested for it. It was something I felt I had to do, though, in order to play well.

Fortunately, after a few months my tolerance levels began to drop and it started having the opposite effect on me. In fact, for a while drinking any alcohol at all just made me feel sick. 'Thank God for that,' I thought. It didn't take me long to realize that it was all a load of rubbish, but for a time I was completely taken in by it. Have you ever heard anything so ridiculous? Next time I think I'll just wee on a corner flag.

MOTD, the Media, Punditry and Presenting

L ike millions of others around the country, watching *Match of the Day* was the highlight of my week when I was young. It was the one night of the week when I was allowed to stay up and the one programme I didn't want to miss. I was always too busy playing football to be that interested in TV, so this was about the only show I was interested in. People like Jimmy Hill and Des Lynam were the presenters when I was a boy, and they were great, but for me Gary Lineker is the best anchorman *Match of the Day* has ever had, and I'm not just saying that because he's my pal. He's got the lot – the experience and the knowledge – and he's good in front of the camera, too. The only part where I think Gary lets himself down is in the looks department, but he can't help that. I think that's why they drafted me in. When it came to actual pundits my two favourites were Alan Hansen and, when he was on, Brian Clough. Even though I was only a kid I could tell that they were just that bit different to everyone else in terms of plain speaking and I think that had an effect on me.

As much as I loved staying up and watching *Match of the Day* as a kid, appearing on it as a player took the buzz to a totally different level. Imagine going to watch your favourite band a few times and then suddenly being asked to get up on stage and play with them. That's what it was like. One minute I was at home watching it with my dad and brother, and the next I was on the screen turning out for Leicester City. It was bonkers! Appearing on the show as a pundit is just completely surreal. I remember taking my seat for the first time. I was a little bit nervous as you can imagine. Then all of a sudden that famous music started and I thought, 'Oh my God! I'm actually going to be on *MOTD*!' It was not only surreal, it was terrifying. I'd done the hat-trick though: I'd watched it as a fan, appeared on it as a player and now I was a pundit. What a privilege.

I sometimes wonder how I ended up becoming a pundit because my first memorable experience with the media almost finished my international career.

In September 1998 I was on international duty with Wales. We were about to play a qualifier for Euro 2000 against Italy and the day before the match took place I was asked to do a piece for Sky Sports.

'What do you want me to do?' I asked.

'I'll tell you what,' said one of the lads from Sky. 'Here's one of Paolo Maldini's shirts. Why don't you toss it into that bin over there and I'll film it?'

Now as well as being attractive, humble and always up for a laugh, I was quite naive back in those days and so without thinking about the consequences of tossing away a shirt belonging to one of the most respected footballers the world has ever known, I just did it.

'Good old Sav, he's always good for a laugh!'

That's what the players said when they saw it on TV, and I thought nothing more about it.

A few hours later I was being thrown out of the hotel by Bobby Gould, the Wales manager.

He was absolutely furious and it didn't matter how many times I told him it was a joke – he wouldn't listen.

'I want you off the premises in twenty minutes or I'm calling the police,' was all he kept saying.

The news was breaking everywhere.

'Robbie Savage has been thrown out of the Wales squad for his behaviour,' said the reporter on *Sky News*. Mum and Dad thought I'd been thrown out of a bar or something. It was a nightmare.

In the end Mark Hughes and Gary Speed tried to appeal to Gouldy's better nature and get me reinstated.

'I'll let him back in the squad,' said Gouldy, 'but he's not playing!'

That was the first of many 'happenings' with the media. That's just me, though. I'll never change.

What it takes to be a football pundit has changed massively over the years. I think it has to be one of the most difficult jobs in the sport.

Go back thirty or forty years and there were very few programmes featuring pundits, but even the ones that did were just discussion shows really, which is what punditry was all about then – offering the odd opinion. It's much the same these days, of course, but there's a lot more analysis involved and the technology seems to be advancing almost by the minute. Punditry was never considered a profession back then. The people who took part were usually ex-players or managers and they did it just to earn a few quid. Today there are dozens of pundits and for many of us it's a full-time job – a job that the majority of us take very, very seriously. You see, a lot of people think that to be a pundit you just have to watch a match, sit down in front of a camera or a microphone and offer an opinion, but that's only part of it.

On *Match of the Day*, for instance, you have a minute and a half to dissect an entire football match and it's no use just stating the obvious: you have to try and tell people something they didn't already know. You have to be informative. Pundits are supposed to be the experts and I think people watch them for three reasons: one, to be entertained; two, to learn something; and three, to disagree with them! If you don't deliver on all three of those points you won't last, it's as simple as that. I get just as much stick as a pundit as I ever did as a player but to me that means I'm doing my job well. I'm dividing opinion and helping to create a debate.

I'll tell you what, though, it's not an easy job, and since going into the media I've had to work on loads of things I never had to worry about as a player. For a start my voice has often been criticized for being too high-pitched, which is a consequence of having a broken nose. What have I done about it? I'm seeing a nose specialist and a voice coach. Secondly, I'm not very good with an autocue. Some people take to it and some don't, and I have to admit that I've found it really hard. But, as opposed to just sitting down and worrying about it, I'll stay behind after a show and I'll practise, again and again and again. It's a slow process but it's the only way. The other thing I often get hammered for is when I get big words wrong; in fact, I've become quite famous for it over the years. Now I take a dictionary into the loo each day and I try to learn a couple of new words. I have to say it's augmented my lexicon immeasurably . . . where did that come from?!

Do you know, some people even have a go at me for getting over-excited when I'm broadcasting? Personally, I don't consider that a problem – in fact, if anything I consider it a compliment – but if I ever thought that it was something I needed to address I would. My philosophy now is the same as it always was – I'll do whatever it takes. I'll never change my character, though.

So presentation's important then, we've established that, but in order to be able to comment on something you have to know your stuff – every stat for every player at every team. I've never done as much study and revision in all my life since becoming a pundit and I have even needed to have an office built at home, but because I love the game it's not a problem. It's what I do.

If you're covering a game on *MOTD* or BT Sport you'll start looking into that fixture four or five days in advance – all the stats and the form, and so on. You do get a lot of help from the crew, by the way. They're forever shouting stats in your ear.

I think it takes a certain kind of person to be a pundit. First of all you need to have experience and you need to know what you're talking about, but just as importantly as that you need to be able to communicate with people. You might the most knowledgeable person in the world when it comes to football but if you can't get your point across in a manner that's entertaining you won't last two minutes. People have got to want to watch, read or listen to you. You're never going to please everybody, of course, but I think that when you first come into the business you have to try and stand out from the crowd.

As a player I did just that, and so I suppose that when the likes of the BBC and the *Daily Mirror* started coming in and offering me media work it was understandable. I certainly don't mean that to sound arrogant, by the way, but they probably knew I would attract an audience because I was starting to become as controversial with my mouth as I was with my feet.

Once everything started to take off I had to make sure that I built on that persona and so for the last few years of my playing career I started telling people exactly what I thought. I wasn't rude – I was just willing to offer a forthright and honest opinion, which is exactly what the media and the fans want.

All my teammates used to take the mickey out of me. In fact, John Hartson used to call me 'Busy'. 'You're into absolutely everything, you are, Sav,' he would say. Isn't it funny that all the ones who used to take the mickey are now working in the media? Only kidding, John!

I love seeing ex-players making their mark in the media, especially former teammates of mine. The people that I don't like seeing in the media are the ones who wouldn't give journalists and presenters the time of day when they were play-ers. That really gets on my nerves. Look, I'm not saying I got on with every sports journalist all the time – I didn't – but it was very rare that you would ever see me blank a reporter, which is what some players did, and probably still do. Sports journalists are responsible for three things: reporting on sport, sportsmen and sportswomen; taking us to task when we don't perform; and celebrating us when we do. In other words, they promote us – our leagues, our teams and ultimately our careers. Talk about biting the hand that feeds you. It's diabolical really. Politeness costs nothing.

As a pundit, just being a big name isn't good enough anymore. It always used to be. So-and-so would turn up, say a few words and that would be it, job done. These days it doesn't matter who you are: if you don't know your stuff, you will fall flat on your backside.

What makes the job really special, at least as far as I'm concerned, is that these days the job is almost completely inter-active and that's something you never got back in the 1970s, or even the 1980s. Social media, the Internet and radio phone-ins like *606* have completely revolutionized the industry to the point where sports coverage is just like the news – it rolls on and on and on. In the old days when a pundit spoke, you listened, and that was it. You either agreed with them or you didn't. So to be able to open up the discussion and pitch a fan against the pundit is just amazing. Hardly a week goes by with-out me getting involved in a spat with some irate fan and I wouldn't change that for the world. What some of them fail to realize is that they wind me up just as much as I do them. They can drive me crazy sometimes! It all makes for good radio, though. I mean, where would we all be without a bit of banter?

One of the most difficult things about being a pundit in such an interactive environment is that, as a neutral, you are constantly talking to people who are not, and so a balanced discussion is sometimes completely off the menu. To be fair, the vast majority of fans who call in manage to put their bias to one side for a bit, but you always get one or two who can't let go. Or at least I do! Does anyone remember Omar, the Liverpool fan who called *606*? What an absolute nightmare he was. He didn't like the fact that I had laid into his team, who, to be fair, had an absolute stinker that day losing 3–0 to West Bromwich Albion. He was like a Rottweiler. After giving me the usual 'you're not qualified to comment' rubbish, he said I should go back to *Dancing on Ice*. Then he said he was going to report me. Who to? The Pundit Police? Nee-naa nee-naa nee-naa. I put him right, though. 'Let's get one thing straight, Omar. It was *Strictly Come Dancing*.'

The one thing that I think threatens programmes like *606* is technology, although I'm talking about technology *on* the pitch, not off it. I think most people are agreed that goal–line technology works as that can tell you, yes or no, whether the ball has crossed the line, and at the end of the day that's what the game's all about. I can even see the argument for using camera technology for retrospective punishments, but only when the proof it provides is 100 per cent conclusive. When you start talking about bringing it in for live, in-game reviews then what the heck are we going to have left to talk about? This is especially relevant to something like *606* as it takes place straight after the matches and so a lot of the points the fans want make are about things just like that. Nothing gets me going like an argument with a fan about a disputed penalty. Please don't take that away from us!

Believe it or not, the biggest ongoing argument I have with fans isn't about penalties, players or a particular team: it's about whether I'm qualified to be a pundit in the first place. Seriously! There are a lot of Omars out there. They think that because I didn't play in the Champions League I shouldn't be allowed to comment on it. What a complete load of rubbish. If that's the case, how can you have players like Gary Neville talking about a relegation battle on TV? They have never been down there so how can they comment? Well, they can comment because they love the game and because they know it – end of story. Just because a doctor has never had measles doesn't mean he can't treat somebody who's come down with it. As I said, it's just rubbish. I've played against some of the best players in the world in my time and against some of the biggest teams. For me, captaining your country and spending so long in one of the best leagues in the world isn't a bad grounding for a football pundit, and the fact that I haven't played in one particular competition doesn't mean anything.

One thing that really annoys me – and to be honest it annoys quite a few other players – is when somebody like myself, who was never a world-beater, goes on TV and talks like they were. Words like self-deprecation don't seem to register with these people and I find it embarrassing. If you've never played at the very highest level and you go on TV and hammer somebody who has, you have to do that with an air of humility, otherwise you just look foolish. I could name at least two who fit into this bracket but I'm not going to.

Something you can't do as a pundit is to turn that round on the fan. Imagine if I said to a caller on *606*, 'I'm sorry, mate, but how can you comment on that Premier League game when you've never played professional football?' I would never say anything like that because I think it's wrong, but you can see my point. Absolutely everybody's entitled to their opinion.

Although I would argue until I was blue in the face that I'm more than qualified to comment on a Champions League fixture, that doesn't mean I don't learn things when I work with some of the legends. Of course I do. That's one of the great pleasures of being a pundit: you get to talk about the game with some of the best. I think we all bring something to the party, though.

I do like to drop myself in it sometimes, especially when I do a commentary. Sometimes my brain and mouth don't engage and, when that happens, I usually end up saying something a bit stupid. Back in my Leicester City days I had a reputation for saying daft things. In fact, my teammates even began labelling them 'Savisms'. One of their all-time favourites was when I asked one of them which train the Kray twins robbed. Well, I didn't know! Does anyone remember my 'Football is easy' comment? I got hit by pelters for that, especially from Gary Lineker. It was an FA Cup match, Aston Villa v. Leicester City, and it was an absolutely diabolical game. Neither team could keep the ball for more than a few seconds. Anyway, as I started to become more and more frustrated while commentating, I said something like, 'Come on lads, football is easy', meaning that it should flow. Within a few seconds of me saying that Gary Lineker tweeted, '"Football's easy" says @RobbieSavage8. I saw you play, mate. Is it really?' After that the floodgates opened. I still can't believe I said it.

I don't know what it is about me, but it doesn't matter what I'm doing, whether it be playing football, being a pundit, commentating or just having a laugh, people can't resist talking about me – even Gary Lineker. It's a gift, I suppose.

The feedback I receive for my match commentaries is pretty much the same as the feedback I receive for my punditry – mixed. Well, at least I'm consistent at getting inconsistent feedback. Believe me, it's not easy. I'm what's called a co-commentator, which means I chip in every now and again with a few carefully chosen words of wisdom, but to be a lead commentator – well, there's an art to it. Everything's instant so you really need to have your wits about you. You get no time to think. Not that many pundits get asked to commentate and those who do don't always say yes. I love it, though. I'm like a kid in a candy shop.

Remember those carefully chosen words of wisdom I just mentioned? Well, my top three would probably have to be:

'Outside the box, that's a free kick but inside the box, I don't think it's a penalty.'

'He's gone in with a two-feeted challenge!'

My best one from *606* would probably have to be:

'You need to take off your rose-scented glasses.'

There'll be more to come, don't you worry.

Unfortunately Twitter's not really a good place to be anymore. Being what you might call a 'personality pundit' and creating some debate does tend to bring out the idiots, more's the pity.

When I say idiots what I really mean are the Twitter trolls. Having an opinion is everyone's right, but when you start making it personal and become abusive – not to mention threatening – you're taking all the fun out of it. It's out of order and just unnecessary. I mean, what do they hope to achieve?

I used to absolutely love Twitter and up until a couple of years ago I was on there all the time. That's what I meant about the job being so interactive. The banter was excellent. Proper football discussions!

As always, though, a few idiots had to spoil it for everyone else, and when I started receiving really bad abuse I decided to cool it for a while. These days I use Twitter more like an information hub, somewhere to log on to first thing and see what's happening in the sporting world, and when I do tweet myself it's usually about what I'm up to rather than expressing an opinion. On the odd occasion that I do dare to tweet something about a team or a match I still receive a barrage of personal abuse, so what's the point?

I don't mind if people think, say or write that I'm rubbish pundit. That's fair enough. Tell me how I can improve. But why do they have to be so offensive? Have they ever met me? Probably not. So how can they judge me?

Yes, I divide opinion, and yes, I'm controversial, but I never resort to personal abuse. One thing I do know about social media is that it doesn't matter whether you're a pundit, a presenter or a player, you're never more than one reckless tweet away from getting the sack, and that's why you mustn't rise to the bait. I just wouldn't want to behave like that, anyway. Why go out of your way to upset somebody? What's wrong with just exchanging a few opinions and enjoying some banter? I don't know what makes the trolls tick, and if that makes me thick then fine, I'm thick, but I'm so glad I'm not like them. I would rather be consumed by football, thanks very much.

As I said earlier, being a good pundit isn't just about stats and first-hand experience: it's also about personality and presentation. People have got to want to watch you, listen to you or read your words, and, like it or not, some people enjoy what I do. I was always known as a divisive player when I was a professional, and it seems nothing's changed now I'm a pundit. I did hear a good one the other day, though. Somebody said to me, 'You're just like Marmite, you are – absolutely disgusting!' That made me howl. You have to be able to laugh at yourself from time-to-time, otherwise you'll never win anyone round. Once again, look at Lineker and Shearer. They're two of the most modest, laid-back people you could ever meet yet within the sport they're like gods. There's nothing worse than a pundit who takes themselves too seriously.

So what does the future hold for Savage the pundit? Well, I've no plans to retire I'm afraid, although these days I'm no longer on *Match of the Day*. That was a tremendous experience but like all good things it had to come to an end. At the end of the day I want to be the best pundit I can possibly be and so when BT Sport came in and offered me a new three-year deal – which included carrying on *Fletch & Sav* – I was delighted. I'll still get to do *606*, with Fletch, which is great. Being part of the *MOTD* team was a great honour, but when one of the big players steps in, puts their faith in you and gives you the opportunity to be part of something exciting and new, it's difficult to say no. We have been doing the *Fletch & Sav* show on BT Sport since the start of the 2014/15 season and it's been great fun. To be fair, it's more of a presenting job than pure punditry and that's something I've had to work really hard at. My limitations as a player meant that I could only ever go so far on the pitch and I was always aware of that, but as a presenter you don't necessarily have those restrictions, especially when you're working alongside people like Fletch. Providing you work hard, watch and listen, you should be able to improve.

It's funny but today I'm in almost the same position as I was as a player, in that to be successful I have to play to my strengths and work a lot harder than most. Sure, I might be progressing as a pundit and as a presenter, but I've had to work my backside off to get there. Yes, I make mistakes and, yes, people are going to have a laugh at my expense from time to time, but that's all part of the game. Bring it on!

I've also been lucky and have had the help of some marvellous people along the way. Lee Dixon, in particular, was very generous at the start, always sharing his research. There's nothing worse than a pundit who won't share their research. Alan Shearer has been great, too, and so have Michael Owen and Ian Wright.

Two other people who have been more than generous to me with regards to offering words of support and advice are Eamonn Holmes and Piers Morgan – two fanatical football fans who are at the very top of their professions. When I first started out as a pundit and co-commentator there were times when I lost confidence and became quite low, and Eamonn helped me through that period. I used to call him up and he would encourage me to keep going. He didn't have to do that. Piers Morgan is another Mr Marmite and, like me, I think he thrives on it. Whatever you think about him, though, he's very, very good at what he does and I love watching him. Like Eamonn he's been a great help to me and we love having him on *Fletch & Sav*.

To be honest, the worst thing about being a pundit is running into people you've had a go at. It happens quite often now and I'm sorry to say that there are several people who no longer speak to me because of something I've said. That's the price you pay for being honest, but it's the only way I can be. Some pundits just sit on the fence when it comes to being asked to put in a really honest opinion and that's their decision. Can you ever imagine me becoming like that? No chance. It's all or nothing.

For me, being offered the contract by BT Sport was like winning a cup-final medal and it is honestly one of my proudest achievements. It came at the end of what had been a very long apprenticeship, too. Do you know how long it took me to get on *Match of the Day*? Four years. I'll tell you what, though, I loved every minute of every game I covered back then, and do you know why? It was because I was learning a new trade within a sport that I absolutely adore.

I think my best moment as a commentator, so far at least, happened after a one-all draw between New Zealand and Italy at the 2010 World Cup. Chris Evans had been listening to the match while he was at the gym and was so impressed by my commentary that he invited me on to his Radio 2 show the next day. That was a massive vote of confidence for me, especially so early on in my career.

It all started for me as a commentator when Jonathan Wall, who is the controller of Radio 5 Live, heard a clip of me having an argument with the former Wales player, Leighton James. Leighton, who was a presenter on a Welsh football phone-in at the time, had often questioned my selection for the Welsh national team and when I eventually fell out with the manager, John Toshack, he naturally took his side. The upshot was that I decided to ring in and take Leighton to task one day and the ensuing discussion, which got quite heated, lasted about fifteen minutes. Leighton and I are fine now, by the way, but at the time our ruck was big news and luckily for me Jonathan not only heard the lot, but was impressed. The following day he asked me if I would like to have dinner with him and Darren Fletcher, and of course I jumped at the chance. We had a great night and ended up having a very long debate about whether Chris Waddle was a world-class footballer. I forget who won but because of that debate Jonathan decided to put Fletch and I together – first on a couple of co-commentaries and then on *606*. I've a lot to thank him for.

One of the first co-commentaries Fletch and I did together was at Aston Villa and I remember leaving the stadium not only with some much needed experience under my belt, but also a flattened nose. This book is full of stories about my nose and every single one of them involves pain.

We were commentating in the press box, which is next door to the directors' box, and separating these two areas is a brick wall. Everything was going swimmingly. It was a decent game and I thought I was doing okay. Then, all of a sudden, Stiliyan Petrov smashed the ball out of play, but instead of my eyes following the direction of the ball, which is what Mr Fletcher's did, I kept my eyes on the pitch. Big mistake! The ball flew past us to our right, hit the brick wall and then smacked me, full on. If Fletch hadn't been watching the ball he would have taken the hit but because he saw it coming he managed to move.

My God, it stung. It knocked my headphones clean off and made my nose bleed. The thing was, though, I just couldn't stop laughing. Neither could Fletch. He and I had known each other for years before we started working together at the BBC, but we had been anything but mates.

It all started way back in 2001 at a Derby v. Leicester match. I was playing for Leicester, Fletch was commentating for the BBC and the game in question was one of the most heated in which I ever played. To cut a long story short, I won a penalty towards the end of the game, which ended up winning us the match, and when the final whistle went instead of disappearing straight down the tunnel I milked it a bit and started kissing my Leicester badge. This, surprisingly enough, didn't go down too well at Pride Park and Fletch criticized me for it on air. A mate of mine told me about this afterwards and so I took him to task about it. We didn't speak for years after that. Now look at us, though. We're football's answer to Ant & Dec really – just a bit taller and a lot better looking.

I genuinely love every single one of my jobs. That's not lip service to my employers, it's a fact, and I like to think that passion comes over in everything I do. From a social point of view, however, co-presenting *Fletch & Sav* for BT Sport is without doubt my dream job and to be honest Fletch and I have to pinch ourselves sometimes. Basically, we get paid for sitting down with some of the greatest footballers ever and having a chat.

It sounds like such a simple format but believe it or not it's the only show of its kind. Yes, you have football shows with guests on, but the interviews are often short and they're just secondary to everything else. *Fletch & Sav* is about two things – the best guests and plenty of insight and banter. You show me a football fan who doesn't want to watch a bunch of ex-professionals arguing about the league and talking about the good old days.

Fletch & Sav came about because of *606*. Darren was the first to join BT Sport but even though Grant Best, who is the senior executive producer at BT Sport, had heard us on *606* and seemed to be a fan of what we did, he had a full quota of pundits at the time and so the suggestion of Fletch and I re-creating our partnership there never really came up. Gradually, though, my name was getting mentioned more and more (in a good way I think!) and so after a while Grant suggested that we all meet up.

Just like Jonathan Wall, Grant Best is football through and through and so we all ended up getting on like a house on fire. The question was though – after we'd finished that first meeting – if we actually were going to try to transfer what we did onto television what would be the best vehicle? After all, neither of us had experience presenting TV shows.

In the end we decided to go with the 'less is more' approach and just go with something very laid back and conversational, and I'm happy to say that it seems to be working really, really well. You see, I probably speak to Fletch at least three or four times every day and, despite us having a bit of a rocky start, we're now the best of friends. This alone took an awful lot of the pressure off at the start of *Fletch & Sav* and because of that we've both been able to grow in confidence.

Our aim now is to make the show essential viewing for football fans, and I honestly think we're going the right way about it.

Some of the guests we've had on the show have been amazing. Gazza was a really big coup for us, as was Russell Brand. I even had Roberto Mancini call me from the top of a mountain on one show and sing happy birthday to me!

Fletch and I are like an old married couple, though. We squabble like you wouldn't believe – always about football – and just when Fletch thinks he's won an argument I'll find a statistic or something that proves I'm right and then take great pleasure in calling him up and telling him. Sometimes this can be about ten days after we've started.

In all seriousness, I can't speak highly enough of Fletch. I'm a big, big fan of his as a broadcaster but to have him as a mate *and* work with him as much as I do is just brilliant.

What Would I Change about Football?

Well, believe it or not, apart from sorting out the current confusion surrounding the offside rule I wouldn't change that much about the modern game. Despite the ridiculous FIFA debacle, I think football is in a pretty good place at the moment. Attendances are good, there's plenty on TV and there are a lot of people talking about the game, and that's how you measure a sport's success. If nobody's talking about it that means nobody's interested and, so as far as I'm concerned, the more websites, TV channels, forums and radio shows there are both discussing and promoting the game of football the better. One thing I would alter, though, is that I would allow players to celebrate with fans when they score. These days they get immediately booked and I don't understand that. As long as it's done safely and as long as the players aren't diving head-first into the stands, what's the problem?

I scored thirty-seven goals in my senior domestic career. That might not seem like many to some but bearing in mind there's no greater feeling in the world than sending tens of thousands of people into seventh heaven, I consider myself pretty lucky. Seriously, scoring a goal is an unbelievable experience and so I can totally appreciate why players want to celebrate with the fans. Keep an eye on things by all means, but why not let everyone just enjoy the moment?

So apart from that rule I wouldn't change much about football, and in particular I wouldn't start using technology for in-game reviews by the officials, except for goal-line technology. Not yet, anyway. I'm all in favour of goal-line technology, but unless they can advance other technological elements to a point where it would only take a few seconds to deliver a completely conclusive decision, forget it. People are always comparing football to rugby and cricket in that respect. They think that because it serves a purpose in those sports it would automatically work in football, but I don't buy that. For a start, rugby and cricket are far more stop-start than football, which means the review process doesn't interfere with the pace of the game so much. Football's such a free-flowing sport and so I think it would be detrimental to have so many interruptions.

In cricket the technology works well because it proves beyond any reasonable doubt whether or not you've nicked the ball and whether it would have hit the stumps. Job done. In rugby, though, it doesn't always work like that and I've seen loads of decisions made that haven't actually been helped by the fact that technology has been available.

If the football authorities ever started using technology where it doesn't always produce a conclusive decision, who would actually make the final decision? Would it be the referee, a second referee or a panel of judges sitting with Simon Cowell in the gantry?

A few days ago Howard Webb told me that the technology is advancing at such a rate of knots that decisions can now be delivered to referees within about ten or fifteen seconds. Apparently you have two officials in a truck outside the ground and they can study the footage immediately. I have to say that I'm still not 100 per cent convinced about this but it's helping me keep an open mind. Both officials would have to be in complete agreement though, and decisions made on the spot every time, otherwise it just wouldn't work. It's food for thought.

Maybe there is one last thing that I would change about the game, which will lead me nicely on to my next chapter, and that's players crowding referees. Don't worry, I haven't gone soft! Most people think that it's wrong and I would have to agree with them. It's a form of intimidation, and you just shouldn't be allowed to intimidate officials. Argue with them if you must, but don't intimidate them. These days only two players are allowed to approach the ref at any one time, as opposed to seven or eight like you used to get, so I suppose that's a step forward. Well it would be if that rule was enforced consistently, but it's not. If you're going to introduce new rules to the game you have to make sure they're implemented, especially when they're supposed to prevent something as serious as intimidation.

I'm not sure where the problem starts, though – with the parents or with the football clubs? The majority of parents in football teach their kids to be respectful to their elders, but then so do the football clubs. But perhaps both parties need to be make sure that respecting the referee is a ingrained part of a young player's game.

Some people would like to see a ban on swearing altogether, but could you imagine what would happen? You'd have games finishing three-a-side! Basic respect should be taught and enforced at every level but whatever you do to combat bad behaviour it's going to take time to filter through. Do I think footballers should just accept referees' decisions and suddenly start calling them 'Sir'? Don't be daft! All I'm suggesting is a few ways of how we could improve things.

Football is tribal, and that's one of the things I love about it. It's also one of the reasons why we all behave like we do – players and fans. Players want to win, which is why they give the officials stick, and the fans want their team to win, which is why they give everyone stick – players, officials, each other, everybody!

During my time as a player I was called all the names under the sun and by all walks of life: doctors, nurses, lawyers, barristers, plumbers, factory workers. Even policemen. They were all united in calling yours truly this, that and the other. And that's the beauty of football: it transcends everything and everyone. It doesn't matter who you are or what you do, only one thing matters: your team.

Referees

This is going to be an interesting one. Don't get me wrong, being a referee is a very difficult job and it doesn't matter how good or experienced you are, mistakes can always be made. No question about it. If it's a fifty-fifty and you've got to make a decision, you might get it wrong. That's okay. But the frustration you feel as a player is overwhelming sometimes, which is one of the reasons why players react like they do. Intimidating a referee or their assistant is wrong, but perhaps if the players had more confidence in the officials and those in charge of them, things might be different.

Believe it or not, I think one of the problems is that referees don't receive enough credit, and because of that they quite possibly lack a bit of confidence. When they perform badly they get criticized by everyone, but when they perform well, which is, to be fair, the majority of the time, nobody says a thing. Could you imagine how players would react to that? It would destroy them. If I played badly I got hammered by everyone, and rightly so. But if I played well I got praised. I couldn't have coped with just the negative criticism. Referees probably usually have smaller egos than players so it doesn't affect them as badly. It's got to eat away at you, though, something like that.

Funnily enough we talked to Howard Webb about this on *Fletch & Sav* and what he had to say completely changed my view on the subject. You see, if he made a bad decision he would get hammered for it, but not just by the press and by the fans like a player would. Refs get hammered by everyone: the press, the players, the fans, the managers, the chairmen, the chief executives. Even their friends and family have a go, according to Howard.

He once awarded Luis Suárez a rather contentious penalty at Arsenal and when he switched on his phone after the game he had literally dozens of emails and texts, all from people he knew and all laying into him big time. That doesn't happen to players, or if it does happen, then only very, very rarely. The only message of encouragement Howard received that day was from his mum! She rang him to say it didn't matter what he did, she'd still be his mum.

That kind of pressure must be very, very hard to handle. And you're on your own, too. Yes, you have the assistant referees, but when the final whistle eventually goes and the reports start to get written it's going to be you who is ultimately responsible.

Howard also confirmed to me that referees are as much affected by confidence as players are, and why shouldn't they be? After all, they're only human. That's something else we forget, though! At the end of the day, referees are football fans like the rest of us and I think they should be applauded for taking on what must be one of the most difficult jobs in sport.

I've tried refereeing before and it's a thankless task. I refereed a couple of youth games a few years ago and by the end of the second one I was all for handing over the shirt to the nearest idiot barracking me and saying, 'Okay, mate, you do it.'

One thing we have to remember, though, is that nobody forces anyone to become a referee, and let's not forget that they're on good money these days and some of them even have agents. Is that good for the game? Well, it should be. You see when referees went professional we all thought that the standards would begin to rise a bit, and I think statistically they have. What doesn't seem to have improved, though, and this is only my opinion, is the amount of game-changing mistakes that are still being made – big mistakes that ultimately cost teams points. You see, when you turn professional certain things are expected of you. You have to train harder for one thing, which they do, and you have to become accountable. To be honest, before speaking with Howard I never really believed that referees were that accountable, but that's not the case. Their performances are scrutinized as closely as that of any player, and if and when they make a mistake or lose a bit of confidence they have people who work with them on setting things right. I think a lot of us were under the impression that if Premier League referees made mistakes they spent a week or two in the Championship and that was it.

You definitely get a different kind of person refereeing these days. Referees used to be strong, silent types who oozed authority. We didn't always agree with them, unless decisions were going our way, but there was a definite respect there. They were people like David Elleray. He was a housemaster at Harrow School when he was off the field, but he was a headmaster on it! He didn't take any rubbish, and we respected him for that. Well, sort of. I actually got on quite well with Mr Elleray and I think he was a very good ref, one of the best. Dermot Gallagher and Paul Durkin were another two I quite liked, along with Howard Webb, Mark Clattenburg and Peter Jones. Peter was excellent. I remember I played in a testimonial that he was refereeing once and I decided to rugby tackle him. We had a right laugh. It's different now, though, and if anything I think it's probably gone too far the other way, and that's the point that Howard was trying to make. We don't see referees as human beings a lot of the time and as a consequence we can't often relate to them. It just creates a barrier between us and them and ends up pushing them into a corner. If things are going to improve that barrier needs to come down a bit and relationships need to be built. I'm not suggesting that referees and players start going out on the town together. That wouldn't work at all. But they have to start becoming more accessible and approachable than they currently are.

When people hear me having a pop at referees some of them say, 'Hang on a minute, it's a hard job being a ref. You couldn't do it.' But I honestly think I could.

You see, I would like to see ex-players be given the opportunity to become professional referees, perhaps on some kind of fast-track system. I've discussed this with Fletch once or twice and he agrees with me.

As a former player your knowledge of the game should be extensive and you would be up to date with the vast majority of the rules and regulations. The chances are you'll also be fit, so why not? It happens a lot in other sports.

Despite my experiences refereeing those youth games it's something I would have been interested in had I not gone into the media.

I may be the wrong side of forty but I'm still as fit as a fiddle. What's more, I know a foul when I see one. Pressure from players wouldn't bother me one little bit and when it comes to the crowd – well, I think I've had quite a bit of experience in that department. More than most refs, in fact.

I've discussed this idea with Howard Webb and it will probably surprise you to learn that he actually agrees with me – up to a point. He thinks that drafting Premier League players into the game might well be a bridge too far as in some cases they could be as well-known as the players. That would obviously create all kinds of problems, not least because the majority of players, managers and fans would already have an opinion about him. Referees are there to run the show, not to be the star of the show. I agree with that.

Howard thinks that perhaps having ex-players from the lower divisions getting involved would work better, and that too makes sense to me.

What about after a match, though?

I would like to see referees come out after games and explain why they made certain decisions. Why not? I've made plenty of mistakes in my time. The thing is, though, I have always held up my hand and admitted it. I got Justin Edinburgh sent off, fair enough, I'm sorry, that was a mistake. Why can't referees do that? If they've made a controversial decision during a match, why shouldn't they explain why? And if they make a howler, why shouldn't they say sorry? That would make them more accountable, and it would also make them more human. Who knows, it might even help them to relax a bit, which might actually help them perform better.

I'm not simply suggesting a witch-hunt by the way – an opportunity for journalists to slag off referees. What I would like to see is a five- or ten-minute session about an hour after the game – once the referee has had a chance to view the high-lights – where they would sit down and answer a few questions. Nothing heavy, just a post-match chat talking about the good points and the bad points of the game. I think it would work wonders for the sport and, you never know, the refs might actually learn something. I know I would. I would love to find out what drives a referee to make certain decisions. I would find it fascinating. Will it ever happen? I doubt it.

England

Even though I'm not an England supporter I find this one of the most frustrating subjects in the modern game. Why? Because the England team seem to have been cursed at some point in the past and are now incapable of realizing anything like their full potential. It's a complete mystery. They've got the resources, the facilities, the players and the fans – everything's in place. No matter how hard they try, though, or who they put in charge, the same thing always happens – failure. That sums up England.

Look at Germany. They probably have a similar set-up to England with regard to players, resources, facilities and so on, yet they're world-beaters – they always have been. I hate to rub it in but in comparison to England's solitary major tournament win in 1966, which tends to get mentioned once or twice, the Germans have won seven: three European Championships and four World Cups, not to mention exactly the same again as runners-up. Astonishing!

Lots of people will say, 'Yeah, but you support Wales. What have they ever done?'

The difference is that we accept our limitations and manage to keep our expectations in check. We also have just three million people living in Wales compared with fifty-three million in England. It's all relative. The point I'm trying to make, though, is that England as a nation – not to mention a football team – has expectations that even Brazil would be proud of, yet time and time again they don't live up to them.

England have qualified easily for the 2016 European Championship because of their ranking. Now, once everybody's pumped up, the headlines will start.

'ENGLAND EXPECTS!'

'FOOTBALL'S COMING HOME!'

'THIS TIME BOYS!'

You know the kind of thing. It sells a lot of newspapers but ultimately it's just tempting fate.

And then, sure enough, once everyone has convinced themselves (me included) that, yes, although they went out in the first week of the last World Cup and made absolute fools of themselves, England could beat Germany, Spain, Italy, and so on to win the European Championship . . . then they'll put in a dismal display and fail at either the first or second hurdle. We've seen it time after time after time – but why? I'm not saying they should be winning everything they qualify for, and to be honest it's debatable whether England have the players to win either of the two big tournaments, but at the last time of asking they were out-performed by Costa Rica, Colombia, Nigeria and Greece, who all qualified for the knockout stages of the last World Cup. It's one of football's great mysteries, I suppose, like why I never got picked up by Real Madrid.

I admire the spirit of the fans massively, and if I were in that situation I would be exactly the same. The fact is that the fans deserve better. There have been a couple of positives along the way, like a fourth place at Italia 1990, but it's just not good enough.

Anyway, let's forget about the past. We can't do anything about that. What about now? What about Roy Hodgson?

Well, there's no denying it, he's got one of the most prolific CVs in football management and I have a massive amount of respect for him. Twenty-one teams including England. That's some going. He's won a few cups, too, and seems to have won the respect of both the fans and the players wherever he's managed. Roy's a decent gaffer, then, there's no denying that. But is he the right man to lead England to glory? I'm not sure. At the end of the day it's one of the biggest and most pressurized jobs in world football so it's no good just having a 100 per cent record in the qualifiers: you simply have to deliver at the tournaments.

I'm sorry, but how Roy survived the Brazilian debacle I'll never know. Let's face it: it really was an atrocious display – one of England's worst ever at a major championship.

The only thing I can put Roy's survival down to is that there was nobody else suitable to take over.

If Sven-Göran Eriksson, Fabio Capello or Steve McClaren had been in charge of England's ridiculously short-lived campaign in Brazil they would probably have been sacked immediately. And quite right, too! Roy was fortunate to keep his job in my opinion.

And I'm not just saying all this because I'm Welsh. I want

England to do well at major tournaments for the simple reason that it's good for morale. Everybody's happy! It's good for the domestic game, too. Sure, my first priority will always be Wales when it comes to international football, but I still want to see England play to their full potential. Or at least get close to it. When was the last time that happened? God, they're frustrating. It's bad enough for me as a Welshman so it must be awful for all you long-suffering England fans out there. I honestly don't envy you.

You can't just blame the manager, of course: the players have to take responsibility, too, and it must be hard for Roy when he hears young players complaining about so-called burnout. That's a massive bugbear of mine and it must have created a real dilemma for Roy. I mean, what on earth can you do in that situation, and what on earth is burnout? I'm not even sure it exists.

Let's look at a few facts, shall we?

When Cristiano Ronaldo was at Manchester United he averaged 4,000 minutes on the pitch every season, which is the equivalent to about forty-five matches. His game is all about explosive pace and sustaining levels of high-performance, yet I don't remember him complaining about being tired. In fact, if anything it helped turn him into the player he is today – three-time winner of the Ballon d'Or.

Sticking with Manchester United for a second, look at the Class of '92. How many times were they rested once they'd established themselves in the first team? They weren't – or at least very rarely – because Alex Ferguson knew he could rely on their fitness, and that getting games under their belts was the best way to help them progress at the highest level.

Of course, managers have to watch their players' workloads. How else are they going to get through busy periods like Christmas and New Year? But honestly, when I hear stories of managers saving young players from tiredness it makes me want to explode.

Is it exclusive to the English game? I'm not sure. Once again though, I don't remember seeing Lionel Messi being rested that much, do you?

Some people think more of the younger England senior players like Raheem Sterling should go on Under 21 duty to get more international experience. Possibly. As a player though, if you've played thirty-eight Premier League games and one or two England senior games, and then suddenly get a phone call asking you to go and play with the Under 21s, wouldn't you see that as a step backwards? I know I would. The reality is that if you're playing Under 21 football on a regular basis just to experience international football, by the time a major tournament comes along you'll be lucky to be on the bench of the senior team. Pulling on an international shirt, regardless of which sport you're playing, should be the most galvanizing thing a sportsperson can do; yet with a lot of England players it actually seems to hinder them. I'm certainly not going to name names here because that would be very unfair but it's been noticeable for a number of years now. Could it be the expectation? Some would suggest that they have the same level of expectation at their clubs, but there's a difference here. When you play for a club you share the responsibility of expectation with your teammates, week-in, week-out, and each one shoulders some of the burden.

Without that camaraderie the stress would be unbearable. When it comes to international football it's very difficult to create the same kind of atmosphere as some of the players don't even know each other. These days, players are superstars and there are egos, agents, social media and rumours at play. I don't think it's impossible to recreate the same club atmosphere, but I think it only happens in very special circumstances. Get that right, though, and I think you're in a really good position.

It's not applicable to the Englands or the Spains of this world, whose players all play in the top divisions, but from Wales's point of view I think having a few players from the Championship certainly helps – players like Chris Gunter, Jazz Richards and Hal Robson-Kanu. That burden of expectation is superseded by pride and enthusiasm and it causes a ripple effect throughout the squad.

But let's get back to Roy. Look at his choices for the 2014 Ballon d'Or: defensive midfielder Javier Mascherano, defender Philipp Lahm and goalkeeper Manuel Neuer. Cristiano Ronaldo and Lionel Messi didn't even get a look in. What does that say about Roy Hodgson's mentality, though, not to mention the fact that in the last World Cup England were defensively poor? If I was an England fan I would be worried.

Look, I'm all in favour of getting behind your national manager, but if you compare the way Roy's been treated to some of his predecessors, it's chalk and cheese.

Martin Glenn, the FA's chief executive, said at Soccerex just recently that Roy had learned a lot from the two tournaments he'd taken England to and that he was far and away the best coach England could have. On the flipside he also said quite recently that if England had a bad Euros Roy would not expect to be kept on, and I think he was right to come out and say that. It's great to be supportive but at the same time you have to be realistic.

If the worst does happen in France next year, that's when it'll get interesting for me. You see, England may have a lot of potential on the pitch, but they also have a hell of a lot of talented people off it, and in my opinion it's about time they began utilizing some of these people.

Starting at the top, perhaps in a director of football-type role, how about Glenn Hoddle? He's one of the most tactically astute coaches I've ever come across. Why not get him to come up with the blueprint for how England should play in future and then filter that down to the Under 21s and so on? In my opinion Glenn is one of the best coaches in the world yet he has nothing to do with the national team. He also commands a tremendous amount of respect and from what I've seen he has a fantastic rapport with players. I've worked with Glenn on *Fletch & Sav* once or twice and you should see the other guests when they meet him. He's a big, big name in the game.

Below Glenn Hoddle I'd have Gary Neville and maybe one or two other the other lads from the Class of '92. And before you say, 'Well, he's never even managed at club level before', look at Mark Hughes. He did a fantastic job for Wales and came within a match or two of getting us to our first major tournament in about a hundred years. He'd never managed at club level before.

Gary Neville inspires confidence in people and he is a strong character – one of the strongest I know. That, for me, is exactly what England lack – character. Gary Neville and Glenn Hoddle would be a formidable partnership in my opinion and would complement each other perfectly.

Seriously though, I'd also bring in Phil Neville and Nicky Butt and maybe even Scholesy if he was up for it. Those lads had a massive effect on English football when they came onto the scene, and I think they could again.

These are just a couple of suggestions, of course, but you see where I'm coming from. This country has a wealth of footballing talent off the pitch, some truly inspirational people. Get them on board!

Look, if England win the European Championship, or at least get to the semi-finals, then we'll talk again. You see, that's the beauty of being a pundit: you can change your mind when circumstances change. I'm afraid I can't see that happening, though. I wish Roy and his lads all the best, I really do, but I just think it's going to be a step too far.

Anyway, that's enough about England. Let's get on to my boys, shall we?

Wales

I've been looking forward to this chapter because as I write Wales are on the brink of qualifying for their first major tournament since 1958 – almost sixty years! In fact, just one win from our last two games and we'll have done it.

In the past Welsh football seems to have gone in cycles. When we were strong in attack, we were poor in defence or had nothing in midfield, and then vice versa, and so it went on. I remember when Ian Rush and Mark Hughes played up front. They were my first Welsh heroes. We had a decent defence back then but not much in midfield, so they never really amounted to anything. By the time I played things had improved a bit. We had Ryan Giggs, John Hartson and Craig Bellamy up front, a world-class midfield featuring Simon Davies, Mark Pembridge and the mercurial Savage, but we didn't have the strongest back four. Sure, we came close to qualifying, and to be fair we should have. That's like coming second, though. At the end of the day it means nothing.

I remember watching Wales as a child. It was disappointment

after disappointment after disappointment. It was the same as watching England really, just with a lot less expectation. If somebody had said to me back then that in twenty years' time Wales would be on the brink of qualifying for the European Championship I wouldn't have believed them. I don't think anyone would.

Today, I would say that Wales are very nearly the finished article. We've got a fantastic core of players, are strong in most areas and, in my opinion, are definitely capable of going places. Hopefully to France for Euro 2016.

Of the twenty-three-man squad Chris Coleman named for the match against Belgium on 12 June 2015, thirteen were plying their trade in the Premier League and one in La Liga. For a country of just over three million people whose first sport is rugby that's not too shabby.

Don't get me wrong, I'm not saying that Wales are suddenly going to charge in and start winning major tournaments. Of course we're not. At least not until the next World Cup! Honestly, we take nothing for granted when it comes to international football in Wales and just being at a major tournament will be amazing.

I'll tell you what, though, I reckon that if Wales played England at the Millennium Stadium in front of a sell-out crowd they would do the Three Lions. I said this a while ago in the media and got slaughtered for it, but I stand by every word. Remember what I said: England are lacking character – and Wales have that in abundance at the moment. Sure, they don't have the strength in depth that England have, but if Chris Coleman could pick his strongest team I honestly think they would win.

Some people think that you can't win or achieve anything without the best players but I couldn't disagree more. Look at Brian Clough. He won two European Cups on the bounce with Nottingham Forest back in the late 1970s – an achievement of Real Madrid-type proportions – and his players were not the best in Europe at the time. In fact, some would say they weren't even the best in England. So how did he do it, then? How did *they* do it? Was it a fluke? What, two European Cups on the bounce? Don't be daft.

As good as the Wales team of today are I still don't think they're as good man-for-man as the team I played with under Mark Hughes when we were on the verge of qualifying in 2003. We performed brilliantly throughout qualifying for the 2004 European Championship but, do you know what, when it came to getting over that final hurdle, we bottled it. It's as simple as that. We had a cracking team, too. The line-up for that final match against Russia was: Paul Jones, Mark Delaney, Andy Melville, Danny Gabbidon, Darren Barnard, Jason Koumas, Me, Gary Speed, Andy Johnson, Ryan Giggs and John Hartson. We really were a very, very solid team but, despite that, we just didn't have the character that these boys have.

How they performed like they did against Belgium – who, let's not forget, are ranked second in the world as I write – is almost beyond me. And I'll tell you what, if they do manage to qualify for Euro 2016, which they will, I think it'll be one of the biggest achievements ever in the history of the Welsh national team.

The majority of people reading this won't agree with me when I say that Wales would beat England if they played now, but I'll bet you any money you like that there'll be more than a few England fans out there who agree with me. You mark my words.

Having the world's most expensive player in your national squad can work either way, and I think it's a testament to Gareth Bale's character that in spite of all his problems at Real Madrid in his second season – not to mention the pressure of being the world's most expensive footballer – he still comes into the Wales squad and performs like he does. Perhaps he sees it as a release from everything. For me, Gareth Bale thrives on being the superstar of a team like he was at Spurs, but I think he gets overshadowed at Real. We've had superstars in the team before, of course – people like Mark Hughes and Ryan Giggs – but neither of them had the spotlight on them like Gareth does. It's a new experience for everybody.

From my point of view, when I played alongside somebody of Gareth's stature – i.e. Giggsy – I fed off it. I've seen players who become intimidated playing in the same team as superstars but for me it's an inspiration – a privilege. I always wanted to impress them. Seriously, when you play alongside the likes of Christophe Dugarry and Roberto Mancini and one of them says 'well done' after a game, it's the best feeling in the world. The Wales lads obviously get that completely.

How about the manager then?

I'm a firm believer that the manager of a national team – regardless of sport – should be from that country: end of story. For me that's been one of England's failings. They've wasted a ridiculous amount of time and money on foreign managers in the past and have treated one or two of their English managers appallingly. It shouldn't be like that, and especially in a sport as big and as important as football. I couldn't think of anything worse than playing for Wales and being managed by an Italian or a Swede. No offence to either of those nationalities, of course, and I'm sure they would be the same. Could you imagine if a Welshman went to manage Italy? He wouldn't last five minutes. No, for me that was a big, big mistake for England and hopefully they'll have learned their lesson.

I think that in Chris Coleman, who incidentally is probably the proudest Welshman on earth, Wales have got a manager who could go on to become their best ever and he too has shown enormous character. There are two things in particular that have really impressed me about Chris. The first one is that this job would possibly have been his last chance in a big managerial role and so to come back after one or two disappointments and do as well as he's done is just amazing. Secondly, taking over from the late and forever great Gary Speed was never going to be easy, especially as he'd done such a fantastic job, and the respect, patience and timing Chris has shown here does him a massive credit. Not many people know this, but just a few weeks after Gary passed away Wales were awarded the title of FIFA's 'Best Movers' of the year, having won more ranking points than any other nation in 2011. That wasn't given out of sympathy; it was won fair and square, and that's obviously one of one of the many reasons why Chris decided to take his time before changing things. When somebody as loved and respected as Gary Speed passes away – somebody who in his case had taken Wales from 117th in the world to 45th – people are going to want to cling on to their way of doing things for a while. It's only natural. Coming in and making your mark immediately would have been disrespectful to Gary's memory, not to mention his talent, and Chris Coleman has done the opposite. Knowing Chris like I do, I wouldn't have expected anything less. He's a true gentleman.

Some people have given John Toshack credit over the years for bringing through some of this current crop of Welsh players but I think you have to thank the clubs for that. As the national manager you'll be made aware of every Welsh player available to you and it's your job to choose the best. It's the clubs who turn them into the players they are. Several years ago John gave a non-league player a run out for Wales, a lad called Steve Evans from Wrexham. I've got nothing against Steve but was that really necessary given the players the manager had at his disposal? I think it was nonsensical.

Do you know what I love most about what's happening with the Welsh team at the moment? The fans. The atmosphere they've been creating at the Cardiff City Stadium has been unbelievable. Even though Wales could probably sell out the Millennium Stadium again I think they should stay where they are. It's a real cauldron when Wales play and I absolutely love going there.

Of the sixteen games Wales have played at the Cardiff City Stadium they've won eight, drawn three and lost five. That's not a bad record for us. By the way, the last time I looked at the FIFA rankings Wales were ranked ninth (yes, ninth!) in the world – two places above Spain and one place above the mighty England. How times have changed, eh?

I'll tell you one big difference between watching Wales at the Cardiff City Stadium and watching England at Wembley: when the players come out for the second half at Cardiff the stadium's full, whereas at Wembley you've got thousands of empty seats. The difference is that there are more obvious football fans in Cardiff and less corporate guests. Even after the game against Belgium the stadium was still packed. There was nobody sneaking off early to catch an early train or a last pint that night. That's another reason why I don't want us to move back to the Millennium Stadium because if we did I think we might lose a bit of that atmosphere.

Incidentally, if I was in charge of international football I would ban friendlies altogether. I loved playing for my country but apart from winning another cap, I just can't see what purpose they serve. As a spectacle they're boring and as a player they're meaningless. Okay, so you get a cap. That's brilliant. But doing what? There are more than enough qualifying games to get experience, and if every national team is in the same boat, what does it matter?

So how does the future look for the Welsh national team? Well, as far as I'm concerned it's never looked brighter, not in my time anyway. We've got Gareth Bale, the most expensive player in the world, Aaron Ramsey, whose been performing brilliantly for Arsenal, and Ashley Williams, who is an excellent captain. The Under 21s are doing okay, too. Seriously, things are looking good for Wales, and it's about time.

My All-time Premier League XI

It won't surprise you to learn that there are one or two Manchester United players in my all-time Premier League XI, but there's no escaping the fact that since the league began back in 1992, United have won more titles than every other team put together. That's madness!

Goalkeeper

David de Gea has been United's Player of the Season for the past two years running yet they haven't won a thing, whereas Peter Schmeichel, the best goalkeeper the Premier League has ever seen, never won Player of the Season at United and they won everything. That's the measure of how good that team was.

What an incredible goalkeeper Peter Schmeichel was. That semi-final replay against Arsenal in 1999 – everybody talks about Ryan Giggs's goal (which was astonishing) but what about Schmeichel's save from Dennis Bergkamp in the last minute? Absolutely world class.

Right Back

I can't look any further than Gary Neville for this position. In addition to the fact that he's quite simply the best right back the Premier League's ever seen he also has to be one of its most consistent players. Four hundred performances for Manchester United over the years and more trophies than you can shake a stick at. The man was a machine.

When I was an apprentice at United Gary Neville wasn't the best full back. That was actually a lad called Chris Casper who unfortunately had to retire from football aged just twenty-four. Gary Neville was playing centre-half at the time, but over the years developed into United's greatest right back.

The one thing I had in common with Gary as a player – and there weren't many, I admit that – was that although everybody apart from our own fans absolutely hated us, most people would want us in their team. I can't pay him a bigger compliment than comparing him to me and now one of us is one of Britain's most loved pundits!

Actually, there is one more thing. Gary Neville has perhaps the driest sense of humour known to man and has over the years come out with some absolute belters. He was responsible for one of my all-time favourites on Twitter. Jamie Carragher tweeted Gary a photo of himself with a couple of young Manchester United fans, and some Liverpool fan jumped in saying, 'if you put on one of them shirts you'll catch a disease' – or words to that effect. Quick as a flash Gary Neville said, 'He might catch that disease called "Winning" and spread it through your lot!' It made headlines all over the world. He could be the next Jack Dee.

Centre Backs

Talking of Twitter, my next choice and I have had some right battles on there over the years, but they are nothing compared to the battles we had on the football pitch. Rio Ferdinand would be my first choice centre back for several reasons. First, just like Gary Neville, he played at the very top of the league for the vast majority of his career, making over 500 appearances in the Premier League. That alone would have to put Rio in contention, but it was his characteristics as a player that, as far as I'm concerned, make him one of the best centre backs the game's ever seen. His style of play was totally different to what we'd been used to in English football. Back then defenders didn't usually 'distribute' the ball like Rio did, they hammered it. When you also take into account his technical ability, his positioning, his pace, his strength and his natural ability to read a game – well, you would be hard pushed to find anyone better. I remember thinking to myself when he first started playing, 'Thank God I'm not a striker!' I did kick his backside in the tunnel one day so in my book that makes me harder than him.

My second centre back would have to be either John Terry or Jaap Stam. Jaap Stam was terrifying to play against. He looked so intimidating. I put in more than my fair share of tackles over the years but I'll tell you what, I can't remember putting in many on him. I may be a bit daft, but I'm not stupid! A few years ago he came an impressive third in *606*'s 'Best Bald Footballer' list, so he certainly made his mark.

If I had to choose between the two, though, I would probably go with John Terry. Once again you can't ignore his consistency: 460 games for Chelsea and probably loads more to come. It's not bad, is it? He's one of those players who seem to get better with age and ever since he decided to quit the international game he's flowered. In fact, the 2014/15 season was probably one of the best of his entire career. What impresses me most, though, is performing like that after he had been all but written off. You see, I know what it's like to get written off, a lot of players do, but not that many know what it's like to come back again. It's a big ask. He did it, and what's more he's been brilliant. Even Rio Ferdinand said that his performances in the 2014/15 season were nothing short of outstanding. Not bad for a thirty-four-year-old. Sorry Jaap!

Left Back

Here, I would go with Ashley Cole, no hesitation. Once again he's consistent, which is important, but he's also probably the best attacking defender the Premier League has ever seen and one of the first modern-day full backs. As far as I know, Ashley modelled much of his game Roberto Carlos and he's been brilliant to watch – but awful to play against – ever since. He was another one I remember seeing and thinking, 'Wow, look at him!' He's also one of the most instinctive players I've ever come across and has no problem reading the game. I suppose you have to if you're fulfilling so many roles. Great player, and very underrated.

Midfield

First on the list in the middle of the park would have to be Steven Gerrard, the man Pelé once called 'the best footballer in the world'. What an outstanding player he is.

Like Alan Shearer, Steven never really got to play with the greatest players in the Premier League, or at least not on a consistent basis, and that to me was a pity. Imagine if he'd played week-in, week-out with players like Roy Keane or Patrick Vieira. The mind boggles! You have to admire his loyalty, though, and it's the same with Alan Shearer. As it was they had to make do with all kinds, yet it didn't make any difference. But to lead a team like Liverpool, who let's be honest have hardly set the Premier League alight, to a Champions League final in 2005 and then actually win the flaming thing after being 3–0 down to AC Milan! Well, it's an achievement that I'm not sure will ever be bettered by an English team in Europe. I know this all-star team is supposed to be about the Premier League but, come on, that was just ridiculous. Yes, he wasn't the only player on the field that day, but he was the one leading them, and if he hadn't been playing I reckon it might have been a cricket score against Liverpool. He was the difference. The reason Liverpool turned it round and won.

We're back to the Manchester United Class of '92 for my next choice – Mr Paul Scholes. For his passing alone you would have to have him in there, but then when you include all those fantastic goals he scored, well, you just can't leave him out.

He was another English midfielder who had the likes of Zinédine Zidane and Edgar Davids falling at his feet, and you can understand exactly why. In fact, when Zidane was once asked what it felt like being the best player in the world, he replied, 'Ask Paul Scholes.' Even the great Brazil international Sócrates was quoted as saying, 'I love watching Paul Scholes. He's good enough to play for Brazil.'

In my opinion he was one of the most talented and versatile midfielders who ever drew breath. Awful dresser, though.

Now for the left side of midfield. Okay, as much as I admire every single player in this list, the one whose name sprang most immediately to mind when I sat down and began putting it together was Ryan Giggs – probably the Premier League's most celebrated player and definitely its most decorated. What's the figure – 8,457 appearances for Manchester United? It's something like that. What a professional: *the* model professional of modern-day football. Seriously, it doesn't matter which team you support, if you have kids who are into football and want to give them a role model, look no further than Ryan Joseph Giggs.

Out on the right I'm going with the one and only Cristiano Ronaldo. It was either going to be him, Marc Overmars or Robert Pirès, and in the end, simply because of what he's already achieved in the game I had to go with Ronaldo. Sorry Arsenal! You do okay with the strikers, though, I promise.

Does anyone else remember Ronaldo's debut in 2003, when Manchester United beat Bolton 3–0? He was astonishing that day, like nothing we'd ever seen before. Pity he let it all go to waste.

Strikers

With so many great strikers in the history of the Premier League you just have to go with two up front, and my first choice here would have to be my old mate, Mr Alan Shearer (even with his tight-fitting shirts on *MOTD*), because he is without doubt one of the finest forwards I have ever clapped eyes on. To score a total of 283 goals for teams like Newcastle, Blackburn and Southampton – who, let's face it, are hardly weighed down with trophies – well, it's ridiculous. And what a striker of a ball he was. Absolutely sublime.

My second striker would have to be Thierry Henry. I have

only one word to describe this man – unplayable. A genius. He can also be as clever off the pitch as he usually was on it, which is annoying. I remember when we were covering the 2014 Brazil World Cup together for the BBC. Thierry, Clarence Seedorf and I were talking to Gary Lineker about the upcoming France v. Honduras game and I was making the point that if Honduras tried to get among the French, just like we used to *try* and do against Thierry and his pals, then they might just do okay.

'We were like flies round you, weren't we, Thierry?' I boasted. 'We wouldn't leave you alone for a minute!'

'We managed,' was his simple two-word reply.

The entire studio fell about, not to mention several million people at home. What a great line, though. My God, he's smooth.

I absolutely hated playing against him, and against his fellow 'Invincibles' at Arsenal. Let's just say that scoring 175 Premier League goals in just 259 appearances makes him absolutely indispensable. Va va voooooom!

The Savage All-time Premier League XI Teamsheet
Peter Schmeichel
Gary Neville
Rio Ferdinand
John Terry
Ashley Cole
Steven Gerrard
Paul Scholes
Ryan Giggs
Cristiano Ronaldo
Alan Shearer
Thierry Henry

Vanity

I'm going to dispel a popular urban myth here – or at least I'm going to try to. You see, believe it or not, I am not that vain. Yes, you read correctly, I AM NOT VAIN! Honestly, I'm not.

The problem is people these days tend to confuse vanity with simple good grooming, which is something I've always taken very seriously. What's wrong with having pride in your appearance?

I'm not saying I've always been on the button fashion-wise, and I probably spent the best part of twenty years as the world's number one Don Johnson look-alike, but I wasn't doing that for anyone else. I didn't want to impress anybody. I was doing that for me, for Robbie Savage.

At the end of the day it's a case of each to their own. Some people are into nice wine, and some people are into fast cars and clothes – and I happen to love fast cars and clothes. I think the way I dress is probably just an extension of my personality. Sometimes I'll be a bit OTT, and sometimes I'll tone it down a bit. Whatever I wear, though, it usually attracts attention and it's the same when I open my mouth – I attract attention. Is it done intentionally? Absolutely not. I have never been asked by anybody I've worked for to act in a controversial manner and I have never gone out of my way to do so. Yes I have *been* controversial, but it's always happened naturally. And it's the same with how I look. Love me or loathe me, I'm just being myself.

Incidentally, you do realize you're reading a book written by a man who was once voted 'third top football babe in the United Kingdom' behind Kirsty Gallacher and Louise Redknapp. Third? I was robbed!

My hair is undoubtedly the star of the show. It's my trademark. It doesn't matter what I wear or even what I say sometimes, my hair will always get the headlines. If you Google the words 'Robbie Savage hair', over 47,500 articles come up. 47,500! That's absolutely astonishing.

Prior to my extremely well-publicized haircut, people used to liken my locks to a lion's mane, which I didn't mind one bit. Once again, though, I was also accused of wearing it like that just to attract attention, which is complete rubbish. As I said, what's wrong with taking 'pride' in your appearance? Sorry!

That haircut, though. What a nightmare! Seriously, I could have been caught robbing a bank and I still wouldn't have got half the headlines my hair did when I got it all chopped off.

I had it cut at the start of the 2014/15 season, but the debate as to whether I should take the garden shears to it started even before that. The *Daily Mirror*, for whom I write a weekly column, ran a poll on Twitter asking if I should keep it and the majority of their readers said I should. 'Phew!' I thought. 'Thank God for that!' But even though I was quite relieved at the time I had been having a few doubts about the old mop. The first seed was planted at an airport one day when I was catching a plane to Portugal. When I got to the check-in desk I realized I'd picked up my wife's passport by mistake.

'A quick shave and some make-up and I'd never have noticed,' said the girl on the check-in desk.

Then, in June 2014, just as I was trying to catch a flight out to Brazil to cover the World Cup for the BBC, it happened again, the wrong passport! This time though I'd actually had a quick look at the passports at home and had mistaken my wife for me. Incidentally, that particular case of mistaken identity says a lot more about my eyesight than it does about my wife's looks. She is an absolutely stunning-looking woman, which means I can't have been that far behind her!

'Nah,' I thought. 'This has gone far enough.'

There comes a time in a man's life when he needs to act his age and not his shoe size (I'm working on it!) and that goes for how he looks, too. I was almost forty at the time and I'd had virtually the same hairstyle for about twenty years. I was a pundit now, not a footballer, and although there are no rules or regulations as to how you're supposed to present yourself as a pundit I thought a change might be as good as a rest. Why not? I was about to buy a new pair of straighteners and some curlers so instead I thought, 'I'll put the money towards a new haircut.'

So off I went to see my hairdresser, Howard Yuill, who has been making me look fantastic for years. We had a few consultations and during one of them he started going on about quiffs and about 1950s pompadour styles. This made me very, very nervous. I thought, 'I'm going to end up looking like The Fonz if I'm not careful!' I trusted Howard, though, and in the end he did a brilliant job. Well, I think so.

And do you know where my mane ended up? You'll never guess. It's in the National Football Museum in Manchester alongside items such as Bobby Moore's shirt from his legendary game against Pelé's Brazil in the 1970 World Cup finals in Mexico, Sir Stanley Matthews shirt and kit from the 1953 'Matthews' FA Cup final, George Cohen's shirt from the 1966 World Cup final and commentary legends John Motson's old sheepskin coat. I'm not kidding you. It's there, pride of place, one of over 15,000 exhibits.

I'll tell you what, though, having shorter hair certainly took some getting used to. The day after the haircut I got in the shower, reached for the shampoo, and before I knew it, I was done! What used to take me at the very least twenty minutes was now taking me no more than ten. It was horrible. 'Oh God,' I thought. 'Bang goes my excuse for being late.'

People sometimes say, 'If you didn't have money, would you still be the same person?' and I always say, hand on heart – yes, I would. It wouldn't matter if I was working at a call centre in Wrexham or on an oil rig in the North Sea, I would still be ribbing people and trying to make them laugh. I would still be getting on people's nerves! As one BT Sport colleague said, 'With Sav, it's just one cheap, inoffensive gag after another.'

And you don't have to have lots of money to take a pride in your appearance, for heaven's sake. You just cut your cloth accordingly. I enjoy buying designer clothes, but at the end of the day I've earned that money, so why not? It's not the be-all and end-all, though. If it all went tomorrow, so be it. As long as I had my family and friends around me I wouldn't give a damn. Honestly.

Having money gives you choices. That's the way I look at it. The trick is not to let it go to your head. Look at Keith Gillespie. I used to room with Keith when I was at Manchester United and as well as being one of the most talented footballers I have ever seen in my life – and a really, really good lad – he was also one of the biggest gamblers. He would gamble on anything. I never saw it as a problem when I was young. I just remember seeing loads and loads of screwed up betting slips by his bed. It was only a few years later that I realized he might actually have had a problem. Keith decided to come clean about his addiction a long time ago; he had apparently lost over £7 million. I don't think having money was the root cause of Keith's problems but it certainly allowed him to feed his addiction. There was nobody there to cure that, unfortunately. No pastoral care, I think they call it. I'll tell you what, though, if you took any young lad who liked a flutter and put him somewhere miles away from home with time on his hands and a shed-load of money, what do you think would happen? It's a recipe for disaster.

So, am I vain? If I was vain don't you think I would have a bit of work done? Of course I would. The truth is it doesn't really bother me. I've got a big nose. So what?

Do I play up to the whole 'poser' image at all? Yes, from

time-to-time, of course I do. It's part of who I am, in a way. But that's because I'm not afraid to have a laugh at myself. I can be as self-deprecating as the next football pundit when I want to be.

Injuries

This could be one heck of a depressing chapter if I'm not careful. I mean, how do you find a positive in being injured?

What I'm going to do is tell you about one of my own experiences, as well as give you a few words on what it's like not being able to play.

I had two career-threatening injuries while I was a player and, unbeknown to me, one of them very nearly killed me. Some of you will be disappointed it didn't but it appears I'm made of sterner stuff.

I can't think of many jobs outside sport where injury is a constant and recurring threat and, believe me, if it's not affecting you physically it affects you mentally, especially if you have teammates who are out long-term.

It honestly doesn't matter if you're a footballer on £100,000 a week or a ten-year-old playing football with his mates, if you get told you can't play the game you love it's like a living nightmare.

The first time I experienced that feeling was when I was about eight years of age. It wasn't down to injury, it was down to my age, but the feeling was still the same.

When I was a kid I was brought up in a cul-de-sac. It was quite an idyllic upbringing. We were a very close family – and still are – and inside our little house lived my late dad Colin, my mum Val, my older brother Jonathan and me. Apart from my family, the only thing I cared about in life was football. *Nothing* else mattered.

I was a decent player from a young age so I used to play a lot with the older lads. I used to love this as it meant I got to play with players more on my level, but the problem was that I had to stop playing earlier than they did and when that happened it was gut wrenching. There I would be, scoring goal after goal in our cul-de-sac and making mincemeat of the opposition, when all of a sudden I would hear our door go.

'Oh no,' I would say to myself. 'He's coming!'

And then within a few seconds I'd hear my dad shout the seven words I feared most in the world.

'Robert. It's time to come in, son.'

My parents were both sticklers for things like manners and routine and so it didn't matter what I said or what I did – that was it – I was in.

'But Daaaaaaad! It's still light. Can't I stay out for another ten minutes?'

'No, you can't. Now I won't tell you again, IN!'

I bet there's more than a few of you reading this who experienced the same thing. It was the worst time of the day and each time it happened it honestly felt like the end of the world.

As I followed my dad back in I would keep looking behind me to see how the other boys were getting on. Then the moment I'd wolfed down my beans on toast and thrown on my pyjamas, I would run down the stairs, straight into the living room, sit on the edge of the settee, rest my chin on the window ledge and then watch the lads until it got dark. As they carried on playing I would be dishing out advice under my breath.

'Shoot for heaven's sake! Awwwww, come on, that was useless!'

The summer evenings seemed so long back then and I would sometimes be sitting there for hours. It was awful and what I should have done was watch *Family Fortunes* with everyone else, but I just couldn't help myself. It was football and if I couldn't play then I would just have to watch. Maybe I was born to be a pundit.

That was my first taste of being denied the game I love and throughout my career as a professional, and for some time after that, whenever I wasn't able to play football I experienced a variation of that same feeling I had when I was a boy.

The first big injury I suffered, the one that nearly killed me, happened at Charlton Athletic on 17 April 2004, although it wasn't until I visited a specialist during the summer that I realized I was injured – sorry, on the brink of death! Did I mention that I am a hypochondriac? Well, I am. In fact, I'm dreadful. One cough and I'm dying.

I once ate some beetroot and the next day when I saw that my pee had turned red I panicked and ran to see the doctor.

'Have you eaten any beetroot?'

'No!'

'Are you sure?'

'Well, I might have eaten a couple of slices. That can't be it, though. I'M ILL!'

See what I mean.

Anyway, we only had seven or eight games to go until the end of the season and we were lying sixth in the Premier League. Not only was it one of the best seasons Birmingham City had ever had but it was also one of the best I'd ever had. In fact, I probably played some of my best football that season.

Sometime during this match against Charlton I fell on my head, and as I hit the ground I felt what seemed to be like a strong electric current run through my arms. I have to say it was one of the most horrible things I've ever experienced and after the game I went straight to see the physio and the doctor.

Stupidly I never went for a scan and instead had my neck manipulated for a few days. After that things were okay for a while but then I started to get pins and needles in my arms and legs. A few weeks on it got so bad that I went to see a specialist. The day before I saw him I'd played in a friendly against Cardiff and the pain was horrific. What's more, for about twenty seconds during the game I couldn't feel anything from my neck downwards. Not a thing. I was terrified.

'I've got to have a scan,' I said to our physio. 'Something's definitely up.'

Talk about understatement of the year. What the specialist told me altered my perspective on life forever.

'I'm afraid it's serious, Robbie,' he said. 'Your disc is 60 per cent impaled into your spinal cord at C5.'

Saying something like that to a hypochondriac is dangerous. I mean, it could have killed me. It was terrifying, sitting in front of the specialist with my physio next to me. And then when I asked if it was career-threatening, he said, 'No, it's life-threatening.'

I honestly almost fainted. My spinal cord was impaled by a disc, apparently, and he said they had to operate immediately.

'If you go home, trip out of the car and fall over, you could die,' he said.

When I told him I'd spent an entire afternoon on a bucking bronco machine at one of my sons' birthday parties a few days earlier *he* almost fainted!

'You did *what*?' he said.

Eight weeks later, after an operation and some time in intensive care, I was heading a ball again, although it has to be said, very, very gingerly. You can't keep a good man down, and just a few weeks after that I was back in contention again.

It certainly put things into perspective, though. I mean, seriously, how important is football when something like that happens? The thought of not being there for my boys, Charlie and Freddie, and my wife, Sarah, still makes me shudder.

So there you are then: I was almost taken out in my prime. Ha! Carry on dreaming.

The other long lay-off I had was down to a broken leg, which I got while playing for Blackburn in 2007. We were away at Watford and during the game Alhassan Bangura had tried to elbow me.

'Right,' I said to myself. 'Next chance I get I'm going to nail you.'

A couple of minutes later the opportunity arose when the ball dropped right between us. I went in fair and square but unfortunately side-footed the ball, which meant my leg was exposed. Imagine side-footing the ball as hard as possible and then following through.

Bangura came in at the same time but straight-legged and with his studs up over the ball. As I side-footed the ball, his leg was there. He caught me, studs up, and that was it. Game over.

There was no yellow card by the way, despite the ref only being yards away, and Bangura wasn't even looking.

After the tackle I thought, 'Something's not quite right.' It was similar to what happened after I broke my neck, except that instead of pins and needles down my arms, I had pins and needles down my shin.

'It's a nerve,' I said to myself.

I've seen the photos since the game and the shock on my face is clear for all to see. I was a deathly white colour. I looked across to my manager, Mark Hughes.

'I've broken my leg,' I said to him.

'No, you'll be fine.' It was Dave Fevre, the physio.

'Hang on a minute,' I said. 'I think it's okay.'

Before Dave could stop me I tried to stand up and, as I did so, all I could hear was this awful grinding noise. Honestly, it was horrendous!

I'd suffered a compound fracture. Worst of all, though, when I pulled down my sock there was some bone sticking out of my leg. As king of the hypochondriacs I can't believe I'm writing this. There was blood absolutely everywhere and, once again, I almost fainted. I'd seen compound fractures before and I knew that they can be fifty-fifty when it comes to recovery. I thought my career was over.

The effect that a serious injury can have on a dressing room isn't good and, as much as a player wants to be around their teammates all the time, it's actually best that they keep contact to a minimum. For one thing, they can make other players feel uncomfortable. I remember travelling back after the game when I broke my leg. We were on a chartered plane and I was put at the back on a stretcher. All throughout the flight my teammates kept coming up to me to ask how I was and each time one of them asked me I just burst into tears. Not very motivational, is it?

Despite the seriousness of the injury I've always been a quick healer and so I was back playing within a few months. During that lay-off, though, I think Sarah suffered more than I did. Being immobile doesn't suit me and within just a few days I became an absolute whingeing nuisance.

The boredom is unbearable. Month after month you do the same thing, day-in, day-out, and none of it involves playing football. You still have to be at the training ground, though, as that's where you receive most of your treatment, and while you're there you can hear your teammates all getting on and having a laugh. Not being part of it is hell and nobody wants to know you, especially not the manager. You feel completely cut off. Sometimes you might watch the lads train or go and see a match, but that just makes things worse. You see, it's no different to being a lad in a cul-de-sac. Not playing is sickening for a professional.

I know that fans get upset when they see footballers get injured on a Saturday, but from a fellow footballer's point of view it's even more devastating as you know exactly what's in store for them.

One thing that really infuriates me is a player who won't play when they have the slightest niggle. Honestly, I have no respect for those players whatsoever. Some use it as an excuse these days and it's diabolical. If you don't feel right or if you have something genuinely wrong with you then you owe it to yourself and your club to say something, but seriously, if every player with a slight knock went straight to the treatment room and declared themselves unfit you wouldn't be able to field a full team. Out of the 600+ appearances I made, I must have walked on to that pitch over a hundred times knowing I wasn't quite right; but at the end of the day I knew it was either something that was just down to wear and tear or something I could get sorted afterwards. One thing I didn't do was cry off. Too many players these days do that and I think it's a massive shame.

Even though they were both serious injuries, I've still been quite lucky compared to some players. I know lads who have had bad injuries right at the very start of their careers and when that happens it's heart-breaking. It the worst possible scenario.

I'm determined to finish this chapter on a high and what better way of doing that than telling you about the time I suffered my first nose injury?

I was a Leicester City player at the time and, between you and me, I could be an absolute pain in the backside. If I wasn't running or tackling I was either winding people up verbally, hiding things, pinching car keys or putting food in places it shouldn't be. Personally, I would call that youthful exuberance, but to some people at Leicester (and Birmingham and Blackburn), it was just annoying.

To be fair, I'm probably doing myself a disservice really as everybody got involved in pranks and most of the time we had a right laugh. Or at least I did!

My mentor at Leicester with regard to joking and playing pranks was Alan Birchenall MBE, one of the first players to command a price tag of over £100,000 and a legend at Sheffield United, Chelsea and, of course, Leicester, where he made 163 appearances in the 1870s. Or was it the 1970s?

The Birch, as we used to call him, was part of the backroom staff at Leicester and was based down at the training ground. He always called me 'Lil', while I was there, as in Lily Savage, and fortunately for me it was one nickname that never caught on.

There's an old saying that's often bandied around, 'Never kid a kidder', and I just wish I'd taken it in while I was playing at Leicester.

The Birch was living on his own at the time and, because he was no good in the kitchen, the canteen ladies would prepare him an evening meal before they left, wrap the plate in foil and the leave it on the desk in his office. One day while Birch was in the gym, I decided it would be a great idea to nick the keys to his office, break in, take the foil off his plate, empty the contents into a bin and then put the foil back on. I never thought for a moment that he wouldn't realize until he got home but that's exactly what happened. The Birch picked up his plate with all his other stuff, drove home, got in front of the telly, peeled off the foil and tucked in to fresh air!

I suppose my reputation must have gone before me

somewhat because the Birch didn't even have to ask who'd played the prank, he already knew. It takes one to know one, I suppose.

I was having lunch in the canteen when he eventually caught up with me.

''Ere, I want a word with you, Lil!'

I tried my level best to appear innocent but it was no good.

Being a consummate joker himself, the Birch thought my joke was hilarious but, as he walked up behind me, he playfully pushed my head forward. Now this was unfortunate for two reasons: firstly, I was leaning over a red-hot baked potato at the time and, secondly, I have a nose that probably needs its own postcode.

Seconds later both my nostrils were full of piping hot potato and I was in absolute agony. The only thing I said that I'm allowed to repeat here is: 'AAAAAAAAAAAAAAAAAAAAAAAAAAAAA AAAAAAAAAAAAAAAAAAH!' Everything else began with either an F, a B or an S.

It was one of the most painful things I've ever experienced. I looked like a red-nosed clown! The club doctor thought it was hilarious, though, as did everyone else at the club. I thought these things were supposed to come back and bite you, not burn you!

Down the years I had shouting matches, shed tears and shared intimate secrets in the treatment room and it's no exaggeration to say physios and doctors saved my career more than once.

At Birmingham, I was indebted to Neil McDiarmid for his

expert care when I broke my neck, and Dave Fevre at Blackburn, not to mention the doctor, Phil Batty, could not have been more attentive when I broke my leg.

Medical staff are so important in the make-up of a football club because you share information with them that normally you'd only tell your family or closest friends, but because their only agenda is to do what is best for the player's well-being that makes it okay. They're definitely the unsung heroes.

A Short Trip to the Seaside

I think it's fair to say that my time at Derby County at the end of my playing career was a game of two halves. Or should I say two managers? Paul Jewell was my first gaffer there and for various reasons we just didn't see eye to eye; in fact, for me personally it turned into a bit of a nightmare.

It all resulted in a stand-off between me and Paul Jewell, which seemed to go on forever. In October 2008, after the chairman suggested that I should try and get myself onto *I'm a Celebrity . . . Get Me Out of Here!* (seriously!) I was then asked if I would like to go out on loan for a few weeks at Brighton & Hove Albion down on the south coast.

'Micky Adams is in charge there,' said Jewell. 'He knows you and he rates you. What do you think?'

What did I think? I hadn't played football for ages and felt like Public Enemy Number One.

'Can I go now?' I asked.

I was at the end of my tether and genuinely felt like I was just drifting out of the game. I needed to prove both to myself and

The 'sixth best goalkeeper in Wales' saves a free kick from Gylfi Sigurðsson during one of his more eventful matches. © *Action Images/Steven Paston Livepic*

(top) Two of the best players Britain has ever known – and Gary Lineker. Only joking! These two were great to work with and I'm proud to be able to call them friends. © *BBC Photo Library*

(bottom) 'My Grandad used to have one of them!' These days Bentleys are all the rage, but when I had one they were anything but. Shows how much I know… © *Mirrorpix*

Not one of my proudest moments. Coming up against Justin Edinburgh during the 1999 Worthington Cup Final. My overreaction that day got him sent off and I've regretted it ever since. © *Daily Mail/REX Shutterstock*

With Russell Grant, my unofficial godfather! He was the life and soul of the party on *Strictly* and we've become great friends. Despite all the hard work, aching muscles, bruises, worry, stress, self-doubt, paparazzi, criticism and constant physical pain, I loved every minute of my time on *Strictly*. *Top © Ian West, PA Archives. Bottom © JABPromotions/REX Shutterstock*

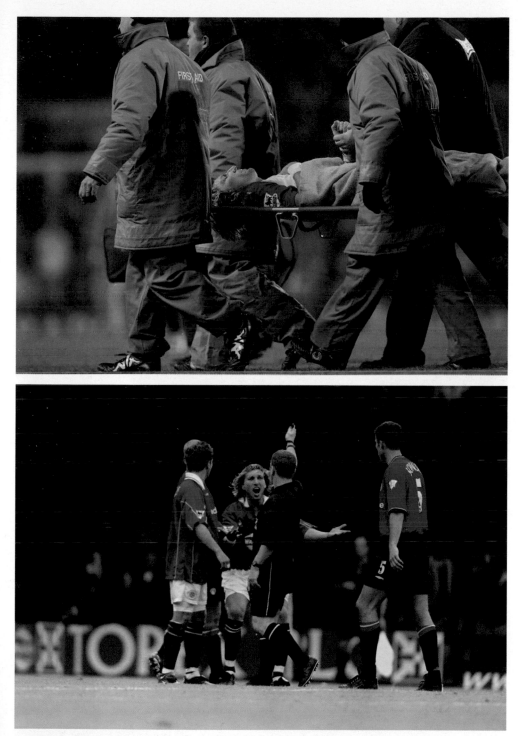

(top) The stretcher was just a precaution this time around, and was called for after a challenge from Rio Ferdinand. I wasn't always so lucky in a Blackburn shirt though.
© *Daily Mail/REX Shutterstock*

(bottom) Paul Durkin booking me – with an imaginary card it seems – during a match against Manchester United. Believe it or not I think we need to be more positive about referees.
© *Mike Egerton/EMPICS Sport*

(top) Hoddle, Lineker, Owen, Gerrard, Wright, Ferdinand, McManaman - FLETCHER! Just some of my extremely talented colleagues at BT Sport. © *C1 Photography*

(bottom) Fletch and his better looking mate Sav, about to go out live from Old Trafford. © *C1 Photography*

Hair today, gone tomorrow. Here I am with my hairdresser and mate, Howard Yuill, handing over my recently chopped locks to Sally Hawley, collections officer at the National Football Museum. I might have been smiling there but I wasn't when it was done.

Main © Mirrorpix. Inset © Jon Super Photography

The most patient woman on earth – apart from my wife and my mother! Teaching me to dance has to be one of the most difficult things you can do but Ola Jordan just about managed it. Here we are entertaining the crowds during a game at Derby County.
© South Ltd/REX Shutterstock

to everyone at the club that I could still do a job and had some kind of future ahead of me.

As it turned out the move didn't have the desired effect on my relationship with Jewell – it would take a change of manager in the form of Nigel Clough to solve my problems at Derby County – although it did produce one of the most enjoyable months I ever spent as a footballer. From a psychological point of view it was exactly what I needed.

Because I'd been all but frozen out at Derby I had hardly spoken to anyone in the game for weeks, so when I first met Micky Adams and the then chairman at Brighton, Dick Knight, it was the proverbial breath of fresh air, or sea air in this case. They made me feel so wanted and just listening to them talk about football and how things were going at the club was like being brought back to life. Then, when I met the lads, it got even better. They had no idea of what had been going on at Derby – they were just pleased to see me, and me them. Laughter, jokes, banter, wind-ups – it was non-stop and I was in my element. It felt just like the good old days at Leicester and Birmingham. I was only at Brighton long enough to play six games for the club but I had a brilliant time there.

Laughing and joking always played a big, big part in my life as a footballer and it was only when I started to experience it all again that I realized just how much I'd missed it.

My first proper day at the club pretty much summed up my time at Brighton & Hove Albion. The day before, Micky had called me.

'We train at the local university, Sav. When you arrive do me a favour, will you, and make a fuss of the car-park attendant?

119

He's a massive fan of yours and ever since he found out you were joining the club he's been grinning like a Cheshire cat.'

Even more love! I couldn't wait to arrive.

The following day when I drove up to the University of Sussex in Falmer, I spotted the attendant straight away. He had strange-looking hair, enormous teeth, thick glasses and an orange jacket.

'Mr Savage!' he said, shaking me very warmly by the hand. 'I've been dreaming about this moment. I'm your biggest fan!'

'That's very kind of you,' I said. 'I'm very glad to be here.'

'I can't believe we've got such a big superstar like you at the club. It's a great day for Brighton. Would you mind signing my autograph book, please?'

'Of course I will.'

He went on like this for about fifteen minutes before he eventually let me park up.

If everyone's going to be like this, I thought to myself, I'm never going to want to leave. I had never received such a warm welcome anywhere.

When I got out of my car and started walking towards the dressing rooms I looked back and noticed that the car-park attendant was now following me. He's probably making sure I know where I'm going, I said to myself. Then, as I walked through the dressing-room door I turned around and there he was, standing right next to me. Oh my God, I've got a stalker!

Just then the car-park attendant and self-confessed Robbie Savage fanatic started to remove his teeth, then his hair and then his glasses. It was the coach, Bob Booker.

'Hi, Sav! Welcome to the club, mate. I hope you'll be very happy here.'

Bob, Micky and all the lads were in absolute stitches. As you know, I'm not always the quickest on the draw but this time I'd really surpassed myself. You should have seen the stuff he was wearing. It was the kind of stuff you would only find in a joke shop! After the initial shock I looked round and thought, brilliant! This is just what I need.

My first visit to the old Withdean Stadium, while not full of wind-ups, did almost cost me a car. I had a Lamborghini at the time, although it was parked back at home, and some of the lads in the dressing room had asked me to drive it down so they could have a look at it. Being a fellow car enthusiast, I was only too happy to oblige, but I honestly wish I hadn't.

Once again this was all down to a car-park attendant, except this bloke was a real one.

'Savage?' he said, looking at me suspiciously while checking his sheet. 'I'm afraid we're full in the car park itself so you're going to have to park over there.'

I looked to where he was pointing and there, about fifty yards to my right, was a patch of grass on a kerb about a foot high.

'I can't get this on there!' I protested.

'I'm afraid you'll just have to, Mr Savage. Now would you mind moving please, sir? You're causing a queue.'

I was already late so had no choice. I drove slowly up towards the kerb. The front of the car was low but I just managed to get the front wheels on to the kerb without it making contact. The victory was short-lived, though, because as I moved forward I immediately heard a scraping noise. I don't know if you've ever heard the sound of Lamborghini on concrete before but, take my word for it, it's absolutely horrible. About ten minutes and half a car later I got out, grabbed my things and made my way to the dressing rooms. I was just releasing a sigh of relief when all of a sudden it hit me. Oh no, I've got to get the flaming thing off again! It was one of many car nightmares.

I was so grateful to Brighton that when I eventually went back to Derby I sent a cheque to the club to help cover my hotel bill. I thought it was the least I could do considering the way the management and players there had made me feel. A few days later I received the cheque back from the club with a note saying, thanks, but they couldn't possibly accept the cheque as I'd been such a good ambassador for the club. What a great bunch of people and what a great club.

Life after Football

You may have thought that this chapter would be all about long holidays and what it's like building a property portfolio. Well, I'll tell you what, that couldn't be further from the truth. This is a subject that is very close to my heart for all kinds of reasons, not least because I know a lot of lads who have found it very, very difficult to adjust to life after football. Basically, they have been dumped by the industry and just left to their own devices.

I, too, have had problems in adjusting to life after playing, and some of those problems still go on to this day. Mark my words, it's a massive issue within football. Seriously, it's very rare that you see a footballer these days making a seamless transition from playing week-in, week-out, to suddenly stopping and doing something new. It hardly ever happens. For a start, the vast majority of professional footballers have absolutely no idea what the heck they're going to do next, and that itself is half the problem.

One of the worst things about retiring from professional football is that as opposed to it happening immediately it creeps up on you over a long period of time, like some kind of giant, expanding cloud. The closer it gets, the more it suffocates you. It's a slow death.

Like watching your kids grow up, the career of a professional footballer seems to go by too quickly. One minute you're one of the youngest players in the dressing room having pranks played on you all the time and the next minute you're one of the old guard. Dad's Army! That gets reflected in the banter. Nicknames suddenly change to things like 'old man' and no matter what you say or do in return there's no escaping the fact that from the dressing-room point of view you really are exactly that – old. You still don't accept things are coming to an end, though. No way. You're a fighter, remember. You keep reassuring yourself that as long as you work hard you'll get another season, or that some fitness guru will come up with a new regime that will extend a footballer's career by two years. Bonkers! You would be surprised by the amount of rubbish you can convince yourself about when the end is in sight. I went through millions of scenarios when my career was coming to an end. The only person you're kidding is yourself, of course, but you don't know that. At the end of the day all you really have is you. Or at least that's how it feels.

Then there are the physical signs. Getting out of bed the morning after matches becomes a nightmare. You can hardly move sometimes. Injuries also become a lot harder to recover from and bit by bit it starts to get to you.

'Your legs have gone, Sav. Haven't they? They've gone. You're finished, mate.'

That's the beginning of the end really, hearing words like that.

The longer it goes on and the closer you get to hanging up your boots for the last time, the worse the feeling becomes.

I was lucky really because, just as my playing career was starting to come to an end, I began getting offers to do media work and my manager at the time, Nigel Clough, was good enough to let me get on with it. He knew himself how hard it can be for footballers on the verge of retirement and he appreciated the fact that all I was doing was trying to build a future. I repaid the gaffer by working my absolute socks off for him and I will always be very grateful to both him and to Derby County Football Club. Thank you.

If I hadn't gone into the media when I finished playing football I honestly don't know what would have happened to me. Even while recovering from my broken leg at Blackburn Rovers, I very nearly went to pieces, so what would I have been like trying to fill day after day after retiring? Within just a few days of my injury, I had become an absolute nightmare. Everything was everyone else's fault and I spent every minute of every day reminding them.

Apart from my family, the game, the club and my teammates meant everything to me: I just couldn't cope with injury, so what about retirement?

I may have been one of the lucky ones but nothing – nothing – can prepare you for the day when you actually wake up as an ex-footballer. It's horrifying. The end of the world as you know it.

It's not just about missing playing the game. That's only the start of it.

Public perception of how professional footballers are treated is probably pretty accurate in that they get very, very well looked after. Rightly or wrongly, that's just the way things are. Racehorses get the best so why shouldn't footballers? If you're ill, a doctor will come and see you straight away, and when it's time for you to go to the dentist someone will remind you and arrange everything. You never have to book a hotel or a plane ticket, and once you've finished training you can sit down and order almost anything you want. Honestly, there's somebody on hand for just about every request imaginable – apart from that! That's problem number two: how do you go from having everything done for you, year after year after year, to suddenly having to fend for yourself? It's not about having to make your own meals or having to book your own appointments – it's about not having that support network anymore and no longer being part of a community.

I know what some of you will be thinking: 'Why should I give a toss about these overpaid idiots?' And that's understandable because on the face of it a professional footballer these days should be able to retire well before they're forty and with a shed-load of cash. What could possibly go wrong? Well, if you scratch beneath the surface you'll very quickly realize that it doesn't matter how much money you've got in the bank, if you have no support or guidance you could be in for a whole heap of trouble.

It's exactly the same with the armed forces, the only difference being money (and that can be as much a hindrance as a help, believe me). You hear hundreds of stories about men and women from the armed forces experiencing difficulties when they have to try and adjust to life on Civvy Street, and it seems that they don't always receive the support they so desperately need – and deserve. Charities like Rugby for Heroes, who were the main beneficiary of the fantastic Rugby Aid match I played in recently, exist specifically to help with issues such as these and do an absolutely tremendous job. Not all servicemen and women experience problems, of course. I mean, if they did, nobody would ever join the armed forces, would they?

A lot of footballers also manage to adjust, and you hear plenty of tales of ex-players going on to build a property portfolio or to play loads of golf, but I'll bet you that even they experience some kind of mental health problems from time to time. Depression, I think, is common within football, whether it's because you're facing retirement, lacking form or injured – in fact, there are dozens of reasons why you might suffer from it. But because it's not really a newsworthy topic, you very rarely get to hear about it. It's only when somebody goes completely off the rails that the media takes notice and that's completely understandable. At the end of the day, when it comes to those players who've retired, you're obviously seen as being an 'ex' footballer, and so if you're not pursuing a job either in the media or in management or coaching, what have you got to offer a reporter? You're yesterday's news, mate. Believe me, it's a horrible feeling.

Why do you think boxers keep coming out of retirement? Sure, some of them might need the money, but I would say that the vast majority of boxers come back either because they miss the adulation and the attention or because they just don't know what else to do. If anything it's probably worse for a boxer because they don't ply their trade as part of a team, which means once you retire, that's it – you're on your own. At least if you're a footballer there's a good chance you might keep in touch with a few people. Mind you, that also works the other way round because footballers have a lot more to miss. Imagine spending fifteen or twenty years being part of a team – or probably several teams – and then suddenly having all that taken away from you. No more camaraderie. No more pranks. No more banter. Take my word for it, from a footballer's point of view retirement is the loneliest and most depressing place imaginable. Even if you're lucky enough to have a loving family around you they're not going to be able to replace what you had as a footballer. They have all got their own lives to live. The kids will be at school and the other half, if she doesn't work, will have her own friends and her own routine. You feel completely and utterly alone.

Another problem you have in football is the fact that some of the people who are supposed to be advising players and looking after their best interests end up taking advantage of them. The vast majority of these people are absolutely spot on, but like in any walk of life you'll always get a few idiots and a few greedy beggars who have to spoil it for everyone else.

I have no problem whatsoever if people make a few quid out of me, providing I'm getting something in return and that it's done ethically. Is that too much to ask?

It's an unfortunate fact of life but if you're well known and have money you're always going to attract those bad advisers and untrustworthy people because everybody wants a piece of you. It's impossible to eradicate. I know quite a few footballers who have retired with only a fraction of what they should have had and all because they've been poorly advised. Some lads have even gone bankrupt because of poor advice and I'm afraid that a lot more will do so in the future. Their experiences leave them feeling angry, not just with those who advised them, but also with themselves for going along with them. Worst of all, though, it leaves them not knowing who they can trust anymore, as quite often the people who recommend these advisors are supposed to be looking after their best interests. Paranoia can be deadly.

Now look, I'm not expecting any of you to start reaching for the violins here. After all, we footballers live predominantly charmed lives. All I'm trying to do is put across the other side of the story because it doesn't matter how rich or famous you are, you're always going to encounter difficulty.

I've been one of the lucky ones – mostly – but I still speak to a doctor-friend of mine called Tim Stevenson about once a month. He helps keep me on the straight and narrow. I've been retired over four years now but I still haven't registered with either a GP or a dentist. I wouldn't know what to do. My wife keeps asking me to do it and says that she'll help me but I keep on putting it off. We all know the saying, 'You can't teach an old dog new tricks.' That phrase could have been invented for retired footballers.

Sometimes I actually forget that I'm no longer a footballer. It might sound daft to some but there are times when I just drift off into a world of my own and suddenly imagine that I'm playing again. The feeling I get when I realize that it's not real is gut-wrenching. Honestly, it's awful, like a short-lived bereavement. That's why I need to speak to Tim occasionally. I still feel a massive sense of loss from time to time. Going to matches can be difficult. As much as I enjoyed watching Wales beat Belgium at the Cardiff City Stadium in June 2015, I couldn't help wishing I was out there playing. That's a massive understatement – I was chomping at the bit! You see, 99 per cent of all footballers live for playing football and that will have been the same since they were probably three, four or five years of age. I'm forty years old now and every day of my life so far (that I can remember, at least) I have wanted to do one thing, and that's pick up a ball and play football. I can't think of many other professions where you start your apprenticeship at such a young age, because although you don't realize it that's what you're doing. You're learning your trade.

The point is that if it's like that for me, one of the lucky ones who has gone straight into the media, imagine what it's like for somebody on the other end of the scale who has no idea what they're going to do.

What I'm trying to drive home here is that being a footballer isn't like most jobs. You live, eat and breathe the game for probably the best part of thirty years and then all of a sudden it stops and nobody wants to play with you anymore. You might get a quick kick around with the kids in the park if you're lucky, but that's about it.

That's the problem as I see it. But what can be done about it? It's difficult to know where to start. You can't just stick an ex-Premier League footballer in an office. It would never work.

My wife Sarah and I went to Barcelona recently and one morning we were in the lift on our way down to the gym when these three blokes got in. They were all suited and booted and after they got in they started chatting about a meeting they were going to and what they were going to say. I just looked at them and thought, 'My God, I couldn't do that in a million years.' For some reason it really scared me watching those lads go about their business. It was all so alien to me.

I know that the Professional Footballers' Association is looking into this problem but it's still something that needs a lot more work. The dilemma you have is that as much as players might need help and advice on living life after football, you have to be very, very careful about when you start offering it to them. If you start talking to a footballer about retirement in his mid-to-late twenties or even his early thirties, he's obviously going to have one eye on the future and not on the game. Managers aren't going to stand for that and rightly so. It's a very difficult balancing act.

I would talk to the players at the very beginning of their careers, just as they are turning professional. When you're seventeen or eighteen years of age, retirement is so far away that there's no chance of it dominating your life. Let's face it, when you're that age you never think it's going to happen to you. All I would be attempting to do with those young players is plant a seed, but that's all they really need at that age – awareness. You can be aware of something without letting it take over your life.

The next time I would want to talk to those players would be as close to their retirement as possible without it affecting their game. If, like me, they retired at thirty-six, I would want to get to them at the start of their final season. I realize that you don't always know when a player is going to retire, which is why you would have to treat each player as an individual. There's no magic cure for this and you're not going to be able to solve everybody's problems. You can only do your best.

This is something I would like to do with Tim Stevenson one day: to help recently retired players adjust. What you would need is a team consisting of ex-players, psychiatrists, agents and basically anybody who might be able to offer assistance. Not every player's going to need help, but I know from personal experience that a lot of players will be crying out for this kind of thing in the future.

And in addition to all those lads who retire as normal, at say thirty-five or thirty-six years of age, what about the kids who get let go in their late teens or early twenties and can't find a new club? I myself very nearly became one of those kids and, despite the fact that I had a few GCSEs to my name, I still think I would have had massive problems adjusting to life in the big wide world. You might only be a young lad but you've still lived in a bubble for several years. You also have to consider the feelings of rejection these young lads experience. This I *do* know from personal experience. When I was let go by Manchester United I honestly felt like my life had come to an end. I was too ashamed to tell my mum and dad because I thought I'd let them down, so instead of going home I arranged to meet my best mate for a game of snooker. He was the only person in the world I felt I could tell at the time. I was so messed up that I wasn't concentrating and I ended up in a really bad car crash. It was totally my fault, by the way. All I could hear as I drove was Alex Ferguson's voice.

'You're not good enough, Robert,' he had said to me. 'Sorry, but you're just not good enough.'

Those words ripped through me like you wouldn't believe and before I knew it I was being cut out of my white Ford Fiesta. That is still one of the worst days of my entire life and definitely one of the worst feelings I have ever experienced – total shame and rejection. So you see, it's not just the old pros with loads of money that experience problems. It's the young ones, too. Football is a community and there should be help and support available for absolutely everybody, regardless of who you are.

Money doesn't guarantee you happiness in life, and people need to realize that there is a lot more to this profession than just kicking a ball, making loads of money and soaking up the adulation. If only it were that simple! Don't get me wrong, being a Premier League footballer has a lot more pluses than it does minuses, providing that you retain two things when you finish playing: support and camaraderie. Lose those and you're in big trouble. We've seen it countless times before. Once an ex-footballer starts to go off the rails it almost always ends in tears. I would love to be able to help prevent it ever happening again.

The Controversial Mr Marmite

I'm pretty sure I can't be football's first Mr Marmite, but I'm probably the first 'mass-market' version.

I can't remember who it was who first called me it but it was my bosses at the *Daily Mirror* who started using it regularly.

'Football's Mr Marmite' it says below my name in the paper each week. 'You'll either love him, or hate him.'

How many pundits do you know who have their own nickname? And it just about sums me up, I suppose. Actually, I can't believe the people at Marmite haven't asked me to do an advert for them. I'd be the perfect ambassador.

It was all fairly straightforward when I was a footballer: fans of the clubs I played for loved me, and everyone else in the world hated me. Everyone! That was it, there was no middle ground. As a pundit it's slightly broader. Yes, people still either love me or loathe me, but now it's for a variety of different reasons. When I played football fans hated me because I got under people's skin and wound them up – players and supporters alike – but as a pundit it's nearly always down to something

I've said, and because I basically talk for a living it could be one of about a thousand things. For me, being called Mr Marmite is probably the biggest compliment you could pay a football pundit as it means you're stirring things and creating debate. You could that say I'm a walking debate. What's the point of sitting on the fence, though?

The way that people express their opinions about me has also become a lot broader since I became a pundit. These days instead of having 30,000 people in a stadium baying for my blood week-in, week-out, now I get people on social media questioning my parentage. That used to bother me quite a bit in the early days as some people on there can be very, very abusive, but you have to learn to just ignore them. Fortunately the vast majority of people on social media, including the ones who give me stick and don't agree with me, are there only for a bit of banter and so they're the ones I respond to. Isn't it funny though that the really, really abusive ones all seem to know exactly what I say and do, and so obviously watch *Fletch & Sav*, listen to *606*, read my column in the *Mirror* and follow me on social media? It's bizarre. People just love to hate me, I suppose.

For every dozen abusive idiots you get on social media you'll also get one or two working in the main media, and that's a shame. They're few and far between, I'm very pleased to say, but they are a lot more difficult to ignore than Twitter trolls – for me at least. They can be just as nasty, too. I've had some awful things written about me in the papers over the years and unfortunately one of these so-called articles (which wasn't in a tabloid, by the way) recently made it into the hands of my eldest son. It was the usual rubbish – 'Why is this idiot on my TV?'

etc. – but just like the trolls on social media the journalist involved seemed to be incapable of presenting a reasonable, intelligent argument and instead went for the lowest common denominator: abuse. Naturally the article quite upset Charlie but I had to explain to him that although it's not nice reading things like that about your dad, it's part and parcel of what I do.

'You've just got take it on the chin, son,' I reassured him. 'I'd much sooner they were writing articles about me than about somebody else.'

'But they don't know you, Dad. Why are they so horrible when they don't even know you?'

It's a question I've been asking myself for years. Honestly, if I had a pound for every time I'd been slagged off as a person by somebody who didn't even know me I would be a billionaire.

That's what a mean when I refer to myself as a kind of 'panto-mime villain'. It's just pretend. It was the same when I was a player. I wasn't a cynical footballer, nor was I a violent one. I just played up to both people and situations, that's all. In fact, if you want the truth about this, I get really badly affected by some of the stuff that gets written about me. I'm still learning, you see. I love it when I get a compliment, the same as I did when I was a player, and I have no problem whatsoever with constructive criticism. It's just the really bad, nasty stuff I can't come to terms with.

Everybody's entitled to an opinion and if somebody thinks I'm no good as a pundit, fine, write an article in your paper explaining why. Don't make it personal, though. That's just pathetic.

There are some people out there who still like Marmite, thank God. I mean, it would get a bit boring if the only feedback I ever got was 'You're talking rubbish, Savage!' The thing is, I only ever get asked about the ones who I get into an argument with but at the end of the day that's understandable. It's newsworthy.

Another word besides Marmite that seems to have become synonymous with my name is 'controversial'. On the face of it, I've got absolutely no problem with this. When I was a foot-baller I was controversial for the same reason I was called Mr Marmite – because I got underneath people's skin and wound them all up big time. But now I'm a pundit it's not quite as straightforward. In fact, I would argue that those who like to label me as being a controversial pundit are under a similar misapprehension to the ones who label me vain, because in my opinion I'm not controversial at all, I'm just honest.

A few of the things I say might be considered controversial by some people but you'll get that with any pundit. Even some of the more non-committal ones are going to come out with something a bit divisive from time to time. The people I object to are the ones who say I'm controversial just for the sake of it or that I say things just to wind people up. That really is abso-lute rubbish. I am only ever 100 per cent honest and it doesn't matter what people think or say I will never, ever deviate from that. It's what sets me apart from a lot of other pundits. I would never let an opinion become personal but at the same time I would never hold back. What would you rather be, somebody who speaks a lot but says nothing or somebody who speaks a bit and says everything? For me there's no contest.

I think there are too many people who are paid to give opin-ions who just sit on the fence because, as I said, they just want to protect a mate or an ex-manager. Funnily enough, I didn't pick up that many friends during my career so it's never been that much of a problem for me. I've got nobody to protect! That's actually true to a certain extent because most of the friends I made in football didn't stay in the game after retirement. People like Keith Gillespie and Darren Eadie all moved on. Even if they had stayed in football, I promise you that it wouldn't make any difference to me. I don't owe anybody anything in that respect, the same as nobody owes me. I'm paid to offer an honest opinion and if that opinion upsets certain people, so be it. I honestly do not care.

Apparently I caused outrage in 2014 because I came out and said that the majority of footballers don't care about the rising price of tickets – but that's the truth! Footballers live in a bubble and have people on hand to do everything for them. Do you honestly think that they're going to sit there saying, 'I see the season ticket prices have gone up again at Chelsea. It's about time I contacted my MP'? Of course they're not, the same as supermarket workers aren't going to complain if the price of bread goes up or gasmen if the price of gas goes up. People need bread so they'll keep on buying bread, people need gas so they'll keep on buying gas, and people need football so they'll keep on buying shirts, season tickets, subscriptions and whatever else takes their fancy. Even I know about market forces. Companies are going to charge whatever they think people are willing to pay, and if they don't pay, the prices will go down.

Sometimes the truth can hurt a bit so in my eyes the sooner somebody said something, the better. I wasn't trying to cause a stir; I was just fed up with people being deluded. Now they know the truth.

I admit that if I wasn't as honest as I am then I wouldn't be anywhere near as successful. I would just be yet another pundit talking a lot but saying nothing. I could probably make a living out of doing that but I would absolutely hate it. I can't be anything *but* honest. You ask my family. It gets me into all kinds of trouble at home. I lack tact, apparently! When it comes to work, honesty is the best policy.

I co-present the biggest football phone-in on British radio in *606*, I have an extremely successful column in the *Mirror*, I am a big part of BT Sport, one of the most exciting sports channels ever to hit our screens, and I've been an ambassador for William Hill now for over five years. Did I achieve all that by sitting there saying, 'Yes, Gary, I thought they played okay in the end'? Did I heck! I did that by putting my neck on the line and telling it *exactly* how it is.

This job means absolutely everything to me, which is why I devote my life to it. I live, breathe, eat and sleep football. If there are twenty games on television in a week, I will move heaven and earth to see every single one of them. What's more, I look forward to the lot. You ask my wife. Sitting down to watch a match – any match – is like going to the cinema for me. I just love it! At the end of the day I believe the majority of fans who either listen, watch or read what I say would do exactly the same. In fact, I bet some of them do.

Can you imagine, though, if absolute honestly was always demanded in football punditry? It would be hilarious and chaotic. There would be fights everywhere.

Who else do I think cuts the mustard with regards to being a conviction pundit? Well, after watching him at the last World Cup, I would say Rio Ferdinand has to be up there. I think he'll go on to become one of the best pundits in the country. There's no flannel or fluff with Rio. He's straight to the point and he doesn't get flustered by others. We actually used to dislike each other years ago but now I can't wait to see him on *Fletch & Sav* because we always have a good bit of banter. Most importantly, he's not afraid of telling the truth. Gary Neville and Alan Shearer are the same. They've got bags of experience, know the game inside out and are not afraid of what people think, say or do. No fear. Paul Scholes is exactly the same. He just says it how it is. They were exactly the same as players. Another pundit who I rate highly is Glenn Hoddle. His tactical awareness is second to none and I've learned an awful lot from him over the years.

The difference between the likes of Rio, Gary, Glenn and then someone like me is that they already had most people's respect when they became pundits – minus the idiots who can't see beyond the club they played for, of course. For me, it's been different. I wasn't what you would call the most popular player on God's earth, nor did I play at the very highest level, so respect as a pundit is something I have to work hard for. A Gary Neville or a Rio Ferdinand could be seven out of ten as a pundit and they would still get through okay, whereas I always have to be ten out of ten, or at least try to be. Whether or not you agree with what I say in the media or like how I say it is completely immaterial here. What matters is that I'm somebody who will always try his best and whatever respect I have as a pundit has had to be earned. What? I'm just being honest!

Me and My Big Mouth

It's amazing but as well as being very, very honest with this mouth of mine I can also, from time to time, be very, very stupid. When I first joined Leicester City back in 1997 I had two nicknames – 'big nose' and 'big mouth'. The nose, I could do nothing about, I'm afraid, and to be honest it was no different with the mouth. I just opened it and things came out. Usually daft things. Don't get me wrong, I rarely set out to offend or annoy anybody – unless I was having a tussle, in which case it was fair game – and on the few occasions that I have, I've regretted it. I think they call it foot-in-mouth disease. Well, I have been a sufferer for a long time.

Believe it or not, the children's TV channel, CBBC, ran a regular feature on the *Match of the Day Kickabout* spin-off called 'Sav's Big Mouth', in which a host of celebrities had to kick as many footballs as they could through my big mouth in thirty seconds. Fortunately for me, I wasn't there in person and instead they used a giant cardboard cartoon of me with an exaggerated mouth – well, slightly. What an honour. Perhaps I could be the new Mr Tumble?

141

I'm afraid that there aren't enough hours in the day or trees in the forests for me to get down on paper every example of how my mouth has got me into trouble, but I'll give you some of my favourites.

Let's start with two of the hardest men in football, shall we? Graeme Souness and Gerry Taggart. I've almost been killed by both over the years, although to be fair I completely deserved it.

I used to have this annoying habit where, if I didn't agree with what somebody was saying, I would just stick my fingers in my ears, close my eyes and say, 'Not listening, not listening, not listening, not listening.' How people could possibly find that annoying I'll never know. It's a mystery. It probably prevented me from getting thumped once or twice because people just didn't know what to do when I started doing that. You can't hit a man who's got his eyes closed and his fingers in his ears, can you?

In October 2004 my team Birmingham were playing host to Graeme Souness's Newcastle. It ended all square at 2–2 and it was quite a fiery encounter if memory serves – exactly what you would expect from a team featuring Robbie Savage and another managed by Graeme Souness. After the final whistle had gone, a bit of banter was taking place on the side of the pitch. Nothing serious, just the usual 'Our team's better than your team.' You hadn't been able to separate us on the field so I suppose we were just trying to settle things off the pitch. As all this was going on Graeme Souness overheard some of it and so decided to get involved.

Now I'm not sure whether this is true or not but I'd read somewhere that Graeme Souness had only been offered the

Newcastle job because the first four candidates had turned it down. He was fifth choice, in other words. True or not, that little fact was being sent over the top and straight into the conversation.

'Well, at least I wasn't fifth-choice manager!' I said.

He looked at me and I could tell by his eyes that I was in trouble, but he just about held himself back. 'Oh yeah, Robbie, because you're such a great player,' he said sarcastically.

We were walking down the tunnel at this point and as I heard him speed up behind me I said, 'Well, I'm a better player than you were!'

And with that I stuck my fingers in my ears, closed my eyes, shouted, 'Can't hear, can't hear, can't hear', and ran like hell towards the dressing room.

He'd only won five league championships, three European Cups and four League Cups playing for Liverpool.

Luckily for me I made it into the dressing room just in time.

When our manager Steve Bruce heard about it, he just looked at me in disbelief.

'Not again!' he said. 'If he'd caught you, Sav, he'd have killed you. That's one man you don't mouth off to.'

When we went up to Newcastle for the return fixture I was absolutely terrified. Honestly, I thought he was going to batter me. When he saw me, though, he just walked up to me and gave me a big hug. I was shaking like a leaf!

Incidentally, Graeme's not the only Anfield legend I've goaded over the years. You can add Phil Thompson to that list, too. This one's an absolute corker. I go bright red just thinking about it.

I was at Leicester City at the time and one afternoon in 2001 we were taking on Liverpool, which Phil Thompson had just taken over as caretaker manager. We were pretty awful at the time and as a consequence Liverpool were thumping us 4–1. It was diabolical. Out of frustration I might have gone in a little bit hard on one of Phil's players and immediately he started having a go at me. Tempers were certainly starting to flare a bit at that point and so instead of just walking away and ignoring Phil, I brought my hand up to my face and gestured that he might – just might – have quite a big nose. Talk about the pot calling the kettle black!

After the match I apologized to Phil and told him that I didn't mean it.

A few years later – as is very often the way – my mouth came back to haunt me. I was in the Sky Sports studios at the time, ready to talk about a game, when in walked Phil.

'You must be Robbie Savage,' he said, reaching out to shake my hand. 'Hi, Robbie, my name's Big Nose. How are you?'

From then on he and Richard Keys wouldn't leave me alone. I had an entire afternoon of it!

So that was 'Legends v. Big Mouth', which had mixed results. Now I'll tell you about – as one journalist put it – 'Savage by Name v. Savage by Nature'.

In 2001 I was playing for Leicester City, at the time under Peter Taylor, and we were approaching the half-time whistle in what would end up being a goalless draw against Arsenal. I remember it well because we had recently signed Roberto Mancini from Sampdoria and he was making his debut that day. What a player he was!

I can't remember exactly why but my teammate Gerry Taggart and I had been getting on each other's nerves for most of the first half and by the time the half-time whistle was approaching things were getting a bit heated. Obviously wanting to see my death-wish through to the bitter end I shouted two words at Taggs, one beginning with 'F' and another beginning with 'O'. Mistake!

That's what I mean about foot-in-mouth disease. It was like goading a Siberian tiger.

'I'll see you in the dressing room,' he said, before clipping me round the ear.

I just stood there and thought to myself, 'Why do you do it?'

Quick as a flash I did what any self-respecting coward would do and apologized, before running like hell into the tunnel and then avoiding him for the rest of the match. Thank God we didn't lose. Taggs hated losing and if we had I have a feeling he'd have wanted another word.

Like Graeme Souness, Gerry Taggart is an absolutely smashing bloke and in my experience is one of the nicest men in the game. I'd still have whipped him, though.

As hard as people like Graeme Souness and Gerry Taggart undoubtedly are, the toughest man I've ever encountered in the game of football is the former striker Geoff Horsfield, who I played with for a while at Birmingham City. He is about six foot two inches tall and at least the same across. Massive! A lovely bloke, though.

Once again I was playing for Leicester City at the time and Geoff was playing for Fulham. It was the quarter-final of the

Worthington Cup and the match had finished 3–3 – time for a penalty shootout. The same thing had happened in the third round of the FA Cup where we pipped Arsène Wenger's mighty Arsenal in the penalty shoot-out after a 0–0 draw. Our regular keeper, Tim Flowers, had been taken off in extra time and so Pegguy Arphexad had come on to replace him. Arsenal's Gilles Grimaldi had stepped up, Pegguy saved it and so we were through. The Professor wasn't at all happy that day!

Now I'd read somewhere that before he became a professional footballer Geoff Horsfield had been a builder. He'd come into the game quite late apparently and until he started scoring goals for a living he had specialized in building patios. He scored that day and had been on really good form.

'I can't be having this,' I thought as we went into the penalty shootout. 'Perhaps I should have a quick word.' And so, just before Geoff stepped up to take his penalty I walked up behind him and whispered in his ear.

'Geoff, after you miss this come back to mine and you can build me a patio.'

It worked, I'm sorry to say. Geoff missed his penalty and we went on to win the shootout 3–0.

No celebrating for me. I was down that tunnel, into that dressing room and on to the coach before you could say cement mixer. He must have been furious.

You see, I never used to think about the consequences before opening my mouth. Sometimes I never used to think full stop! In addition to playing home and away fixtures in the league against Fulham, there was always a slim chance that one day Geoff and I might play for the same club. What then?

Sure enough, two years later I signed for Birmingham City, and who was playing up front? Geoffrey Malcolm Horsfield, a one-man army with a talent for scoring goals and – according to me – building patios.

I've always said I'm one of the luckiest people in the world, and on this occasion I think that was proved. Geoff not only saw the funny side of what I said but we also became really good mates. He did have a laugh at my expense, though, as on the first day of training he walked into the dressing room, saw me, walked slowly over, put his face right up to mine and growled:

'Now then, Savage, about that patio.'

I almost fainted.

And what do you think Geoff did during the summer while he wasn't playing football? He built patios! You couldn't make it up, could you?

I was at Derby County towards the end of my playing career, but I still hadn't learned my lesson as on separate occasions I ended up mouthing off to one hard-nut and one giant.

We were on one of the worst runs imaginable at the time, with just one win in twenty-nine league games. It was diabolical. We'd just been crushed 6–1 by Chelsea at Stamford Bridge and were about to entertain Manchester United at Pride Park. Nobody could envisage anything other than a United drubbing that day, but I was having none of it. I'd had a torrid time at Derby until then because of my problems with the gaffer Paul Jewell and we were staring relegation in the face. It was awful. Tempers were fractious to say the least.

I didn't have a bad record against United, though, and

obviously had history with the club. 'This is my big chance,' I thought. 'If we can put in a good performance here, who knows?'

I gave one of my best ever performances in a Rams shirt that afternoon and we were unlucky to lose in the end. We were undone by a fantastic goal – a Cristiano Ronaldo special.

Part way through the game Andy Todd, who I'd played with at Blackburn and knew really well, came on as a substitute. To cut a long story short the ball went down the line and as opposed to heading it out, Toddy thought he would let it run out for a goal kick. It was a nice idea but unfortunately he was robbed at the corner post, it was played back in and Ronaldo scored.

Even by this point in the season I'd said very little either on the pitch or in the dressing room as I hadn't been playing that well, but after putting in a good show against United I was starting to get some confidence back.

'You really should have got rid of it,' I said to Toddy after the game.

It was a fair point, but as opposed to leaving it there I went on – and on – and on!

We'd come so close to getting a result against United that I just couldn't let go. God, I wish I had!

All of a sudden Toddy turned round, chucked his bottle of water at the wall and started to walk towards me. I thought, 'That's it, I'm dead. He's going to kill me.' And he was, too. I looked at his eyes as he approached me and they'd completely gone. Everyone else in the dressing room stood up expecting the worst but just as he got to me . . . he stopped. I looked at him and I could tell that he'd had to force himself not to leather me. We were both shaking at the time, but for two very different reasons.

Naturally I apologized to Toddy and we went straight back to being mates again. 'If that had been anyone else, though,' he said afterwards in the showers, 'I'd have ripped his head off.'

Most people would do that the other way round so I was lucky we were such good mates.

It was totally my fault. What a berk! I'd had one good game and thought I was king of the world.

Why did I always pick on the big ones?

Next on the list was another teammate, Darren Moore, a six-foot-three centre back who made almost 600 appearances as a pro. He must have weighed at least fifteen stone and could keep strikers well outside the box just by looking at them. Or growling. Not a man you want to upset, then, unless you're me, of course.

We were playing at home against Arsenal at the time and the score was 1–1 when, while under a bit of pressure, I fed the ball back to Darren. I could tell he didn't look too comfortable and as he went to pass the ball it went straight to Nicklas Bendtner and he scored. The Gunners went on to win that game 6–2. Another dream shattered!

The next match was at Blackburn and we lost it 3–1. Nine goals in two games! Out of pure frustration and because of what had happened the previous week I had a go at Darren. 'We're leaking far too many goals. What the hell's going on, Mooro? It's ridiculous!'

As the dressing room fell silent I once again got a funny feeling that I may have said something I shouldn't have.

The looks on people's faces said only one thing: 'You idiot!'

I looked back down at Darren and he started to stand up. The thing is, he didn't seem to stop. He just went on and on. I know he's tall but, honestly, that day he seemed more like ten foot three. I'd goaded Goliath! Nice one, Sav. I tried desperately to remember a prayer of some kind but nothing sprang to mind.

Once Darren had reached his full height he pointed a finger at me.

'I'll see you on Monday,' he said.

I looked around the dressing room. Everybody was staring straight at me, except this time their eyes were saying, 'Get back home, pack your bags and leave the country.' And at the time that's exactly what I wanted to do. My God, I was scared.

I tried to apologize to Darren before we left but he just ignored me.

All through Sunday I felt like the condemned man.

On Monday the inevitable happened and Mooro pulled me to one side. 'For those about to die,' I thought. 'We salute you.'

'You're lucky, Sav,' he said. 'I very nearly lost my temper with you, and if I had you'd have been in trouble.'

I hadn't experienced so much relief since using Graham Poll's toilet. Which, for those of you that don't know, I did in 2002. Suffering from a terrible stomach bug and absolutely desperate for the loo, I ended up using the toilet in the referees' changing room without permission before a Leicester City game with Aston Villa. Mr Poll and the officials weren't too happy about that, and I ended up being fined two weeks' wages. Talk about spending a penny!

One of the best wind-ups that I ever had played on me as a player had quite a bit to do with my big mouth. It was 2008 and I was on loan, enjoying a great time at Brighton & Hove Albion.

Not long after the car-park attendant wind-up that had happened on my first day's training, some of the lads pulled me to one side.

'Just a word of advice, Sav,' they said. 'Leave off Tommy Fraser.'

Tommy played in midfield for Brighton and is still a pal of mine.

'What do you mean, leave off him?'

'We just think that you should, that's all.'

They knew exactly what they were doing. You see, if you tell me not to do something the chances are I'll do the opposite. It's just my nature.

Sure enough, I couldn't help myself and almost immediately I started hammering Tommy. I hammered the gear he wore, I hammered him in training. It was all good fun, of course, but I kept at it.

The other lads pulled me to one side again.

'Sav, we've told you, mate, just lay off him.'

'Yeah, yeah, whatever.'

'No, we mean it. If you don't lay off Tommy he'll set his granddad on you.

This just made me worse.

'His granddad! Are you having a laugh?'

Anyway, a couple of days later the lads got me into the dressing room.

'That's it, Sav. Tommy's had enough. His granddad's coming in to have a word with you.'

This actually seemed genuine.

'Why is everybody looking so serious?' I asked.

'You don't know who Tommy's granddad is, do you? We did try and warn you, Sav.'

By this time I was terrified!

'No, I don't. Go on, who is he?'

'Have you ever heard of "Mad" Frankie Fraser?'

'What, the gangster? Yes, of course I have. Hang on, you mean he is Tommy's granddad?'

They looked at me as solemnly as they could. 'That's right. We did try and tell you, Sav.' Then, all of a sudden they began to laugh.

My face must have been an absolute picture. I honestly thought I was for it!

I hardly said a word to annoy Tommy after that. I knew it was a wind-up, but I'm a massive worrier.

You know why I've enjoyed writing this chapter, even if it brought back memories of my life being in danger? Because every single one of these lads – Mooro, Toddy, Hors, Taggs and even Mr Graeme Souness, Esq. – are still mates, and they all know that despite me once having a mouth the size of the Channel Tunnel I haven't got a nasty bone in my body. Anyway, there was no point hitting me because I would have decked all of them.

The Fans

This subject could be as long as it is wide. I reckon I have the most unique relationship with football fans that this country's ever known, for the simple reason that I can evoke every emotion known to man – or woman. Think about it. How many other players or pundits do you know who can receive boos, cheers, death threats and invitations to attend kids' parties all in the same day? None, that's how many!

I can make people laugh and I can make people smile, but my God I can make them angry.

Yes, I'm supposed to be this pantomime villain-type character that people love to hate – but the fact is, that has as much to do with the fans as it does me. Without them I'm nothing.

If you're a football pundit you need listeners, readers or viewers; otherwise you're out of a job, but you also need them to respond to you and engage with you. I rely on people responding to me and engaging with what I say for two reasons: first, it tells me how well I'm doing, and second, it makes it more fun. If they just sit there and listen, where's the atmosphere? It's all about interaction with me. You have to try and form a relationship with the fans right from the start, and that's exactly what I did as a player – I generated a response and formed a relationship. They weren't always friendly relationships, of course, and it's the same now I'm a pundit, but that simply broadens the audience. If I had a choice of playing a game of football or broadcasting a radio show to a crowd of either 50,000 adoring fans or 50,000 people who, shall we say, were somewhat mixed in their appreciation, I'd go for the mixed audience every time!

I never set out to develop a rapport with the fans. I mean, most players just keep their heads down and try and get on with it, don't they? You let the crowd in when you're doing well, and you try and block them out when you're not. That's how it was with me until the day I got Justin Edinburgh sent off. That was the moment I let the crowd in, and what a time to do it. I actually fed off the anger that day and from then on I knew that as opposed to trying to ignore the crowds I could actually use their different moods to my advantage – and have a bit of a laugh occasionally.

What I love now I'm a pundit, and what still surprises me to this day, is that people ring up shows like *606* and ask specifically to speak to me. It's just surreal. When I hear it I always immediately say to myself, 'Why do they want to speak to me?' It's the best feeling. About half the time they're going to shout at me, of course, but that makes absolutely no difference. The fact is, they want to have a debate with me. It doesn't matter to me whether I'm being hammered on the terraces or on the radio, just so long as people care enough to hammer me. It is a relief sometimes when people call up and agree with you, but at the end of the day they're not really what a show wants. If you agree, nod your head and open up another can of beer – and if you don't, ring in and let me tell you why you're wrong!

When it comes to people getting angry at you, the difference between being a footballer and being a pundit is simple. When you're a pundit you can have a go back and it's a level playing field, but when you're a footballer or manager, you can't. Personally, I think it should be a level playing field and players and managers should be allowed to have a go back. In fact, there's nothing I'd have loved more when I was a player than to have had a pop at some people, especially the ones who spat or threw stuff. I'm not talking about goading entire stands, just the ones who try and spoil things for the majority.

Even when we were off the pitch we weren't supposed to retaliate, and sometimes you really had to stop yourself. I remember two situations when under normal circumstances anybody in their right mind would have retaliated. The first time was at Old Trafford. I'd gone there with my family to watch Manchester United v. Spurs and just as I was walking to my seat somebody ran up behind me and punched me in the back of the head. Now some people will probably think, 'Ha ha, it serves him right', but I was actually holding on to the hand of my son Charlie at the time, and he was only two years old. The second time was while I was at Birmingham City. This time I was holding Charlie in my arms when a so-called fan came up and spat in my face from close range. My boy was absolutely terrified.

Anyone else would have been free to retaliate to a couple of cowardly idiots like that, but I wasn't allowed to do a thing. Look, I'm certainly not condoning violent behaviour here but we should be allowed to stick up for ourselves and for our families the same as everybody else is, especially when people use either threatening behaviour or violence against us. At the end of the day it's self-defence.

Honestly, I've had the lot over the years. I've had death threats made against me and just about every member of my family. Even my kids! I've even had people turning up outside my house at four o'clock in the morning wearing masks – and all because of a game of football. It's supposed to be a form of entertainment, for heaven's sake.

I've got no problem with people calling me all kinds of everything from the stands, but I should be able to leave that stadium on a Saturday evening and not feel intimidated.

Some people think that because I used to wind people up on the pitch I should expect that kind of behaviour. Have you ever heard anything so ridiculous in your life?

Social media has been a bit of a game changer as it allows fans unrestricted access to players and pundits alike – providing they decide to use it, of course. You can understand the ones who don't!

One of the things I've learned about social media over the years is that in some ways it's actually no different to being on the terraces. You go to a match, you have a few drinks, you watch the game, you shout a bit of abuse at the players, and then you go home. It's the same on Twitter. People either watch or listen to the football, have a little bit too much to drink and then get on their computers or on their smartphones and start mouthing off. Or should I say 'typing off'? The difference is that on the terraces it's all forgotten about in a second or two. Not so with Twitter. Comments tend to follow you around.

There was a guy a few years ago; he got drunk one evening and started tweeting some comments to me that he later wished he hadn't. It was really abusive stuff. Unfortunately for him he put his work email address on one of the tweets and so when I decided to re-tweet it, which is what I tend to do with a lot of the extremely abusive stuff, a load of my fans and followers decided to complain to his boss, and why not? The following morning I received a string of messages from this guy pleading with me to speak to his boss.

'I'm going to get the sack if you don't,' he said. 'Please call him and tell him it was a mistake.'

And that's what I did. I called up his boss and he got let off the hook. Now you mark my words, not many people would have done that. Why would they? Come on, be honest. If somebody sent you a string of abusive messages and then asked you to get them off the hook you would tell them to do one, wouldn't you?

Look, I'm not excusing the idiots on social media. No way. All I'm saying is that you have to judge each case individually. That bloke made a mistake and he apologized. Is there anybody reading this who has never made a mistake before? Exactly! Some fans do take it too far occasionally and end up making idiots of themselves, but then so do players. Not pundits though. We're far too reserved and well behaved. It's true! As I said earlier in the book, you're only ever a word or two away from getting the sack and that applies to fans, to players and to pundits.

That's enough about the idiots. What about the silent majority, eh? The ones who are in it for the sport and for a bit of banter? Well, for a start they're not that silent some of them. When I went to the World Cup in 2014 I met thousands of fans from all over the world, but it was the England supporters who gave me the best laughs. Everywhere I went I got the same thing:

'SAVAAAAAAAAAAAAGE YOU W*****! COME AND HAVE A DRINK WITH US!'

I may not be the biggest drinker in the world but do you honestly think I'm going to turn down the chance of having a laugh and a bit of banter? No way. Each and every one of those fans was as good as gold and I promise you we had an absolute blast. We all had one thing in common, you see – football. How good's that, though, an ex-Welsh international having a laugh with a load of England fans? It doesn't get any better.

Fans are usually quite surprised when they meet me. They think that because I have strong opinions about football I'll have strong opinions about everything, but I don't. I don't really care about anything else. Ask me about current affairs – no idea. Ask me about the environment – no idea. Ask me about politics – no idea. In fact, when I was at Leicester City many, many years ago I once got diagnosed with having concussion because I couldn't name the current Prime Minister.

'Robbie's been hit,'

'Okay, look at me, lad. Who's the Prime Minister of Great Britain?'

'Absolutely no idea.'

'Get him off, he's concussed!

The thing is when they asked me the same question a few hours later I still had absolutely no idea.

Apart from spending time with my wife and kids (obviously), I'm never happier than when I'm having a laugh with people like me – football fans.

I've been the subject of some absolutely classic chants over the years, as I'm sure you can imagine. Two spring to mind, both quite funny. The first one happened while I was at Derby. It was a pre-season match at Torquay and as I went over to take a throw-in the crowd started chanting, to the tune of the lyric 'Where's your mama gone?' from the song 'Chirpy Chirpy Cheep Cheep', 'WHERE'S YER CARAVAN? WHERE'S YER CARAVAN?'

I looked back at them and shouted: 'It's in Monaco next to my yacht!'

They absolutely wet themselves at that and so did I. It created a really cracking atmosphere and we ended up having a great laugh.

The next one happened while I was commentating for BT Sport. We were at Stoke one night and when the fans realized that I was covering the game they sang, 'HE LOOKS LIKE A GIRL, HE LOOKS LIKE A GIIIIIIIIIIIRL, THAT ROBBIE SAVAGE, HE LOOKS LIKE A GIRL.'

Not exactly complimentary, but it was all good fun.

Fortunately, despite some people hating my guts, the vast majority of chants I've had sung at me over the years have been in good humour. But when it starts to go the other way it can be horrendous and I think the worst time I ever had as a player was when I was at Derby. Although I ended up becoming captain at Derby and finished my career there on a high, there was a time at the start of my tenure there when we were performing badly and because I was supposedly the star player I was the one who got it in the neck. Take my word for it, when the worst chants at a home game are directed at you it can be totally demoralizing, and at the time I used to dread going on to the pitch.

That's just a worst-case scenario though, and unless you're either unlucky or just very, very bad at what you do, the majority of chants are actually okay.

Most people, quite naturally I suppose, seem to have a lot of pre-conceived ideas of what I'm like as a person, based on either how I behaved on the football pitch or how I am on the TV and the radio, but that's just me doing my job.

Even some journalists have been pleasantly surprised when they've met me. It's true! I went to the 2015 Champions League final with BT Sport and ended up spending an entire weekend with five journos I'd never met before. I could tell some of them were thinking, 'Oh my God, it's HIM!' but we all ended up having a really good time together.

If you have a drink and a chat with me and you still come away thinking 'What an absolute idiot' (or words to that effect) then fair enough, but at least give me that chance. I'm really not a bad bloke once you get to know me.

The most satisfaction I ever had as a player with regard to the effect the team had on the fans was when I played for Birmingham City. The big derby for them was against Aston Villa and since the beginning of time Birmingham had always been the poor neighbour.

When I arrived at Birmingham from Leicester City I already had a fantastic record against Villa: in my five seasons there I never once came away on the losing team.

Some of those matches had been carnage by the end and the Villa fans and I already had a certain 'understanding', shall we say? Or in other words, I used to wind them up and they used to go absolutely mental at me.

The fans at Birmingham City knew all about this and couldn't wait for the first derby featuring me.

'You must hate going to Villa Park, Sav,' they used to say. 'I've heard it's like a cauldron once you start winding them up.'

Yes and no. Of course I didn't like having cigarette lighters and coins thrown at me but the atmosphere they created once we started to 'engage' with each other used to just make me play better. It was like receiving constant shots of adrenalin. If the Villa fans had just sat on their hands and ignored me for ninety minutes I probably wouldn't have played half as well. Who knows, Villa might even have won a match.

What happened in my first season at Birmingham? Yes, you guessed it, we did the double over Villa and to the Birmingham fans it was like a hundred cup finals all rolled into one. They'd always been in Villa's shadow and so helping them get one over on their big rich neighbours was fantastic. Imagine all those years of being second best. It meant the absolute world to those fans. Despite leaving St Andrew's under a bit of a cloud I had a wonderful time at Birmingham and probably played my best football there.

★

Signing autographs is something I enjoy doing a lot as it reminds me just how privileged I am. I do get embarrassed, though. I just can't believe I'm being asked sometimes. It's not false modesty. I just can't! You've also got to remember that nothing lasts forever and that one day all these requests are going to stop.

Autographs are actually becoming a thing of the past now, as nowadays the majority of people ask for selfies. These can be fun, when they work, but because people sometimes get a bit nervous when it comes to taking the picture they end up turning their phone off instead. By the time they've turned it back on again you've been standing there for three or four minutes. No, give me a good old-fashioned autograph any day!

What I really can't abide are people who refuse to sign them. That's like sticking two fingers up to the people who pay your wages. It's massively disrespectful. If you're on the beach with your family or something then fine, ask them to come back when you're on your own, but there are loads of people I've seen who instead of stopping and signing something for a fan will just barge their way past with their noses in the air. Idiots like that should pull their heads out of their backsides and remember where they came from. It drives me mad.

I, on the other hand, just can't say no, and that drives my wife mad.

We can be out shopping sometimes when suddenly I might have five or six people round me talking about football, asking for autographs and taking selfies. It's great! Sarah calls it 'The Robbie Savage Show'.

I remember we were out at a restaurant called Australasia in Manchester once. I was just tucking into my edamame beans when all of a sudden four girls came over to the table and started chatting and asking for autographs. 'No problem,' I said. You should have seen the look on Sarah's face. If, as the saying goes, looks could kill, I would have died a really horrible death that night.

At the end of the day she's punching well above her weight being with me so she should just be grateful.

JOKE!

I've signed autographs in some very strange places over the years – geographically, I mean! One of the most bizarre places was on the hard shoulder of the M1. I'd pulled in with a puncture and was standing there wondering what to do next. As much as I love cars I'm useless when it comes to maintenance. After about fifteen minutes a lorry pulled in next to me.

'Thank God for that,' I thought. 'Saved at last!'

When the driver got out of his cab he walked up to me and handed me a piece of paper.

'Hi, Robbie. Would you mind signing this please?'

'Of course,' I said.

At the time this seemed like a good deal to me. I sign a bit of paper in return for having my wheel changed. The thing is though, as opposed to asking me for the jack and then getting me mobile again, he just shoved the piece of paper in his pocket, got back in his cab and drove off. I felt like a right lemon.

As he drove slowly back on to the motorway a car-load of football fans spotted me and began waving at me and telling how much they liked me. Actually, that's rubbish. There were lots of back-to-front Winston Churchill impressions and cries of 'Oi, Savage, you w★★★★★!'

Thanks a lot, lads!

On the whole I absolutely love football fans. I've had some funny experiences over the years but at the end of the day it takes all sorts, doesn't it? The most important thing to remember is that it doesn't matter who you are, we all have our place within the game – a game we all love – and as long as we don't let the idiotic few spoil it for everyone else we'll carry on just fine.

Savaged on *Strictly*

Football has got nothing on *Strictly Come Dancing* with regards to what's required of you, not just physically, but mentally too. Being a footballer is a bit like being a pop star: you get long periods of boredom followed by short bursts of intensity. I must have spent years of my life sitting on my backside praying for the next match to come along. It can be hideous sometimes. *Strictly*, by comparison, is just relentless. Totally full-on. From the moment you sign the contract to the moment you get voted off it never, ever stops.

When I first got asked to do it I thought somebody was having a laugh with me. I'd never danced before, not even in nightclubs or at weddings. I was just too embarrassed. It didn't matter how many times you asked me, I would always say the same thing, 'Just leave me alone!' Actually, that's not 'strictly' true because Sarah and I did have the first dance at our wedding. That's honestly about it, though. It just wasn't me.

Once I realized that the approach was genuine I went to meet some of the producers on the show. I still couldn't understand why they'd asked me.

'Why me?' I said.

'Why not?' they replied. 'You've got a big personality and we think you'd do well.'

'But I can't dance!'

'And? Neither can half the other contestants. That's the whole point, Robbie. You have to learn.'

'Ah! Got you.'

You see, sometimes it takes me a while to click.

I talked it over with Sarah and a few friends and in the end I thought, 'Why not?'

I'm competitive, I like a laugh and I'm not afraid of hard work. I also wanted people to see first-hand that actually I'm not such a horrible person after all. There's no harm in a bit of positive PR every now and then.

But do you know the main reason why I signed up to appear on *Strictly*? My mum and dad. Dad was getting very ill with Pick's disease at the time and because he needed a lot of care, he and my mum hardly ever went out. Dad was in his own world for much of the time but Mum, who didn't want him go into a home, had to stay with him and it was a really hard time for her. She in particular absolutely loved *Strictly Come Dancing* and so I thought, what better way of keeping Mum entertained through such a difficult period than seeing her youngest son on her favourite TV show? She was absolutely over the moon when I told her and ended up being invited by the late and much missed Colin Bloomfield to go on BBC Radio Derby while I was on the show to talk about how I was doing. She became a bit of a celebrity.

Despite all the good intentions regarding my mum, nothing could have prepared me for what was to come. Words like 'hard work' don't even touch the sides.

Before I go any further I would just like to say how very, very lucky I was to be paired with Ola Jordan. That woman has the patience of a saint. Well, you would have to teaching someone like me. It must have been awful for her but she never let on. Well, not much. Ola's husband James, too, was also a big, big help and I'm so glad we've all stayed friends.

You know when you do something physical for the first time, say like rock climbing, and the morning after you're usually a bit stiff. Stiff? I felt like I was a thousand years old the morning after my first practice session with Ola. It was murder. Every muscle in my body had just seized up. The session itself had gone okay. I had a bit of rhythm according to Ola and could shake my hips a bit.

'You've got potential, Robbie,' she said.

Potential for what? Making a fool of myself in front of millions of people?

All kinds of things went through my mind when I started. At least when I was playing football I had some confidence in what I did. With *Strictly* I had almost none and that played havoc with my head. All those feelings of self-doubt and insecurity that I used to get in football were back, just a lot worse. I know it's only a television show but at the end of the day you want to do as well as you can. And what about all your friends and family? You don't want to let them down.

When I was in football, friends and family used to avoid coming to watch me play, mainly because of all the abuse I got. That was their excuse, anyway. Now, though, they had no excuse and they couldn't wait to switch on the television on a Saturday evening. I still got abuse, of course, but this time it was mainly from Craig Revel Horwood. Actually, I'm not sure what's worse, 35,000 angry football fans or him!

Can I let you into a secret? After the first show when Craig had given me just two out of ten for my cha-cha-cha I went straight back to my hotel room and cried. I did! I called up my parents and just burst into tears. It wasn't just what Craig had said, it was the whole build-up – the rehearsals, the time away from my family, the media circus, the doubt, the worry, the pressure – and then to go out there in front of eleven million people and only get a miserable two? Well, I'm afraid it just tipped me over the edge. The following week he said I danced like a rabbit with the trots.

I threw my toys out of the pram and threatened to quit the show after the cha-cha-cha debacle, although I soon backed down and decided to come out fighting again. That's how much it meant to me. Honestly, it's serious stuff. I'm so glad I didn't quit the show because the sense of pride I got from working hard and getting a seven from Craig the following week was tremendous. What a relief that was. Mum was absolutely thrilled but not half as much as I was. I'd been so conscious about letting her down.

I'll tell you what though, Bruno Tonioli can be just as harsh as Craig sometimes. What was it he said about my dancing style? 'I love the way you strut your stuff. You're like a cross between Kate Moss and Russell Brand.'

Another time Bruno said I was like a kangaroo with lead feet, but that description was probably quite accurate.

I think the worst feedback I got for a dance – even worse than for the cha-cha-cha – was when we did the samba or, as Len Goodman called it, the 'sham-ba'. We used a gimmick for the dance – I whipped off my trousers to reveal a pair of football shorts with the number eight on – and unfortunately it went down like a lead balloon. The dance itself had gone okay but all the judges talked about were the shorts.

There was one upside, though, as according to Bruce Forsyth it was the first time a male dancer had shown his legs on the show. What an accolade!

I was definitely more of a ballroom man that I was a Latin man. It was the whole hips thing that got me. I was hopeless. They just wouldn't move the way I wanted them to! Being told I had to learn a Latin dance the following week honestly used to fill me with absolute dread. All I saw was Craig holding up twos!

The rehearsal process for *Strictly Come Dancing* is absolutely relentless. Eight hours a day, five days a week, so all in all you probably rehearse whatever dance you're doing about 200 times. It's such an emotional roller-coaster. When you get a dance right for the first time it feels fantastic, but the frustration you experience getting there can be overwhelming. Sometimes we would get to Friday, the day before the show, and I still wouldn't have got the dance. That's when panic started to set in – panic and pure fear.

I can remember on at least two occasions going into the show on a Saturday having not completed one good dance in rehearsal.

Talk about flying by the seat of your pants! I also remember forgetting the moves once or twice. My mind would just go completely blank. I remember stopping Ola one day just before we went out to dance.

'Oh my God,' I said to her. 'I've forgotten what I do!'

She thought I was joking but I wasn't. How I managed to get through it I'll never know.

The thing is that in a football game, whatever happens on the pitch there'll always be ten other people to share the blame or the responsibility. On *Strictly* it's just you. Yes, you have a dancing partner but at the end of the day they're not the ones being judged. It's your mistakes that the judges are going to point out and there is no hiding place. What makes matters worse is that if you do make a hash of it people can watch it back as many times as they like.

How the professional dancers manage to hold it all together astounds me. I certainly wasn't the best dancer they've ever had on the show but I also wasn't the worst. Poor Ola had her work cut out trying to turn me into a dancer so imagine what it must be like if you get lumbered with somebody even worse. It would do your head in.

What didn't take me quite as long to work out as the dance moves is the fact that doing well on *Strictly Come Dancing* has as much to do with your personality as it does your dancing ability. This means that the short films they show just before you dance, which you film during the week, are actually just as important as the routine itself. You've got two shop windows and you have to make both count.

The only thing I really didn't like about being on *Strictly* was the fact that the attention you receive from the press is just as intense as the rehearsal process. There's no let-up.

Talk about being out of your comfort zone. Let me take you through a typical day for me. First I get up and help get the kids ready for school. Then, once they've been dropped off, I go straight to the gym. All quite normal so far. On the way I might get the odd wave or the odd 'salute' from somebody but that's about it. It's all good fun. There are certainly no photographers.

Once I get home I'll have a look on Twitter and see what's occurring. I may tweet the odd pearl of wisdom about the beautiful game but within a few minutes I'm bored so I go and get ready for work. That could be anything from doing my podcast for William Hill, my column for the *Daily Mirror* or an appearance for BT Sport. Come the evening there's not a lot going on and that's exactly how I like it. It's just me, the wife, the kids and the dogs. Perfect. You don't see me on the red carpet much, do you? Although I do like going to the odd sporting event if I get invited. I went to the 2015 British Grand Prix and had an amazing time. That's about as glitzy as it gets, though. Sure, I've got a few celebrity mates – people like Freddie Flintoff – but so what? He's just a normal lad like me. To be fair, Freddie could probably be classed as a national treasure, and I feel privileged to have him as one of my best mates, but there's nothing starry about him.

See, it's not exactly A-list, is it? That's my comfort zone. I'm a tiny fish in a big pond with regards to audience. Once I signed up for *Strictly Come Dancing,* though, I got followed everywhere by paparazzi and then headlines were splashed across the news-papers to accompany the photos. I was used to getting a para-graph or two on the back pages, not the front. It was relentless.

I remember once we were arriving at a hotel in Cheshire after a particularly tiring training session. Sure enough, the moment we got out of the car the paparazzi were there – snap, snap, snap. We were both absolutely exhausted and probably looked a bit dishevelled, but instead of reporting what was actually occurring that day the headline was something like 'Robbie's partner Ola looks glum as they arrive at a hotel – TOGETHER!'

I've got some wonderful memories from appearing on *Strictly Come Dancing*, and also some quite poignant ones. Gary Speed came to watch me one Saturday night and that was the last time I ever saw him alive. I was so pleased he'd come to see me and all the way through the show I kept on looking over to him. All he did that evening was smile. That's a wonderful memory.

That was the night I broke my nose on a TV camera. We were doing a jive to Otis Redding's 'Love Man' and everything was going really well. Actually, it was probably going a little bit *too* well, which is why I got a bit carried away. At the end of the routine I had to slide towards the camera. That's slide *towards* the camera. Unfortunately I got a bit over-excited and ended up sliding straight into the flaming thing. You should have seen my nose afterwards. It was a right mess. I got a standing ovation, though.

McFly's Harry Judd, who went on to win the show, has become a really good mate of mine. I've since found out that he's actually one of the most competitive people on earth but at the time he hid it brilliantly. I wish I'd seen through that. I might have tried a bit harder!

Russell Grant was the life and soul of the entire show. People call him my 'godfather' these days because as well as speaking to each other most weeks we've got a lot in common. First of all we're Welsh, of course, but Russell is also a massive football fan. He's into non-league football mainly and is patron of his local club, Wealdstone FC. He too has lost a relative to a form of dementia and is a fellow supporter of the Alzheimer's Society.

I have to say that despite all the hard work, aching muscles, bruises, worry, stress, self-doubt, paparazzi, criticism and constant physical pain, I loved every minute of my time on *Strictly* and I met some absolutely amazing people on the show. It still hasn't changed how I feel about dancing, though, so if you ever see me at wedding or in a nightclub, don't ask.

Roy Keane and the
Answerphone Message

I should have really called this chapter 'How I Unwittingly Turned Roy Keane's Autobiography into a Massive Success' because that's exactly what happened.

In October 2014 I got a telephone call from a mate of mine.

'Hey Sav, have you seen Roy Keane's new book? There's a story about you in it apparently. Everybody's talking about it.'

My first thought was, 'Here we go. What's he going to accuse me of?' Then after mulling it over for a second I realized there wasn't anything. Nothing I could think of, anyway. Roy and I weren't mates so there were no social tales to tell. What about on the pitch then? Well, I'd certainly had a few battles with him over the years, and he'd even got me round the collar once while I was playing for Birmingham, but it was nothing he hadn't done to virtually every other player he'd come up against.

I rang my mate back.

'Have you any idea at all what it's about?'

'Something about a Budweiser commercial.'

That helped – not!

I wasn't kept in the dark for too much longer because the moment I logged on to Twitter that morning it all became apparent. Talk about a deluge! It was absolutely everywhere. I was in every newspaper every day for over a week.

Just in case you have been living on another planet for the past year or so, in October 2014 Roy Keane published his second autobiography and inside it there was a story about him trying to sign me while he was the manager of Sunderland in 2006–8. He obviously knows his midfielders then!

I was at Blackburn Rovers at the time but I wasn't figuring much for the first team. Roy had contacted Mark Hughes who was my manager at Blackburn and Sparky had given him permission to contact me. Anyway, I'll let Roy tell you the rest:

'Sparky gave me permission to give him a call. So I got Robbie's mobile number and rang him.

'It went to his voicemail: "Hi, it's Robbie – whazzup!" – like the Budweiser ad.

'I never called him back. I thought "I can't be f****** signing that."'

As you probably know by now I don't really follow fashion, I create it, and as soon as people got wind of what had gone on everybody started having that as their answerphone message. It was my gift to the world, if you like!

Anyway, once I knew what had gone on I got straight on Twitter and posted: 'Oh come on Roy whazzuuuup!!!! Hahahaha.'

I even re-recorded the message for William Hill and that went viral.

You see, that's the difference between me and the majority of other ex-pros. Most people wouldn't know what to say if someone like Roy Keane came out and wrote something like that about them. In fact, they would probably go into hiding. I just saw it as an opportunity to have a laugh. Why not? I didn't feel embarrassed in the slightest. At the end of the day Roy Keane, one of the greatest midfielders ever to play in the Premier League, had wanted to sign me as a player. As far as I'm concerned that was a massive compliment. In fact, it's probably the ultimate accolade for a midfield player. He's considered one of the best and so to be singled out by him like that – well, it doesn't get any better. One of the few regrets I have from my time in the Premier League is that I never got to play against a fully fit Roy Keane when he was in his pomp. I played against Patrick Vieira in his prime, which was fantastic – if a little bit challenging – but to play against Keane and in that situation was probably the ultimate test. God only knows what he'd have done to me!

In hindsight I probably would have been a little bit more sensible with my choice of voicemail if I had known who was going to call me. That's just me, though. *C'est la vie.*

Challenging for League Titles

Competition is what keeps all sport alive. The Championship has to play second fiddle to the Premier League, but it shouldn't be underrated because, in addition to being one of the most well-attended football leagues in the world, it's also one of the most wide open and that, as far as I'm concerned, makes it all the more attractive. I don't have any statistical analysis to hand but I think the Championship got more headlines and column inches in the 2014/15 season than it has in a very, very long time. I've certainly been talking about it a lot more. Last season there were eight teams vying for the title and hardly any of them were early favourites. That's massively exciting in any league.

A lot of people think that kind of unpredictability is what's missing in the Premier League, but I would have to disagree with that. Yes, of course it would be great if teams outside the top five or six could challenge for the title occasionally but rightly or wrongly that's not how it goes. Just thank your lucky stars you don't follow a team in the German Bundesliga – apart from Bayern Munich or Borussia Dortmund, of course. One- or two-horse races aren't good for football. Things are a bit better in Spain now that Atlético are challenging, and in Italy hopefully the two Milan clubs might start causing Juventus a few problems again.

So compared to the other three big domestic leagues in Europe the Premier League's doing pretty well. There are five teams in the running whereas the others have between one and three. I remember when the Premier League was a two-horse race between Manchester United and Arsenal – although usually Manchester United won. I got bored with it, to tell you the truth. It was great if you were a fan of Manchester United or Arsenal, but not everybody was. Nah, give me the modern-day Premier League any day. Even though we had what seemed like hundreds of genuine world-class players back then I still prefer it like it is today. Competition is what keeps the game alive and the more the merrier. I know there'll be Arsenal and United supporters out there saying 'I preferred it like it was', but what's better for the game, Manchester United or Arsenal romping home in January or February or any one of six teams clinching it on the final day? That's one of the reasons the Premier League is still such a big deal globally – it can be wide open.

When I went abroad either on holiday or to play football in the 1990s or early 2000s all you saw were Manchester United or Liverpool shirts. It didn't matter where you went, locals would be wearing those two shirts. These days when I go abroad I see four primarily: Manchester United, Arsenal, Chelsea and Liverpool. You do get the occasional City shirt but it takes time to get an international following. That's as many team colours as you see from the other European leagues put together. What other shirts do you usually see apart from Barça and Real? Exactly.

But can a team outside the current top five or six ever win the Premier League? I have to say that I think it's doubtful, although you should never say never. I mean just look at Manchester City.

What I think is more likely to happen is that certain teams could perhaps make it into the fringes of the top six, given the right circumstances and investment. Those teams are West Ham, Everton, Aston Villa and Leeds.

Before you all take to Twitter and abuse me just let me try and explain myself.

First of all, it's not all down to money these days. Domestic European football is absolutely crawling with billionaires all trying to outdo each other and so this brings up the problem of location. If a multi-billionaire even richer than Mike Ashley came to Newcastle, how's he going to get the right players to move up north if there are at least four or five other billionaires running even bigger clubs closer to the capital?

Some Newcastle supporters might say, 'Hang on, look at Cheshire where all the Manchester players are based. That's hardly next door to London, is it?'

A good point, but ultimately quite a weak one. Cheshire is home to a whole host of footballers and their families, not to mention managers, chairmen, chief executives, and so on. The point being there is an established footballing community living there, which makes it easier for players to settle. On top of which you have great shops and a massive airport on your doorstep in Manchester. Bingo!

And that's one of the reasons why I've put Everton on my list, apart from the fact that I was supposed to sign for them once or twice.

If somebody with Manchester City's money went to Everton and built a new stadium they could be knocking on the door of the top six within a few years. Everything's in place. You've got a big potential audience and a great location. What else do you need besides money and talent?

Aston Villa speak for themselves really, an absolutely gigantic club with seven titles, seven FA Cups and a (proper) European Cup to their name. They're the biggest team in the second-largest city in the country and only an hour or so from London, depending on who's driving. Once again, as long as they can get the big money, the big new stadium and the talent – they too could be in contention for a top-six place.

As for West Ham, in five or six years' time they really could be up there, providing they get the investment to go with their new stadium. I have the utmost respect for the chairmen, David Sullivan and David Gold, and I believe that they are the right men to take them forward. They were joint chairmen at Birmingham City when I played there, and despite the troubles that hit that club, they're proper football men. What's more, they're dyed-in-the-wool West Ham supporters and so I know that they'll only ever have the club's best interests at heart.

That just leaves Leeds, who are already a big club but have the potential to be massive. Leeds is the country's biggest single-club city and has over 800,000 people living there. It's a fantastic location, just an hour on the plane to London, and has places like Harrogate just on the doorstep. It amazes me that none of the billionaires have been in to buy Leeds as I reckon with the right stadium you could get 60,000 there every week. Think about it, there are about 80,000 people who go and watch Liverpool and Everton every other week and from a population of less than half a million. Leeds is a proud football-ing city and although it doesn't have the success of say an Aston Villa or an Everton, it's still a massive club. Another Manchester City if you ask me. Leeds were also the last team to win the old First Division title back in 1992, so they know what it's like to win the big one – just!

For me there are only two scenarios that could change the Premier League status quo beyond what already exists today or what I've suggested above. The first one is if somebody takes the financial aspect to yet another level. At the end of the day that's exactly how Manchester City did it and Chelsea before them. How things have changed, eh? I remember in 1999 seeing Paul Dickov score an equalizer for Manchester City against Gillingham in the Second Division playoff final, and before we knew it they were signing players like Robinho. What a shock that was to the Premier League.

You see it was different for Manchester City than it was for Chelsea. Chelsea were doing okay when Roman Abramovich came in and it was already quite a big, fashionable club. City on the other hand was just seen as being Manchester's second team – the perennial strugglers who never seemed to have much luck. Well, that certainly changed, didn't it?

The only other thing that could change the situation, and this is probably even less likely to happen, is if some or even all of the current billionaires decided to pull out of the game. I can't think of many reasons why they would except for some kind of global financial crash, but everything goes in cycles. Maybe these people will become bored of football one day. You just don't know.

Do I think any of the above will ever happen? It's unlikely in my lifetime. For the time being we're all just going to have to try and accept things the way they are. But even though it's difficult to see beyond the current top five or six I would sooner it was five or six than just one or two. I mean come on, is that really such a bad thing? The first *and* second tiers of English football are thriving at the moment and I don't see any reason why that shouldn't continue for a very long time.

The Greatest Team to Play
in the Premier League

Now you might think this choice is a bit bizarre, especially as only one player from this team features in 'My All-time Premier League XI', but that was just fantasy football. This is the real thing, a team (rather than individual players) that set records, won championships and intimidated just about every other team in the division by doing one thing and one thing only – playing amazing football. No prizes for guessing who I'm talking about. I still break into a sweat just thinking about them! Yes, ladies and gentlemen, my choice for 'The Greatest Team to Play in the Premier League' is Arsène Wenger's 'Invincibles' of 2003/04, not to mention his Arsenal team leading up to that astonishing year. How can I best describe them? Well, as far as I'm concerned as a long-suffering but admiring member of the opposition, they were just a glorious nightmare.

It didn't matter who your manager was, what belief he had or how good he was at motivating people, once you set foot on that pitch the feeling was always the same. 'Oh God, it's Arsenal.'

In fact, for me those feelings of impending doom usually started a bit earlier than that – about a week earlier! You'd look at the fixtures when they came out and the first one I looked for was Highbury. Then I'd think, 'Go and book yourself a hair appointment for that day – quick!'

I don't know if any managers do it now but when I was at Blackburn Mark Hughes used to split up the fixtures into groups of say six and then try and work out how many points we might get from each group. I caught a peek at one or two of these predictions and whenever you had a group with Arsenal or Manchester United in it there were just great big zeros scrawled next to them.

I remember going to Highbury once when I was at Leicester. It was December 2000, when the foundation of the 'Invincible' team was already being put in place, and we'd had quite a good season so far: we had won ten, lost four and drawn five. Not bad for us. I don't know why but on the coach going to Highbury you could smell the fear. Actually I do know why: I knew we were in for a drubbing! Everybody was a bit uneasy and there was no laughing or joking like there usually was. Even Peter Taylor, who was usually such an optimistic guy, was subdued.

Arsenal obviously had a fantastic reputation. After all, they were *all* world-class players – but what made it worse that day was that they were coming into the match on the back of a four-goal stuffing at Liverpool and all week we'd been listening to the press and the media going on about how mighty Arsenal would be desperate to turn things round. We played dreadfully that day and in the end Arsenal whipped us 6–1. To be honest it could very easily have been ten. Yes, we were pretty bad, but God they were good. I'm surprised we even scored one. It was an Ade Akinbiyi rebound from Trevor Benjamin's header. That meant we were only 2–1 down at the time but at no point did it feel like there was a comeback on the cards. Henry scored within minutes and after that it went from bad to worse.

Actually I don't think I can talk about it anymore. It's too upsetting!

Physically they had the edge over everyone. They were bigger, stronger and, when the need arose, harder. You just couldn't get near them.

Even when you played all the great Manchester United teams featuring the likes of Cantona, Keane and the Class of '92, you still went in there thinking you had a chance of getting one over them, and sometimes we did. With Arsenal it was different. I've honestly never seen confidence like that in my entire life. They just oozed it.

I think the best result I ever had against one of Wenger's classic teams was a goalless draw while I was at Birmingham. Not exactly aspirational is it, a goalless draw? I'll tell you what, though, against that team it was like winning a cup final.

It was May 2004 and Thierry Henry had just been crowned PFA Player of the Year. Arsenal were just a couple of weeks away from being crowned Premier League champions (not to mention the 'Invincibles', having gone the entire season undefeated) and there was a real party atmosphere in Highbury. Luckily for us that seemed to unnerve the Arsenal players and in the first half they didn't have one shot on target. They didn't seem nervous as such, just a bit overwhelmed by everything, and who can blame them? They were standing on the edge of greatness.

We came close three times before Arsenal eventually threatened, but in the end it just petered out. What a relief. We were on that bus within half an hour of the full-time whistle going, just in case the ref changed his mind. A point at Highbury!

I remember Martin Keown coming on as a substitute in about the ninetieth minute and I was really moved by the reception he got. He was no longer a first-team regular by then and I think he needed to notch up ten appearances to get a championship medal. This brought him one game closer to the target and the crowd went absolutely berserk.

I got some decent write-ups for that game. In fact, according to the BBC, 'Birmingham were well-organised and resilient, with Robbie Savage working tirelessly in midfield.' Not bad, eh? Thanks very much indeed.

As fantastic as teams like Arsène's Invincibles were, they belong to a bygone era really and I don't think we'll ever see their like again in the Premier League. Part of the reason they were able to play like that was because there were fewer teams who were likely to win the league. Don't get me wrong, they were all world-class players and they were beautiful to watch, but the game's moved on a lot since then and they wouldn't get anywhere near as many opportunities. It's a match I'd love to see though, the Invincibles team of 2003/04 versus the Chelsea team of 2014/15. I think Arsène might actually get one over on José there, for a change.

The 2003/04 Invincibles Teamsheet

Lehmann

Lauren

Campbell

Touré

Cole

Vieira

Gilberto

Ljungberg

Pirès

Bergkamp

Henry

Subs: Edu, Parlour, Wiltord, Reyes

Foreign Players

In my opinion you get a lot of clubs – not just in the Premier League but in the Championship, too – who will look for players abroad before they look closer to home. In my opinion the reason for this harks back to the early days of the Premier League.

Back then foreign players were still a bit of a novelty in the Premier League and the players we did have over here were invariably game changers – people like Dennis Bergkamp, Gianluca Vialli, Juninho and Gianfranco Zola. They were all so technically gifted and that was exactly what was missing from English football.

They were a breath of fresh air, not only for the season-ticket holders and the viewers at home but also for the likes of me. When I was at Blackburn I played with Tugay Kerimoğlu, the Turkish international who is without doubt the best player I ever played alongside in midfield. He was so incredibly gifted that I knew it didn't matter where he was on the pitch, if I passed it to him he would, a) receive the ball without getting dispossessed, and b) do something fantastic with it. All of a sudden I had options. And that's what foreign players brought to the Premier League: skill, refinement and bags of technique. Things would never be the same again. You can say that again!

You see, I can only speak for midfielders but until then the mentality of the British players (or what we'd actually been taught) was to get the ball up to a centre forward as quick as you could. Once the foreign players arrived you had other options open to you – in fact, hoofing it up to the forward became the last thing you wanted to do. The problem I experienced was that when I went to play international football for Wales I didn't have a Tugay playing alongside me and I think that was the case with a lot of British domestic players. We went from playing a more modern style of football in the Premier League to a more old-fashioned style of football with our international teams, and so the more foreign players you had arriving in the Premier League the more difficult it became to adjust. It was like trying to speak a foreign language.

What you have now is just an extreme version of those early days. It's gone from an appreciation of foreign players and continental football to an obsession.

It's understandable, in a way. I mean, what would you rather watch, football *c*.2015 or football *c*.1976? It's a no-brainer. But then why do they always have to take it to extremes? These days you've got teams made up almost entirely of foreign players – in British teams, remember. How can you as a supporter turn up to watch a British team and not be able to watch more than one or two British players? I don't get it.

Some people call it progression, but how can it be? It does

nothing whatsoever for the home nations' international game. In the 2014/15 season only a third of players who took to the field in Premier League matches were British and that for me is unacceptable.

This could change daily, of course, but at the time of writing the Barcelona first-team squad has nine Spanish players, but a further seven who speak either Spanish or Portuguese.

In my opinion one of the reasons why the Premier League has so many foreign players is because many of the managers are only ever really a game or two away from getting the sack – especially the ones at the lower end of the league – and so they can't possibly put together a 'genuine' long-term strategy. In an ideal world they'd give a couple of kids a run out, but instead they end up on the phone panic-buying foreign players who've got a bit of a pedigree. Seriously, who would be a Premier League manager?

I'll tell you what, though, at the end of the day foreign players have brought a tremendous amount of good to English football in terms of style and quality.

If you had to make a list of the Premier League's twenty greatest moments over the past twenty-three seasons since it began, I guarantee at least half would involve foreign players. All right, maybe a third, but that's still massively impressive and in my opinion is testament to the effect that the likes of Tugay, Henry, Bergkamp, Ronaldo, Zola, Vialli, Drogba, Di Canio, Schmeichel, Suárez and Ginola had. Oo-ah, Ginola. It was my ambition to become his nemesis when I was a young player because when I was at Leicester and he was at Spurs it was always my job to man-mark him whenever we played each other. This was back in the late 1990s and early 2000s so I was young, fit and keen. Before every match we played against them I'd get the same instructions from the gaffer.

'Robbie, don't let him out of your sight!'

Sometimes I did okay against him but more often than not he just ran the entire show.

He was *such* a dangerous player and could run rings round entire teams, let alone the poor devil man-marking him. I remember playing Spurs at Filbert Street back in April 2000. They fielded a class team that day with players like Sol Campbell, Darren Anderton and Stephen Clemence, but then we also had a pretty decent squad featuring the likes of Andy Impey, Muzzy Izzet, Tony Cottee and Frank Sinclair. All things considered then it should have been pretty even, but there was one thing separating our two teams: a tall, reasonably good-looking Frenchman with more talent in his little finger than the majority of us had in our entire bodies.

He was a proper game-changer; somebody who could surprise teams by doing something mesmerizing just when you weren't expecting it. That day at Filbert Street was no exception. It wasn't a brilliant game by any stretch of the imagination and both Leicester and Spurs had created precious little by way of chances. It was quite a scrappy affair. Then, all of a sudden, Ginola received the ball in the box and before any of us, Spurs players included, knew what was happening he'd scored. We just stood there, shell-shocked. His speed, accuracy and vision was the difference that day and although we lost the game it was massively impressive.

The one other player I have to mention here is Gianfranco

Zola, one of the most creative forwards ever to grace the Premier League. Like David Ginola, Zola also had the pleasure of having me man-mark him once, except that on this occasion I came out on top. I was still at Leicester City at the time and Martin O'Neill had just left to join Celtic. Peter Taylor had been appointed as his successor and although we'd all been very down about Martin leaving he still managed to bring us all round and make us laugh.

The game in question took place at Stamford Bridge at the start of the 2000/01 season and when Peter Taylor told me that he wanted me to man-mark the great Gianfranco Zola I gulped. 'But how?' I thought to myself.

God only knows how I did it but I stuck to Gianfranco like glue that day and we ended up winning the game 2–0 with goals from Stan Collymore and Muzzy Izzet. We didn't often win games at Stamford Bridge, but to go there and successfully man-mark one of the best players in the world was amazing.

He was such a brilliant player to watch. Coming into the Premier League – one of the most physical in the world – and making such a massive difference so quickly was a towering achievement; but then this was a man who'd learned his trade playing with Diego Maradona at Napoli. Didn't it show?

Players like these two, and the rest I've mentioned, have helped to make the Premier League what it is today.

And who have we got to thank for bringing these players into our lives? The managers.

Inviting foreign players into the English game *has* been progressive and I applaud the Premier League for allowing it to happen. But please let's try and redress the balance a bit and get the amount of home-grown players who regularly get a game back up to where it should be. In Spain it's about 60 per cent at the moment, which I think is admirable, so why not aim for 50 per cent? Let's have foreign players *complementing* the Premier League again and not just swamping it. Okay?

The Art of Being a
Modern Footballer

The role of each position on the field has changed since I was playing, so I'm going to explain the 'art' of being a goalkeeper, a defender, a midfielder (I might struggle a bit with that one) and a striker in the modern game.

What qualifies me to lecture the world on what it takes to be a great footballer? Well, when it comes to the world's most versatile players you don't really have to look any further than yours truly. Yes, you did read that correctly, I said yours truly. Now, before you all start tearing out these pages and setting fire to them, just give me a second and I'll prove it.

As a midfielder, which is what I spent the majority of my career doing, I was a straightforward box-to-box man and while I was on the pitch I had two jobs to do – run and tackle. I didn't pass the ball much and I didn't score many goals but I ran miles and miles every game and I put the boot in more times than there are words in this book. Fair enough?

If you want to see a modern-day version of me you would probably go and watch someone like Yaya Touré. We're almost identical in every way except for the fact that he can pass, score goals and is great on the ball. Oh yes, and he also has vision. I was better at tracking back than him, though, and I had nicer hair. Anyway, that's just a tip for you.

So now you're probably saying, 'Being a midfielder with limited ability does *not* make you versatile. In fact if anything it makes you the opposite.'

Thanks very much.

But what about my professional career as a striker, or as a defender, or as a goalkeeper! You see, you didn't know I'd made professional appearances in those positions, did you? Well, I did.

Here's the lowdown on my credentials. When I got taken on first as a schoolboy and then as an apprentice by Manchester United I was actually signed as a striker. Not many people know that. I didn't score many goals to be fair and I was competing against the likes of Mark Hughes and Brian McClair, but that was my first position as a player. It wasn't until I was playing for Bobby Gould in the Wales squad a few years later that it was suggested – by Bobby – that I might try out in midfield. By that time I was playing professionally for Crewe Alexandra and although I wouldn't be troubling Ian Wright or Alan Shearer anytime soon, I got my name on the scoresheet once or twice. I even scored a hat-trick at Burnley once. There was a right-footed volley from a corner (that was a peach), a left-footed tap-in and a screamer from thirty yards. Not bad, eh? As I said, I was versatile.

After making my debut as a midfielder for Wales, Bobby Gould must have called Dario Gradi at Crewe because the next time I played domestic football was in the centre of midfield – my new home.

Funnily enough, when I first signed for Leicester City a year or so later Martin O'Neill played me as a right wing-back in a five-man defence. Talk about confusing! I could run all right but I didn't really have a lot of tricks in my locker and so never really felt comfortable there. Martin still stuck at it for a while, though, and it wasn't until my second season at Leicester that I managed to convince the gaffer that I could do a job for him in the middle of the park.

So that just leaves goalkeeper. Well, believe it or not, I once spent over forty-five minutes between the sticks for Derby County and I only let in two goals. That's not bad!

And what was the extent of my experience? Well, my apprenticeship as a goalkeeper came in two stages: on the concrete on our estate a few times when I was little (and only when it was my turn) and then a few chats with big Stephen Bywater who I roomed with at Derby. Honestly, that was it. I'd never even had a go in training.

We were playing Reading at the Madejski Stadium in March 2010 and Mr Bywater, who was our first-choice keeper, had been taken off with a back spasm. Not long after that his replacement, Saul Deeney, got sent off for bringing down Jay Tabb in the area and so all of a sudden we were in trouble.

The gaffer, Nigel Clough, had a plan.

'Sav, you're not getting a kick in midfield. You go in goal.'

'Really? Okay then.'

And so that was it. I put on the shirt and the gloves and into battle I went. The Reading supporters gave me heaps of stick and, surprisingly enough, I gave them some back! It was great fun.

To give you a clue as to how I got on that day I'll just give you the headline from the following day's *Daily Telegraph*:

'Robbie Savage shines in goal for Derby County.'

I was brilliant.

Underneath the headline they wrote:

Savage was required to stand between the sticks for over 45 minutes, and during that time he unfurled a range of saves (including a sublime tip around the post from a *Gylfi Sigurdsson* free kick which was lancing straight into the top right corner), let in only two goals, and afterwards appeared so taken with his performance in the new position that he joked that he might even make it into the Welsh national squad as a goalkeeper.

Did I really say that? In fact, when I turned on my mobile phone after the match I had a text from Eric Steele, the Manchester United goalkeeping coach, saying, 'You're the sixth best goalkeeper in Wales!'

Two of the other messages were from Craig Bellamy, who said I'd wasted my career in midfield, and from Roberto Mancini, who said he needed a new keeper and was I available?

When the press asked me if I'd had any experience in goal I said, 'No, lads. I'm just a natural sportsman.' Classic me, eh? Always humble.

The one thing the *Telegraph* forgot to mention was that I also even saved a penalty. Well, what I mean is that I managed to put Shane Long off *scoring* a penalty. It's the same thing in my book.

I got so carried away by it all that the Derby lads even joked that a Robbie Savage clean-sheet would have been too much to bear and that they were glad that I let in two goals.

So there you are then – Mr Versatile – the only man who is truly qualified to advise you all on what it takes to be a great footballer.

Read on . . . and learn!

Being a goalkeeper has to be one of the most boring jobs in the world.

In my short but nevertheless eventful career as a keeper I spent half my time trying to think of ways of keeping warm, which brings me nicely on to my conclusion as to what kind of person makes a good goalkeeper.

Basically, goalkeepers are a different breed. Perhaps it's all the bravery involved. I mean, let's face it: diving head-first into the feet of an oncoming fifteen-stone centre forward isn't what the majority of us would choose to do for a living, is it? No, it takes a certain kind of person to want to do that.

But then what about the cold and the boredom? The cold, as football is a winter sport, must surely become a problem sometimes. I had forty-five minutes in early March in Reading and, for heaven's sake, almost froze to death – *and* I had quite a bit of goalmouth action. Imagine playing out a 0–0 draw in Sunderland on a Monday night in February with the wind

Brothers in broadcasting. Jonathan Wall at Radio 5 Live and Grant Best at BT Sport have a lot to answer for. © *C1 Photography*

(top) Playing for Wales alongside the great Gary Speed was one of the highlights of my entire career and I think football misses him massively. © *Mike Egerton/EMPICS Sport*

(bottom) Taking some advice from Mark Clattenburg, in my opinion one of the best referees we've ever had. © *Nigel French/EMPICS Sport*

(top) A better looking version of Ant and Dec – you'd never know we used to be enemies, would you? © *REX Shutterstock*

(bottom) Ola Jordan and I on the sofa on breakfast TV. The media attention you receive when you're on *Strictly* is relentless, from the moment you sign the contract until the day you get voted off. © *Ken McKay/REX Shutterstock*

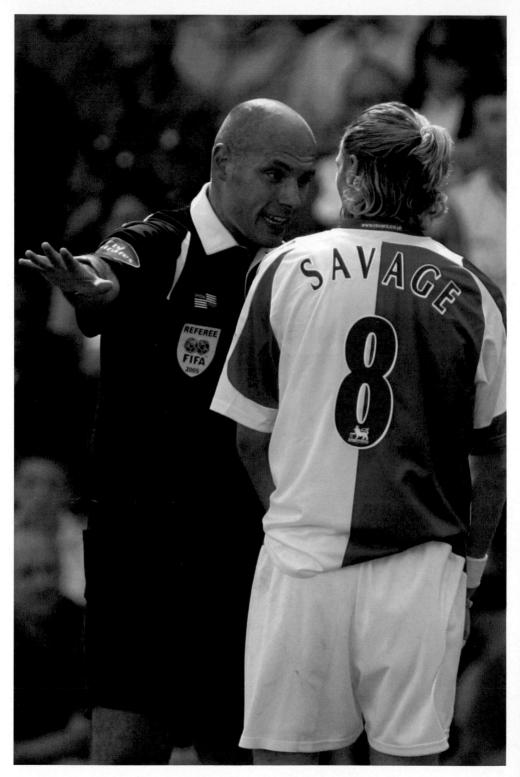

Since becoming a regular on *Fletch & Sav*, Howard Webb has completely changed my opinions on refereeing – and, in some cases, even referees! © *Simon Bellis/EMPICS Sport*

(top) Wazzuuuup Roy! I still can't believe that happened. Can we move on please. © *Mirrorpix*

(bottom) 'Get up, you!' Me versus Ronaldo during his career at Manchester United. © *Action Images/Michael Regan*

Playing against one of my biggest heroes was a strange experience, but given how good Gary Speed was it was also a privilege. I have so many great memories of him. © *Mirrorpix*

Not a bad way to make a living! *Fletch & Sav* is about two things – the best guests and plenty of insight and banter. *(bottom)* Myself, Fletch, Wrighty and Rio chatting to Captain Marvel himself, Bryan Robson – according to Paul Gascoigne, the greatest footballer of his generation. © *C1 Photography*

(top left) Me and the family. © Author's own

(top right) Before and after. You have to stay in shape being a pundit and after twelve weeks with my trainers, Josh McHale and Steve McElroy, I managed to get down to 12st 12lbs. © Josh McHale and Steve McElroy

(bottom) Me, vain? You're having a laugh… © Author's own

blowing a gale and the temperature at minus three. What the heck do you do for warmth then? Wet yourself? But the boredom must be just as bad.

I have the attention span of a three-year-old, which is why I was always happiest playing as a box-to-box midfield player. Good or bad, win or lose, providing I was up for it (which I always was) there was never a dull moment. Imagine the opposite of that, standing there like a lemon waiting for something – anything – to happen. Surely it would drive you mad. What makes matters worse is that while all the action is going on elsewhere you have to remain focused, alert and ready for action.

Being serious for a second, the role of a goalkeeper has definitely changed over the years as these days there's a lot more focus on distribution. That's makes sense up to a point, but what about Manuel Neuer becoming what's known as a sweeper-keeper? As far as I know it was Pep Guardiola's idea – an experiment really – and also involved turning Philipp Lahm from a full-back to a defensive midfield player. Could it be a sign of things to come? I doubt it, for the simple reason that Manuel Neuer is a very rare kind. As well as being a fantastic goalkeeper he is also a very gifted outfield player and is as confident with a ball to feet outside the box as he is with a ball to hands inside. Now how many goalkeepers do you know with that kind of ability? Exactly. The only keeper I ever played with who could do that was Neville Southall; in fact, he was a magnificent outfield player.

The only way you can play a sweeper-keeper is if you have a Manuel Neuer and as far as I'm aware they haven't got around to cloning him yet. More like him are bound to come along eventually, but they're never going to become the norm. Not in my lifetime anyway. I always cringe when I see a goalkeeper come out of his box because nine times out of ten it ends in tears. They always look terrified, too.

It doesn't always work for Neuer, by the way, and there have been times when he's taken the role to extremes.

Look, as I said, because of the way the game has changed I admit that goalkeepers today need to be able to distribute the ball effectively, but if you are going to come out of your box every five minutes and start involving yourself in open play you have to make sure you have both the confidence and the ability to pull it off. At the end of the day I would want my goalkeeper to concentrate on keeping the ball out of the net and if he could do *that* effectively – fantastic.

So there we are then; although the role of goalkeeper has evolved a bit over the years the *art* of being a keeper is still the same as it always was – keep the ball out of the net. I still wouldn't advise anyone to take it up, though.

Defenders, like goalkeepers, are a special breed. They are the unsung heroes. There's still more than an element of bravery involved, of course, especially for the centre backs. It's just more physical more of the time. There's nothing scarier than being set upon by a six-foot-four centre back who you've upset – nothing. In my day it was the midfielders who got all the headlines – people like Roy Keane and Patrick Vieira – and yes, they were both as hard as nails. I was never scared of them though. If you want to talk real physical intimidation look no further than lads like Gerry Taggart and Darren Moore. Those two honestly put the fear of God into me and they were on my team!

These days, like just about everything else in the game, the role of the defender has changed. You don't have to be quite as physical as you used to be because the rules state that you're not allowed to tackle so aggressively, nor do they allow grappling in the box so much. Mobile phones and social media have been the catalyst because whatever you do on that pitch will be either seen or recorded by somebody and, since that's been the case, the powers that be have been able to reflect and take action. Back in the day, defenders used to get away with all kinds of stuff – punches, digs, elbows, stamps. After all, what's the best way to put off striker from making runs into the box? Take him out of the game! You knew where the ref was and so if you thought you could get away with it, you would floor the striker. You can't do that today, of course, and the game's much better for it.

Forward players are also a lot quicker these days, as is the style of play, and so in order to be able to defend against them you have to be a bit more like them. The big, slow centre backs of yesteryear are still as big, but they're not quite as slow.

Rio Ferdinand was probably one of the first of that new breed of modern defender, in this country at least. He was quick, comfortable on the ball, physical when he needed to be and could distribute the ball well. It's those kinds of attributes that have led to a new generation of defender coming through: players who are quick, have a turn of pace and who can read the game. Some of the big defenders used to base their entire game on putting in big tackles but that's no longer good enough.

Firstly, you would get sent off but, secondly, you probably wouldn't catch anybody.

Look at the way Spain played when they won the World Cup and the European Championship. Everything was built from the back, which meant the centre halves had to have skill and be comfortable on the ball. Every position's changing really. Look at full backs. They're all bombing forward, overlapping, getting balls in *and* defending – but that's what they're expected to do these days.

To summarize then, in order to be a successful defender in the Premier League you need to be strong, athletic, good on the ball, quick, relatively skilful and be able to read the game. If that doesn't demonstrate just how much the game has changed in this country, then nothing will.

In the middle of the park things are very different. In my day if you were playing four–four–two one midfielder would play box-to-box and the other player would sit and defend, and you'd cross over where necessary. These days with varying formations it's different. In today's Premier League, especially away from home, you're seeing a lot more managers playing a four–two–three–one formation, where the two midfielders are expected to sit and protect the back four. These players have to be good defensively, of course, but they also have to be good technically because being able to receive the ball in tight areas and link play is essential to their role. This is where Claude Makélélé excelled and, because of the formation he played in, he basically did the job on his own. What a tremendous player he was.

Nowadays teams generally play two in that role, examples being Fernandinho and Yaya Touré at Manchester City, Eric Dier and Ryan Mason at Tottenham, Gareth Barry and James McCarthy at Everton, and Morgan Schneiderlin and Bastian Schweinsteiger at Manchester United. I was going to include Matić and Fàbregas on the list but in my opinion playing someone like Fàbregas in that role, who is not a defensively minded player, can leave you exposed and so is not as effective.

Physically, midfield players are generally more diminutive today (apart from the likes of Touré and Matić) and so put that together with the fact that they're also more technically gifted, and it really is all change.

Regarding the three players in front, the question is are they attackers, midfielders or number tens? Basically, they're all three. Players still have defined roles, of course, but as far as the midfield is concerned these roles are far more closely linked with the players both behind and in front of them, and in my opinion this has improved the game massively.

If centre-back and centre-midfield roles are currently evolving, centre forwards must be just about extinct, especially the big, old-fashioned number nine. You need to be so quick these days, which is one of the reasons I didn't make it. I could run all day, but I had no pace. That's probably my only regret in football; that and not being given a chance to play in midfield at Manchester United. Saying that, even if Eric Harrison or Alex Ferguson had realized I was more suited to a midfield role I might not have got in. Nicky Butt would probably have been first on the sheet but Scholesy did not start to come in until after us so I might well have got a game or two. Anyway, that's all by the by.

If I had to blame anybody for the demise of the old-fashioned centre forward I would probably point the finger at Lionel Messi, Barcelona and that all-conquering Spanish national side. Look at that Barcelona team of six or seven years back. They didn't play one centre forward. Instead, they had Lionel Messi leading a three-man line comprising of himself, Samuel Eto'o and Thierry Henry. I'd rarely seen anything like that before in domestic football – three forward players linking up – and I remember being blown away by the movement, pace, skill and interplay. It completely revolutionized football for me. It was the same with the Spanish national team when they left Fernando Torres on the bench and played without an out-and-out striker. It was unheard of in this country.

Even now things aren't much different at the Nou Camp. I know Barcelona have got Luis Suárez now, who's classed as an out-and-out striker but even he can (and does) operate in any one of the three forward positions. And that's the beauty of the modern game: it just screams skill and versatility. Most top teams now play a four–three–three formation at home and a four–two–three–one formation away, which is where a small element of the old-fashioned centre forward comes into play, showcasing players like Christian Benteke, Zlatan Ibrahimović, Olivier Giroud, Romelu Lukaku, Robert Lewandowski and, to a point, Diego Costa. Win the battle in midfield, though (easier said than done, of course), and you've got three players in front of you, all with instructions, but basically playing a free role. You've got options galore. Seriously, don't you think it's fantastic to watch?

I'll tell you one thing that makes me laugh about formations: I was at a kids' football match not too long ago and towards the end of the game the manager of the team that was losing suddenly shouted, 'Okay, let's go for it, let's go with two up front!' Playing with two up front is almost unknown these days. How things have changed . . .

Some of the best football I have ever seen played in the Premier League was when Manchester City had Sergio Agüero in the middle, David Silva on the wing, Carlos Tevez in and around Agüero and Yaya Touré just in behind them. What an unbelievable team that was. Best of all, though (for me, at least), the four–three–three formation has even started filtering through to the mighty Wales team. When we lined up against Belgium in June, Chris Coleman and his opposite number Marc Wilmots both played a four–three–three formation and it was quality. In fact, it was like watching Brazil v. Argentina. Honestly, it was! Well, maybe Arsenal v. Chelsea, but I would settle for that. The point is that the formation's not just being played by the big countries or the big club teams. You need to have the right players, of course, but if that's the kind of football that clubs, managers and players are aspiring to play (and we're aspiring to watch) then as far as I'm concerned the future's bright.

I'll tell you one thing that hasn't changed since I was playing up front and that's goal celebrations. Last season somebody had a moan about Real Madrid's loan-signing Javier Hernández because he thought his goal celebration was a bit over the top. Sorry, but what a load of rubbish. I know I didn't score that many but believe me there's no better feeling in the world. If somebody wants to keep things low key and just run down the touchline and wave at the crowd then fair enough, that's their prerogative, but if somebody else wants to jump up and down and start swinging from the chandeliers then you just let them get on with it. It's supposed to be a 'celebration'. The clue's in the name.

As a result of the changes in the way the game is played, I find it difficult to be anything other than positive about today's football and especially about what's to come. It's taken us a while to catch up with the other European countries but thanks to the strength of the Premier League and the influence of foreign players and foreign managers I think we're just about getting there. Incidentally, did you know that last season alone over 800,000 fans from overseas came to watch Premier League matches and spent over £680 million? That's astonishing.

Seriously, it's a good time to be a football fan. I have a whinge about stuff on the telly and on the radio, but at the end of the day that's all superficial. What matters is that football in this country is strong, both off the field and on it. I've already mentioned one or two tweaks I would like to make – after all, nothing's perfect – but I'll tell you what, I always cannot wait for the next round of matches. The Premier League is the most competitive major football league in the world – fact – and I expect to see some absolutely blistering football, week-in, week-out. And as strong as the top four or five are you still get some brilliant surprise results from time to time. Look at the 2014/15 season. Each one of the established big five clubs suffered a shock result or two. Manchester City lost to Burnley and Crystal Palace while Stoke beat Liverpool 6–1. My personal favourite was Leicester City beating Manchester United 5–3 but look at Swansea City; they beat Manchester United *and* Arsenal home and away. Even the mighty Chelsea suffered a 3–0 drubbing at West Brom. The point is, it doesn't matter who you are, every team in that league is fallible and that's why I think the Premier League is the best in the world.

Could a much lower team from La Liga or the Bundesliga beat Barcelona, Real Madrid or Bayern Munich 5–3 or 6–1? I doubt it.

Freak results are so good for the game and if I could pay a few quid to guarantee at least a few of those every season I would get my cheque book out straight away. How about Bournemouth 5 Manchester City 1? I would love that.

When I was first approached about writing this book I was asked if I could write a few words on what I considered to be the 'Golden Age' of football. I think what the publishers had in mind was a chapter about all the teams and players I used to watch as a kid, which is fair enough. When I sat down and thought about it, though, I realized that *this* is my 'Golden Age' of football: not the 1980s or the 1990s. It's the two thousand and noughts and teens that do it for me. Didn't I just say that some of the best football I'd ever seen in my life was played by Arsène's Invincibles and that title-winning Manchester City team featuring Agüero, Silva and Touré? Well, that's the truth, and I could give you 101 other examples of great football from the same period. I think we spend too much time in Britain going on and on about how much better it was in the old days, but I don't subscribe to that at all. Things move on and I think we should too. Respect the past and learn from it by all means, but don't obsess about it. What's that saying, 'There's no future in the past'? Absolutely spot on.

The Best Games in
Which I Ever Played

This is an easy one, as even though I made a respectable thirty-nine appearances for Wales and over 500 appearances for domestic clubs, there are a few matches that are as clear in my mind today as they were the day I played in them.

One of the best domestic matches in which I ever played was the first home match I started for Leicester City back in August 1997, almost twenty years ago. Just in case I needed any more motivation we were entertaining the mighty Arsenal that day, and it ended up being one of the most eventful and exciting matches ever played at Filbert Street.

Unfortunately we started off poorly and within just ten minutes the mercurial Dennis Bergkamp had put one past our keeper. Here we go, I said to myself. I feared the worst, as did the 21,000 Leicester fans. We managed to keep them at bay after that, well, until about the sixtieth minute. It was him again, Bergkamp. Two-nil to the Arsenal and all the hopes I had of getting off to a winning start were all but fading. After the second goal went in I remember seeing Martin O'Neill going absolutely berserk with us on the touchline and that seemed to really stir the crowd, which in turn stirred us up. It was exactly what we needed.

Waiting until the last quarter of a match to start playing against any Arsenal team would normally signal a cricket-score defeat but for some reason by the time Emile Heskey got one back in the eighty-fourth minute, they'd still only scored two. You can say what you like about Emile Heskey, but as far as I'm concerned he was an outstanding player and has been seriously underrated over the years. Anyway, with one goal back and the crowd well and truly behind us it was game on, and despite Arsenal outplaying us for the first eighty minutes of the game, we out-passioned them for the last ten. Actually, make that the last sixteen minutes because in the third minute of stoppage time Matt Elliott scored an equalizer with a twenty-yard shot that was deflected off Grimaldi. Hang on, didn't I say sixteen minutes? That's right, there was still to be a twist in the tale – two, in fact.

In the ninety-fourth minute Bergkamp completed his hat-trick – 'The best I've ever seen,' according to Alan Hansen on *Match of the Day* – and the Gunners at last thought they were home and dry. No chance! Less than two minutes later, as Arsène Wenger, the away supporters and every Arsenal player pleaded with the ref to blow his whistle, Steve Walsh ran unmarked into the Arsenal box and managed to head home the equalizer. Cue several minutes of absolute pandemonium!

Everyone bar the crowd was on the pitch. The Arsenal players were furious because referee Graham Barber added six minutes of stoppage time and the headline in the *Daily Mirror* the following day read 'It's A Clock-Up!' Arsène Wenger was also going mad, and for some reason, although I honestly don't know why, Ian Wright was furious with Steve Walsh. Let's face it, from a spectator's point of view there's no better way of rounding off a six-goal thriller than a bit of argy bargy and that night the *Match of the Day* viewers were in for a real treat. In the red corner, Mr Ian Wright – five foot nine, and in the blue corner, Mr Steve Walsh – six foot three. Thank God they managed to keep them apart!

Saying that, things like height or build meant absolutely nothing to Ian Wright, which is one of the reasons why I loved him as a player. He could score the odd goal too, of course. What a legend. Not only was he totally inspirational as a footballer but he's also a fantastic bloke and, as many of you will know, he's now a regular on *Fletch & Sav*. Like a lot of players, myself included, Wrighty could fly off the handle occasionally. The difference was that the vast majority of perpetrators – again, myself included – would take their foot off the gas and try and calm down once we'd been reprimanded. With Wrighty that wasn't often the case and unfortunately it got him into all kinds of trouble.

Last season he and Joey Barton were guests on the same episode of *Fletch & Sav* and we had quite a long discussion about what separates the likes of me, who might well do something rash but were rarely dangerous, and the likes of Ian or Joey, who quite often found it difficult to draw a line. They were both totally honest about what made them do it and I think it was Wrighty who said that, unlike most people, they simply don't have an off switch. If something happened that made him angry he reacted without thinking and before he knew it he would have a fine and a ban for his trouble. It was only when he took up golf, of all things, that he managed to find a way of responding to those difficult situations instead of just reacting to them. If you play golf you'll know exactly what he means. I play and I lose my temper every time I hit a ball! To be a really good golfer, you need self-control.

The other domestic games I remember from really early on in my Premier League career were when I came up against Manchester United for the first and second time. This was obviously going to be quite a strange experience as not only would I be facing the club that had decided that I wasn't good enough for them all those years ago but I'd also be up against a lot of my mates – the Class of '92.

The first game took place on 27 August 1997 and, even though they were the great Manchester United, I still felt like we were meeting them on equal terms. Leicester City were a really solid Premier League team and there was as much pride in our dressing room as there was anywhere else in the country, let alone the Premier League. After all, we were in fourth place at the time. Not too shabby, was it?

Even though the match ended up 0–0 it could easily have been three apiece. Emile Heskey, who played out of his skin that day, came close on at least three occasions and Manchester United, who I honestly think were quite surprised by how good we were, hit the woodwork three times. I almost scored, too. A ball went out towards the corner flag and I remember racing past Roy Keane to collect it, bringing it back into the box, running past my teammate Steve Claridge – who probably wondered what the heck was going on – and then taking a shot, only for Peter Schmeichel to save it. Just! Not long after that we won a free kick just outside the box and I remember saying to Garry Parker, 'Can I take it?' I was so up for it.

I did and it *just* clipped the top of the wall. Otherwise it would have gone in. What a game!

Afterwards Martin O'Neill said to me, 'You were fantastic today, Robbie, well done.'

I was like the cat that got the cream. It was such a proud moment.

I think I probably exorcized a few demons that day. The next day when I looked at the papers I'd been given nine out of tens across the board, and in one paper, 'Star Man'.

The next time we played Manchester United was at Old Trafford the following January and do you know what? We won 1–0! This result brought to mind some of the last words Sir Alex Ferguson said to me the day he let me go.

'You aren't ready for here, but you'll make it somewhere. One day you'll come back to haunt me.'

Well, bearing in mind I had a hand in the winner that day, which was scored by the brilliant Tony Cottee, you could say that he got it spot on.

At the end of the game my emotions got the better of me a bit and I have to say that Giggsy and all the other lads were brilliant to me. Really, really kind.

A few years later in 2002 I was lucky enough to play in my first ever second-city derby. I hadn't long since joined Birmingham City and had heard a lot about the rivalry between them and Aston Villa. Villa were the rich, successful all-stars, of course, whereas we were seen as the working-class grafters. That suited me absolutely fine. I loved playing for the underdog and couldn't wait.

Villa's Olof Mellberg started the war of words in the run up to the game and all I can say is, 'Thanks, Olof.' He came out and said that he hadn't heard of any of the Birmingham squad, despite me making their life a misery while I was at Leicester, and I remember our manager Steve Bruce telling us all to remember what he'd said. We remembered all right.

On the day of the match, the atmosphere at St Andrew's was bordering on explosive to say the least and the fans on both sides were going absolutely berserk. It was a proper cauldron and I think even the police were intimidated by it.

Clinton Morrison scored the opener for us after a howler from Mellberg and just before Villa kicked off again I remember looking round and seeing fights breaking out everywhere. Oh my God, I thought, this is worse than an Old Firm encounter.

Our second goal has to go down one of the most bizarre goals ever scored, not to mention one of the funniest. Olof Mellberg took a throw-in back to his keeper, Peter Enckelman, but instead of Peter stopping it and then clearing it with his foot it rolled straight underneath it and into the back of the net. I still don't know for sure if Peter made contact with the ball, and the goal shouldn't have stood if he hadn't, but the look on his face suggested he had. Anyway, the goal was given – 2–0! Immediately after that a fan ran onto the pitch and slapped poor Peter across the face, which was completely out of order. There were police running absolutely everywhere. It was chaos!

From then on there were tackles flying in all over the place and poor old David Elleray had a hell of a job keeping control of things. The mighty Geoff Horsfield wrapped things up for us in the eighty-third minute when, in an absolutely brilliant move, he stole the ball from Alpay near the edge of our box, drove forward and then shot low past Enckelman: 3–0! After that all hell really was let loose. The police didn't know what to do! It was every man for himself that night.

To cap off what had already been an incredible evening I was awarded man of the match. It still gives me goose-pimples thinking about it again.

What an absolutely brilliant result and what a great night for the Birmingham fans. Their club had spent forever being in the shadow of Aston Villa so to see how much joy that result brought them and to have been a part of it was just awesome. And it was all facilitated, don't forget, by a few words from Olof. Thanks, mate.

The headline for my favourite international game reads as follows:

'WALES 2 – ITALY 1'

As long as I live I will never, ever tire of seeing that scoreline. Nor will I tire of reading about the game.

Allow me to set the scene. It's 16 October 2002 and there are 72,000 at the Millennium Stadium. The roof's closed, the Manic Street Preachers are playing live and the legendary John Charles – or *Il Gigante Buono*, as he was known to the Italian supporters – has just been paraded in front of the crowd.

We stood a good chance of qualifying for Euro 2004 at the

time and although we eventually fell at the last hurdle our previous five games had yielded some very impressive performances – not to mention some interesting results. Draws against Argentina and the Czech Republic had been followed by a win against the mighty Germany. Not bad, eh? Then a draw against Croatia followed by an extremely impressive 2–0 win against Finland in Helsinki brought us up to date. We were as solid as any international team in the world at the time and were being managed by one of the best young managers in Britain – Mark Hughes. The atmosphere in the stadium was incredible and it made the hairs on the back of your neck stand on end. It galvanized us.

When we took to the pitch I noticed something that I'd certainly never seen before, but also something I never thought possible. The Italians were intimidated. You could tell by their body language: it was all wrong. I don't think it was any one thing in particular but if you took into account our previous form, the atmosphere and the fact that despite us only being little old Wales we actually had one or two genuine world-class players among us, you can understand it. Their fear only really surprised me when I looked back on it, because at the time I just thought to myself, 'Hang on, this lot are scared. We could win this!'

I think every single Welsh player on that field thought the same. We might not have been favourites with the bookies but if Mr William Hill himself had been on that pitch a minute or two before kick-off he would have had us odds-on to win.

Sure enough the Italians started shakily and, although we didn't exactly fly out of the traps, it didn't take us long to get up to speed. John Hartson – who put in a performance that many said was worthy of John Charles himself – and in particular Craig Bellamy were absolutely immense that night. Although a deflected free kick from Alessandro Del Piero on thirty minutes gave the Italians an equalizer and, on paper at least, a chance of winning the game, they were always on the back foot and there was only ever going to be one winner. Craig Bellamy had set up Simon Davies for the first goal – a beautifully placed shot across Buffon from the left – and then scored the winner himself – sidestepping not only the keeper but also two defenders before slotting the ball neatly into the back of the net. I talk a lot about atmosphere in this book, and I've been lucky enough to experience some pretty special ones over the years, but I'll tell you what, to beat one of *the* great Italian teams in your own back yard and in front of 72,000 of your own supporters – well, that's what the game's all about.

Let's have that scoreline one more time shall we?

'WALES 2 – ITALY 1'

Beautiful!

The Wales Teamsheet

Jones

Delaney

Melville

Gabbidon

Speed

Davies

Savage

Pembridge
Giggs
Bellamy
Hartson

The Worst Game in Which I Ever Played

I experienced more than my fair share of disappointments as a footballer. It doesn't matter whether you play football for Barcelona, Blackburn or Barnet; they're guaranteed to make an appearance at regular intervals during your career and can come in all shapes and sizes. It's the same in any sport. The setbacks you can't really influence, such as injuries, can have far-reaching effects if they're serious, but in a way it's the things that you *could* have prevented that actually hurt more.

One of the biggest disappointments I ever experienced as a player was when I was released by Manchester United, but in the end that acted as a catalyst for me to work hard, keep my head down and prove them all wrong, and I did. It was the same when I experienced injuries: You have to try and come back stronger. Most players are chomping at the bit by the time they're ready to try and get back in the team so you can usually find positives.

What's really difficult to come back from is when you let yourselves down as a team, especially when you're playing for your country and are just a game away from qualifying for a major international tournament for the first time in decades.

No prizes for guessing which match I'm going for, then.

It all happened at the Millennium Stadium in Cardiff on 19 November 2003 when Wales hosted Russia for the second leg of our playoff final for Euro 2004, which would take place in Portugal. The qualifying campaign had started off tremendously with four straight wins, including the 2–0 win away at Finland and the 2–1 win at home over Italy. What a great start! The trip to Finland had been complemented by a night out with John Hartson after the match. We managed to find a bar absolutely full of Wales supporters and the last thing I remember is seeing Harts doing cartwheels along the top of the bar and hearing the supporters singing, 'One Robbie Savage, there's only one Robbie Savage.'

The entire country was buzzing and after the fourth game, a 4–0 win at home over Azerbaijan, we were five points clear at the top of the table with four still to play. Surely we would be on our way to Portugal. Mark Hughes had transformed the Wales set-up since becoming manager and he was starting to get something back. He'd brought in a nutritionist, a guy called Tony Quaglia who's a really big mate of mine, and had persuaded the Welsh FA to spend a few quid on improving things like travel and accommodation. That kind of thing means a lot when you spend a great deal of time away and I think we all really appreciated it.

In my opinion there are few who can rival Mark Hughes as a man-manager, and what made the difference was always what he said as opposed to how he said it. I remember once during qualifying he gave us a night off a few days before a match.

'Can we go out then?' asked Gary Speed.

'Yes, you can go out if you want,' replied Sparky. 'I know you'll make the right decision.'

The right decision, clearly, was to stay in. He knew exactly what he was doing.

Not long after Tony Quaglia joined the set-up he asked if any of us fancied a ride in a police car. One of his mates was a policeman and so he thought it might be fun. Giggsy and I were the ones who were really into cars at the time and so we jumped at the chance. A few days later we were sitting in the back of a police car on the M4 doing about 150 mph! I turned to Giggsy and said, 'Can you imagine what Fergie would say if you rang him now? "Hi, boss. I'm in the back of a police car with Robbie Savage and we're doing 150 mph." He'd go mad!'

That game against Azerbaijan was bitter-sweet for me as just as few minutes after setting up the opening goal I had to come off with an ankle injury. Fortunately, it wasn't anything serious and so I was back for the next game, a 1–0 defeat away against Serbia and Montenegro. It was the first time a Welsh team had played in Belgrade for over fifty years and what should have been a decent enough game turned into quite a scrappy affair with nerves probably getting the better of us. I'd also rather stupidly promised myself that I wouldn't get booked that game and so played with one eye on the referee. It was one to forget.

We still led the group by two points but now had Italy, our next opponents, breathing down our necks. Having beaten them at home, we were left with no doubt whatsoever that the

Italian boys were out for revenge within just a few minutes into that corresponding fixture at the San Siro; and, unfortunately for us, they got it. At half time, when the score was 0–0, we honestly thought we stood a chance. Giggsy had just hit the post and I was full of confidence. We all were.

Within the next half an hour Filippo Inzaghi scored a hat-trick and Alessandro Del Piero bagged a penalty. Despite us creating one or two more decent chances, we were completely outclassed.

The worst thing for me about that game was that I got myself suspended, something I obviously desperately did not want to happen. The trick in Belgrade about consciously trying not to get booked hadn't worked, in that I hadn't played that well, and so I just had to let nature take its course. At the end of the day, I am who I am.

Anyway, it looked like it was going to be the playoffs for us.

The next two games made sure of that as, after a spirited 1–1 draw away to Finland and a disappointing 3–2 home defeat against Serbia and Montenegro (I couldn't play in that game either due to injury), we were confirmed as finishing second in the group behind Italy.

The ten teams involved in the draw for the playoffs were Wales, Slovenia, Norway, the Netherlands, Latvia, Scotland, Spain, Turkey, Croatia and Russia. Drawing Russia wasn't the end of the world – after all, it could have been Spain or the Netherlands – but it wasn't going to be easy.

We were drawn away in the first leg and so on 13 November 2003 we all boarded a plane bound for Moscow where we were to play the first of two absolutely massive games. We did the usual things when we arrived – bought Russian hats, walked round Red Square and had our photos taken – but mentally we were anything but tourists. We were history makers.

Jason Koumas was outstanding in that game and forced what was probably the only save from the Russian goalkeeper. As we had expected, Russia dominated possession but we were a very disciplined team and our defenders were able to cope with everything that was thrown at them. Paul Jones also played a blinder and as Russia laid siege to our goal in the final ten or fifteen minutes he pulled off a string of unbelievable saves. He was such a good keeper.

Taking a clean sheet back to Cardiff for the second leg was an outstanding achievement, and it was probably more than some were expecting.

Advantage Wales, then, or so we hoped.

Four days later when the Russians arrived in Cardiff the entire country was alive with talk of Portugal and of our first major tournament since 1958. The Italian home game had been big, as had the recent match in which we had drawn against Argentina. This was the big one, though.

Sparky is a hero to millions of Welsh people, with me being probably his biggest fan. If he had got us through to Euro 2004 there would have been a statue of him in every town and village from St David's to Holyhead and from Wrexham to Newport. As it was, I'm afraid, he just had to settle for being a national hero because, when it came down to it, I'm afraid we just couldn't get over that last hurdle.

We had three gilt-edged chances during the game and on any other night we would have put them away easily, but sometimes things just don't work out. To be fair to Russia, they raised their game from the first leg whereas we went the other way and therein lay the difference.

To make matters worse, the only goal of the game was scored by Vadim Evseev, a defender who had been at the centre of a clash with Giggsy during the first leg. That had been a disgrace of the highest order and had seen the Russian team outrageously try and prevent Giggsy from playing in Cardiff. About midway through the second half Evseev had gone in on Giggsy with the kind of tackle that would normally result in two things – a stretcher and a red card. Fortunately Giggsy hadn't been injured but because of the severity of the tackle he had retaliated. Bearing in mind that Ryan Giggs has the patience of a saint it must have been one heck of a bad challenge, and it certainly looked it. Anyway, about five seconds later Evseev had suddenly gone down like a sack of potatoes and after that all hell had been let loose. The Russian Football Federation had complained to UEFA about what had happened and asked for Giggsy to be banned for the next match. Their demand had been ignored, of course. The incident showed how good Ryan Giggs was. Teams were terrified of him.

When Evseev scored from a header in just the twenty-second minute of the second leg we were both devastated and terrified: devastated because we'd done so well in the first leg and terrified because we were now on the brink of letting all the hope, promise and excitement we had experienced since starting our campaign back in September 2002 just slip through our fingers.

Sure enough, about seventy minutes later our worst nightmare was confirmed and so instead of booking our tickets to

Lisbon and taking on the best in Europe like we'd hoped, we all ended up going back to our day jobs and considering our international futures.

I felt most sorry for Sparky. He came into the dressing room after the game and apologized to us and thanked us for all our hard work. What a gentleman and what a great manager. We all loved playing for Sparky and had so much respect for him. We'd let him down, though. And we'd let the fans down. Carrying the hopes of a nation on your shoulders can be testing at times but ultimately it's a privilege. It's not that we didn't do our best; we just didn't play our best.

You see, that's the difference between a situation like that, where it's ultimately up to you whether you succeed or not, and something like an injury. Like it or not, we could have prevented it from happening. Mark my words, that's a horrible feeling.

The Class of '92

There's been a lot said and a lot written about Manchester United's FA Youth Cup-winning Class of '92 over the years. In fact, I think they even made a film about it, didn't they? Well, about the players who became Manchester United superstars anyway! I knew there was a reason why I didn't get asked to appear. (You just wait until they make a film about Crewe Alexandra's A-team of 1994. It's only a matter of time before I become a film star.)

Instead, I thought I would have some fun and do something a little bit different regarding the Class of '92. First of all, I'm going to tell you a little bit about some of the lesser-known members of Eric Harrison's now legendary group, such as what they're doing now and what they were like back in the day. I still bump into some of them from time to time. And then I'm going to go through each of Fergie's superstar fledglings one by one, tell you exactly what they were like as youngsters and give you their transfer value based on today's money. Okay?

Kevin Pilkington

Kevin Pilkington was our main goalkeeper in the Class of '92 and what a great lad he was – a real gentle giant. He was one of those few people who just seemed to get on with everyone he met and just went with the flow. You would be hard pushed to find anyone who has a bad word to say about him.

My earliest memory of Kevin is watching him howl with laughter every time Alex Ferguson shouted, 'Savage! Get your hair cut, boy!' I would sit there and go red while Kevin almost wet himself.

Kevin was an excellent keeper and was tipped for big things at United, and, unlike many of us, he ended up making a few first-team appearances for the club. I think he made five or six in all, which to some people might not sound like many but when you take into account who Kevin was up against at Manchester United everything suddenly becomes clear. He didn't have any old Tom, Dick or Harry in front of him, he had Peter Schmeichel, the Great Dane – and if you had someone like him in front of you not only would he block out the light but also any chance you had of become a first-team regular.

I've recently read one or two interviews with Kevin and he's very philosophical about his time at United and is proud of what he achieved. Quite right too, Kev. There's no shame in being kept out of a team by the greatest keeper ever to grace the Premier League.

Kevin had six years as a professional at Old Trafford, which isn't bad at all, but once Raimond van der Gouw was signed in 1996 I think he knew that his future lay elsewhere and he ended up at Phil Taylor and Robbie Williams's favourite team, Port Vale. He then won a permanent contract at Mansfield Town where he made 170 appearances between 2000 and 2005. You see, I've done all my homework. I know more about Kevin than he does.

After leaving Mansfield he spent the next five years at local rivals Notts County before returning there as a coach in 2012, and he works there to this day. Ironically enough, Kevin's first stint at County was eventually brought to an end when they signed a young keeper by the name of – no, wait for it – Kasper Schmeichel! You couldn't make it up, could you? The curse of the Schmeichels strikes again.

Kev's a great lad and was a really good, solid keeper.

John O'Kane

John O'Kane's career at Manchester United was progressing quite steadily until the day when Alex Ferguson suggested that a certain Gary Neville should swap from being a centre half to a right back. Until then John had made that position his own in the Class of '92 but it wasn't long before it became obvious that Gary Neville had taken it to a new level. Saying that, John still made a couple of appearances for the first team before going on to have a decent career at clubs like Everton, Bolton Wanderers and Blackpool, before ending up at Hyde United where he saw out his career, eventually being forced to retire in 2006.

The last time I saw John was in 2014 when some of the Class of '92 turned out for Salford City FC in a charity match at the AJ Bell Stadium. We lost 5–1 and, to be fair, it could have been 15–1! It was great seeing John again and he looked in really good shape. Best of all, though, he's happy and is now employed as a support worker in Lancashire.

George Switzer

Recently I was having lunch outside a restaurant in Alderley Edge in Cheshire when all of a sudden I heard a horn blasting out and a voice shouting, 'Oi, Sav! How's it going, you muppet?'

I didn't need to ask who it was; in fact, I didn't need to look up. I knew straight away it was George Switzer, the left-back extraordinaire who not only had similar coloured hair to Paul Scholes but also played with the same amount of energy, commitment and passion. He was a brilliant player in his day and out of all the lads who didn't make it in the game I think he was one of the biggest surprises. Like me, George didn't get to make any first-team appearances for United and ended up playing a few games for Darlington before dropping down into non-league football.

What a character, though. He's a courier these days so he's still getting rid of things for people. Just not balls.

Chris Casper

Chris made just two senior appearances for Manchester United yet he, like George Switzer, was another lad who was always tipped for great things. He went out on loan a few times and always impressed but he was still unable to break through into the first team. Let's face it, though, being 'good' or being 'promising' at Manchester United in those days just wasn't good enough. You had to be either mesmerizing or just a flaming genius! Like me and the rest of us mere mortals, poor old Chris was neither and it's a pity because he really, really wanted to succeed. His dad, Frank Casper, had enjoyed a long and successful career as a professional and Chris was obviously desperate to emulate him.

Unfortunately worse was yet to come for Chris as on Boxing Day in 1999, after working hard to cement a regular first-team place at Reading, he suffered a horrific leg injury that basically finished his career. Although short, his career as a footballer wasn't without its highs and as well as being an integral part of Manchester United's FA Youth Cup-winning side of 1992, alongside a young and very handsome second-half substitute named Robert William Savage who almost scored, Chris served as captain of the England youth team for a while and was a member of the European Championship winning side in 1993. That's not bad for a short career, is it?

Since he retired Chris has had a few different jobs and all of them in football, I'm pleased to say. He currently works for the Premier League where he helps academies in the north-west implement educational schemes.

Good luck to him.

Simon Davies

Together with Keith Gillespie, who I'll come on to in a second, Simon Davies really is 'the one that got away' because as well as making around twenty senior appearances for United he also scored a goal for them in the Champions League against Galatasaray. Unfortunately that just happened to be the same game in which David Beckham scored his first ever goal for the club and so Simon's achievement was somewhat overshadowed. Once he was in the first team nobody could really see him coming out, but in an extreme version of what Kevin Pilkington encountered Simon had not one but two United legends in front of him in Ryan Giggs and Lee Sharpe. Who would be a midfielder at Manchester United, eh? Well me, if I'd had the chance.

Simon and I were both involved in an unusual relationship with a mop when we were at Manchester United. Seriously!

When I signed as an apprentice at Manchester United I learned that in addition to impressing Eric and the gaffer on the pitch we also had to fulfil certain roles off the pitch, but I soon realized that these were strictly for the amusement of the senior players.

Before I give you the details of one or two of the dares I had to perform to give the senior players a laugh, you should be warned about some of the punishments that were dished out should you make the unwise decision to decline the offer or, as some of the lads did, hide in the kit van. First there was naked golf, which could be interesting. One for the exhibitionists, I think. Thank God they didn't have mobile-phone footage back then! If you didn't fancy that you could always ask to be put into one of the big tumble driers for a while, which would then be turned on. It's a good job they didn't put Scholesy in there. He'd have disappeared!

After that you had the dreaded 'Bongs', which involved having a ball that had been wrapped and then twisted inside a towel bounced repeatedly off your head. Believe me, it was a lot more painful than it sounds. Not painful enough for you? Okay, well how about lying on a treatment table with your head sticking off the end and then having people take pot shots at you. That resulted in a succession of bloody noses, not surprisingly. The last one I can remember involved having the Manchester United logo rubbed onto your chest with a wire brush and shoe polish. That brought tears to your eyes.

Whenever I saw a first-team player around The Cliff training ground, someone like Steve Bruce or Bryan Robson, I used to go red and run a mile. They were superstars, after all, and I was in awe of them. But when it was time to perform a dare I was always the first to stick my hand up. 'Pick me, lads! I'll have a go.'

My favourite was something called Funny Movements, in which you had to dance to no music for one minute. Some of the players used to hate doing this but I loved it! I used to have the lads in stitches.

Each Friday the senior players would hold a kind of joke court session, and if you hadn't completed a job you'd been given or if you'd left your kit out or something, you would be tried and then punished. The dressing room self-policed in that respect and it worked brilliantly. There was no jury, just three senior players as judges, and if they decided that you were guilty, the rest of the room would decide the punishment.

The only time I almost came unstuck with regards to dares was when they made me spend an evening of passion with a mop.

For this dare, first I was told to leave the dressing room.

'We need to prepare things, Sav,' I was told in a very serious tone. 'You wait outside and don't come in until we say so, okay?'

Well that put me, at ease – not!

After about five minutes I got called back in.

'Okay, Sav, we're ready.'

As I nervously walked through the door I immediately noticed the lights were being turned on and off.

'You're in a nightclub, Sav. Okay?' came a voice.

If you say so!

'Now you see that mop over there?'

I looked over and there in the corner of the dressing room was a mop that had been done up to look like a woman. I say 'done up'. In actual fact it had just been turned upside down and had a coat hanger put over it which was supposed to represent her shoulders. Her? What am I saying?

'Chat up the mop,' said the voice.

'What?'

'Chat her up! You're in a nightclub, you're having a dance and all of a sudden you see her, the most beautiful mop in the world. Now show her your moves and chat her up.'

I had two choices: either I could turn on my heels, run like hell to the kit van and start crying, or I could stay put, try to get off with a cleaning instrument and impress a load of sporting superstars.

'Hi, I'm Robbie,' I said, shuffling my way towards the girl – sorry, mop.

For an inexperienced sixteen-year-old that was actually a killer line.

'Why, hello there, handsome!' came a squeaky-voiced reply.

It could have been any one of about fifteen players, all of whom were wetting themselves laughing. I couldn't see who it was because I was in a nightclub, obviously.

'Do you clean here often? Sorry, I mean, do you come here often?'

That was my best yet.

'Yes!' she, he or it replied. 'Do you?'

'It's my first time.'

By now I was fact-to-face with the mop and had my hands draped across her shoulders. Surely it was only a matter of time?

'Would you like to dance?' I asked.

'Ooh, yes please,' she squealed.

So, with the mop's permission I picked it up and we slow-danced around the dressing room. The only thing missing was Chris de Burgh's 'Lady in Red'. I was really getting into the part now. Perhaps a bit too much.

'I hope you don't think I'm being forward, but would you like to come back to my place?'

'Ooh, yes please! You will be gentle with me though, won't you?' squealed a famous voice.

So, to cut a long story short, I made mad passionate love to a mop on a treatment table in a dressing room at The Cliff, surrounded by several million pounds' worth of international footballer. I wasn't exactly what you would call skilled when it came to that sort of thing and although I knew the basics about the birds and the bees my own experiences didn't go any further than a story in the dressing room. I know it sounds a bit outdated but that was how it was then. I was dedicated to my football! I had absolutely no idea what I was doing but I definitely pretended to do something. Anyway, it certainly made everybody laugh and did no harm to my reputation with the seniors.

I never did get her name, though, unfortunately. I wonder what she's doing now.

At a later date, when Simon Davies was asked to do the same thing with the mop he just went quiet and started shaking. The poor lad was petrified! Those senior players were all heart and so instead of making him chat up and then sleep with a mop they simply made him hold a cup of water. He was shaking so much that it went absolutely everywhere. It was hilarious! From them on he was nicknamed Shaky.

What a great life it was, though. After training every day we'd go back to the digs, have dinner, and then we'd play again with the kids in the evening. From 10 a.m. until about 8 p.m. (with a couple of breaks in between) we did nothing else but play football.

Simon retired from playing in 2007 after a long career in the lower leagues and short stints with Chester and Airbus UK (where's that?). Then, after managing Chester City, he became the assistant manager of Manchester City's Elite Development Squad and he's been there ever since.

Even though he too never made it big as a player it's great that Simon's stayed in football as he's obviously an excellent coach. He's a cracking lad.

Colin McKee

Colin, who was one of my fellow strikers in the Class of '92, was originally spotted playing for Scotland Schoolboys in the late 1980s and, unlike me, actually made the starting line-up of the 1992 FA Youth Cup final.

Although he won both a contract and a squad number after that final, Colin only made one appearance for the club and ended up playing for Kilmarnock, which he did from 1994 until 1997. After plying his trade at a variety of other clubs Colin retired in 2001, aged just twenty-seven.

Ben Thornley

David Beckham may well have become a global fashion icon and international sex symbol but in Manchester in the early 1990s it was Ben Thornley – or Squeaky as he was known on account of having a very high-pitched voice – who was setting the female pulses racing. He had everything: talent, good looks, fan mail, female adulation . . . bodily hair! We never had any of that. To make matters worse, Ben also made an early senior appearance. What did he have that the rest of us didn't? Back then, just about everything.

Every Christmas at The Cliff they used to put on a Manchester United pantomime. They don't do it now, of course, although if it was up to me I would bring it back.

The most memorable panto I was ever involved in was *Snow White and the Seven Dwarfs*. Jim McGregor, the Manchester United physio, wrote the script and all the schoolboy and academy lads played the parts. This was performed, by the way, in front of Alex Ferguson and all the senior players. The entire club, in fact. Ben Thornley played Prince Charming, Scholesy played all the dwarfs (only joking!) and the role of Snow White was played by me. Yes, that's right, me. I actually scrubbed up rather well, even though I do say so myself.

As part of the story Prince Charming obviously has to kiss Snow White and so that is how Ben 'Squeaky' Thornley became the first bloke to kiss Robbie Savage – without tongues, I might add.

Unfortunately Ben was another member of the Class of '92 whose career became hampered by injuries. He was very highly thought of by everyone and if you speak to Gary Neville he'll tell you that for a time Ben was probably the best out of all of us. He was the first one to make a senior appearance in the Premier League yet was younger than the majority of us. The world was his oyster.

Just nine Premier League appearances later Ben sustained a knee-ligament injury in a reserve match against Blackburn Rovers that basically spelled the end of his career at Old Trafford. Yet another example that the effect an injury can have on a footballer's life can be devastating.

What really impresses me about Squeaky is that as opposed to letting such a bad injury finish his career all together, he worked hard, pulled himself round and went on to have a decent career at clubs like Huddersfield and Aberdeen. Okay, so he didn't fulfil his potential at Old Trafford. Welcome to the club, mate! But to come back from that kind of serious injury and still establish yourself as a good professional footballer is just as big an achievement if you ask me.

I still see Ben from time to time – in fact, whenever I go to Old Trafford to watch a match I see him there hosting some of the corporate lounges. You see, although he only made a few appearances for the club, Ben is part of Manchester United folklore. I suppose we all are.

Keith Gillespie

I don't need to tell you what happened to Gilly either on or off the field as it's already been very well documented. What I would just like to say is that in addition to being a great lad he is also, in my opinion, one of the most talented wingers ever to have come out of Great Britain. He was one of eight members of the Class of '92 who were awarded four-year contracts (as opposed to my one!) and was regarded by many, and with some justification because he was from Northern Ireland, as the next George Best. He had everything – pace, power, skill, vision, the lot – and at the time when all the contracts were being offered out he was even more highly thought of than Becks.

Sure, you could go on for weeks about what went wrong for Keith, what with the gambling and so on, but for the sake of this book I would like to just say that in addition to being one of the best footballers I've ever had the pleasure to watch and play with, he's one of the nicest lads you could ever meet and I wish him all the luck in the world.

So what about 'The Chosen Few', the ones from that youth team who really made it? Somebody asked me the other day what I thought the Class of '92 would be worth in today's market and I thought, wow, what a question! We had a chat about it and chucked around some figures, like you do, but later on that day I thought, hang on, why not do this properly? I did something similar to this in my *Daily Mirror* column about five years ago but as none of the lads, including me, had actually retired from playing football at the time it was really more of an ongoing discussion than it was a retrospective. You see apart from Becks, who, let's face it, is God, I still see the others on a fairly regular basis and am still able to teach them a few things about punditry and life in general. Joke! I suppose I'm like a father figure to them, which means there's nobody better qualified to assess their careers and work out their current market value.

Before I go on, let's just the try and grasp the enormity of the task ahead, shall we? You see, if Raheem Sterling is worth £50 million in today's money, how much would the equivalent of Ryan Giggs be worth in his pomp? We're going to be talking telephone numbers, aren't we? You've got to be looking at a total of around half a billion for the Class of '92.

One thing this does drive home is just how unique that set of players was. To have that much talent in just one intake is something that we will never see again. Giggs, Beckham, Scholes, Butt, the Nevilles – they, with a bit of help from lads like me, Gilly and Squeaky, destroyed youth teams week after week, and I mean destroyed them. We were like Arsenal's Invincibles in that respect. Teams genuinely feared us, and with good reason.

Looking back, they were obviously players on the verge of doing something great in the game, but at the time we were all completely focused on one thing: football. Credit for that – for keeping everyone's feet on the ground – has to go to the youth-team boss Eric Harrison, because if it wasn't for his guidance, wisdom and, it has to be said, discipline, some of those players might not have made it. Seriously, he was a manager, mentor, teacher, mother, father and friend all rolled into one.

Eric was firm but he was also very fair. I'll tell you what, though, if you made a blunder on one of the training pitches at The Cliff and he was watching – which he usually was – you would suddenly hear the windows of his office bang and as you looked round he would be standing there shouting God only knows what. I used to freeze when I heard the banging start. 'Oh God, was it me?'

It didn't stop there. Once Eric realized he couldn't

actually smash through the glass he would make his way round to the outside of the pitches and that's where the rollicking – sorry, I meant to say the quiet words of advice – would really start! No one was exempt from Eric's wrath and he would go on until he was satisfied that he'd got his message across.

So, you see, instead of becoming a bunch of mollycoddled millionaires, we had our feet almost nailed to the ground. We didn't know the meaning of the word ego. We weren't allowed.

After I've told you a little bit about each of 'The Chosen Few' I'll give you their current market value based on the 'Savage Footballing Index'.

Phil Neville

A Manchester United (and Everton) legend with not only fifty-nine international caps to his name but also a shedful of medals. You don't make over 500 Premier League appearances by accident so taking into account the current market conditions – not to mention how much Manchester United paid for Luke Shaw – I would value a young Phil Neville at £25 million.

Gary Neville

The thinker among Fergie's fledglings and the one most likely to become Prime Minister. Commonly referred to as 'the best right back ever to play in the Premier League' and by Sir Alex Ferguson as 'the best right back of his generation', Gary always looked good in a pair of Marks & Spencer tracksuit bottoms, which is what we all used to wear back then. Seriously, they were the most comfortable things we could find. Given all of the above, and the fact that he knows a lot of big words, I would say Gary would have to be worth at least £40 million.

Nicky Butt

Nicky Butt is as hard as nails. I once saw him knock somebody out in the showers at The Cliff and thought, okay, I'd better be nice to you! We did end up having some fierce battles on the pitch, though, and I used to love playing both against him and with him. Nicky was an old-school box-to-box midfield player who could defend and score goals and he was one of the best midfield players I have ever laid eyes on. In fact, along with Keith Gillespie, he was probably our best player in the Class of '92. Given that I'm going to put him at £30 million.

Paul Scholes

Now the last time Paul Scholes and I appeared on television together (he was a guest on *Fletch & Sav* in 2015) he ended up calling me a very rude name live on air. I can't possibly repeat what he said but suffice to say it attracted one or two headlines here and there. Actually, if you put his name, my name and the offending word into any popular search engine you'll get over 3,500 articles come up. See what happens when you're short on talent? You have to resort to swearing. Even so I'm not going to let Scholesy's outburst cloud my judgement of him and will try and keep it fair.

We really are getting onto the business end of things now as Scholesy is quite rightly regarded as one of the greatest footballers who ever drew breath – not just in this country but the world over, with Zidane, Davids and many others ranking him among the best. Let's face it, when people like that start telling you that Scholes is one of the greatest you have to sit up and listen.

Although Scholesy joined Manchester United in the same year as I did, we didn't really play together until a bit later on. What a footballer. I remember watching him and thinking, 'You're a genius!' As a fellow player you couldn't feel anything other than admiration – and jealousy.

Despite being a bit of a potty mouth Paul Scholes was a bona fide footballing genius and if he was around today I think he would have to be worth at least £90 million – maybe, just maybe, £100 million. Actually, if Manchester City were still trying to up their quota of home-grown players it could be as high as £150 million!

David Beckham

What can you say about David Beckham that hasn't already been said over and over? I've got something. If you think my mop dare was bad, that's nothing compared to what Becks had to do with a Clayton Blackmore calendar. He relived the ordeal during an interview to promote *The Class of '92* film and I have to say it made me wince when I heard it. Some of the things those senior players used to think up! They certainly had vivid imaginations.

Today David Beckham is one of the most famous people in the world but back in the early 1990s at Manchester United he was just Becks, a hard-working, modest but extremely promising young midfield player. The one thing I had in common with the young genius was fitness. We were probably the two fittest players in the Class of '92 but as time went on and I began to struggle to hold down a place, he started to become a force to be reckoned with. By the time I made my Premier League debut with Leicester City he was half-way to becoming a genuine Manchester United and England legend.

Because of Becks's status these days as a businessman, A-list celebrity, model and so on, it's easy to forget about his prowess as a footballer. But once you strip away all the fame and notoriety you'll always be left with one of the biggest talents world football has ever known and for that I would put Becks's value at an impressive £70 million.

Ryan Giggs

Before Giggsy made it big doing things like writing the foreword for my autobiography, which he very kindly did a few years ago, he spent almost twenty-five years at Manchester United and in that time played a big part in helping them win the following major trophies: thirteen Premier League titles, four FA Cups, three League Cups and two Champions League titles. That's just obscene! How he never won the Ballon d'Or I'll never know.

Giggsy was absolutely incredible when we were kids – a year older than most of us but light years ahead in terms of talent. He also conducted himself impeccably both on and off the pitch and is probably the most dedicated player I've ever known.

From a respect point of view – at Manchester United at least – Giggsy is probably on a par with the likes of Sir Matt Busby, Sir Bobby Charlton and Sir Alex Ferguson, and rightly so. In fact, the sooner he joins them on the Knights' Table at Old Trafford the better. It's only a matter of time.

As one of the best players ever to have played in the Premier

League, and given the fact that Gareth Bale and Cristiano Ronaldo were sold for upwards of £80 million (Ronaldo's worth more now, of course), I would have to value Giggsy at a cool £120 million.

Before I unveil the magic number according to the 'Savage Footballing Index' I'm also going to tot up the also-rans because, when all's said and done, we were all in the Class of '92. If they hadn't been so unlucky with injuries, Chris Casper and Ben Thornley would have been worth a few million. I'll go for £4 million apiece. Our keeper Kevin Pilkington, defender John O'Kane and forward Colin McKee would add another couple of million each as would the man with the van, George Switzer. Add to that a further £25 million for Keith Gillespie and £150 million for yours truly (Joke! I'm going for a very modest £8 million), that makes a grand total of £484,000,000, getting on for half a billion.

This is only fantasy football, of course, and I know there'll be loads of you out there who think I should have valued myself at a lot more, but it's still interesting and once again drives home just how astonishing that crop of players was. Will it ever be repeated? I doubt it.

I had some absolutely fantastic times with all the players I've mentioned in this chapter and it was a privilege to have been even on the fringes of that class. But do you know what also makes me proud? Whenever I see any of them now either in a TV studio or at a match it doesn't matter who they're talking to, their manners are absolutely impeccable (except for Scholesy's very occasional swearing) and that is, in no small part, down to

Eric Harrison and Sir Alex Ferguson. I dare say the parents had a lot to do with it as well – as did my own mum and dad – but you get my drift. Once kids leave home they're exposed to all kinds of influences and they're not always that healthy. Things like politeness, good manners and respect meant as much to Eric Harrison and Sir Alex Ferguson as fitness and dedication. It didn't matter how talented you were or how famous you were: if you didn't conduct yourself correctly in public you wouldn't have lasted two minutes at Manchester United and that's stuck with all of us. You can't put a price on manners and I for one will always be very grateful to them. Treat people how you would like to be treated. It's not rocket science.

My All-time Wales XI

I know what all you English boys and girls will be saying. 'Is it possible to put together an all-time Welsh XI?' Well, actually you might just be surprised. It's not all Robbie Savage and Ryan Giggs, you know!

Despite me extolling the virtues of 4–3–3, I'm actually going to go with a 4–2–3–1 formation here.

One last thing to bear in mind before I start is that this is *my* all-time Wales XI – players I've either played with or have seen play – and so I can't really include any members of the 1958 World Cup team. As tremendous as those players obviously were, their heroics aren't something I can really comment on as, believe it or not, I wasn't there.

There's only one candidate for goalkeeper and that's the legend that is Big Nev. Not only is Neville Southall an absolute legend in the world of football, and in my opinion one of the best goalkeepers there has ever been, he's also quite a well-known wit. This was evident a few years ago when both he and I appeared at a live event for Radio 5 Live. We did episodes of things like *Fighting Talk* and *606* and we also put on an awards ceremony. It was a really good day out.

As you would expect the banter was always in full flow and in one of my cheekier moments I asked Neville – who it has to be said has a reputation of having a bit of an appetite – if he would like a pie.

'No, thanks,' he said. 'Would you like a medal?'

Game, set and match, Mr Neville Southall, MBE, winner of two league titles, two FA Cups and the Cup Winners' Cup.

I went redder than a Wales shirt!

Fortunately for Everton – and for Wales of course – Neville Southall was as quick in the goalmouth as he was at that event and for as long as I played alongside him he always seemed to have an aura about him – one that only real legends have. The phrase 'safe pair of hands' could have been invented for him because that's exactly what he was. As long as he was in goal you always felt like you had a chance. Total legend.

My two first-choice centre backs would be Ashley Williams, the current Wales and Swansea City captain, and Kevin Ratcliffe, who, in addition to winning fifty-nine caps for his country, made over 300 appearances for Everton. Ashley Williams has already made over fifty appearances for Wales and is looking like becoming one of the country's all-time greats. He's a born leader, not to mention quite a decent footballer, and together with Kevin I think they would equip themselves admirably at the back. Confidence is key in a small-nation team and, just like Big Nev, they would have no shortage of that. Exactly what you want from your two centre backs.

Right back would have to be Simon Davies. Not Simon 'Shaky' Davies, although he did win a cap for Wales. No, I'm talking about the other Simon Davies, the one who played for Fulham and Spurs. Simon's natural position was as a winger but he made quite a few appearances for Wales at right back and always did very well. Look at his experience, too: fifty-eight caps for his country and around 300 Premier League appearances. Even if right back wasn't his most natural position, I would still like to have him in my team. He's a great lad and a fantastic pro. Wales through and through.

At left back I'd have chosen the late and extremely great Gary Speed, one of the best players ever to put on a Wales shirt.

I, like many millions of others, was totally devastated when I heard about Gary's passing in 2011 and rarely does a day go by when I don't think about him. You see, Gary had such a huge impact on the game of football that it's impossible not to be reminded of him, and long may that continue. He made an unbelievable 677 club appearances during his career and eighty-five international appearances. Not even Giggsy, who played until he was fifty-six, can hold a candle to those stats. The biggest shame about Gary's death from a footballing point of view is that he was such a bright young manager and obviously had an amazing future ahead of him. Would he have become as good a manager as he was a player? I honestly think he would. The effect that Gary was having on the Wales team at the time of his death was far-reaching and I'm sure it would only have been a matter of time before he was picked up by a big club.

He, like Giggsy and Mark 'Sparky' Hughes, was the epitome of a model professional and set a tremendous example to others.

Everybody in the game – and I mean everybody – had the utmost respect for Gary Speed and that's one of a hundred reasons why I think he would have gone on to become one of the managerial greats.

When I first started playing for Wales I wanted to be just like Gary Speed and in many ways I still do. Just like the Manchester United lads, he had perfect manners and would help anybody if he thought he could.

I miss him like mad, so thank God for the memories. I have many of Gary and I'll treasure them forever.

As much as I would like to be playing in this all-time XI I think Aaron Ramsey probably just pips me to the post in the centre of midfield. I absolutely love watching Aaron Ramsey play. Sure, he might not be that explosive pace-wise but his movement between the lines is superb and he has an absolutely sublime first touch. As far as I'm concerned he's one of the best midfielders in Europe and I for one would have loved to have played alongside him.

Next to Aaron I'm going for one of my first and biggest heroes, Mark Hughes. I've already spoken about the respect I have for Sparky but that was more to do with Mark Hughes the manager. Mark Hughes the player could have the same effect on a team as Neville Southall, in the sense that he inspired confidence and made you feel like you had a chance. That means a lot to smaller countries like Wales because when you're playing the likes of Germany, Argentina or Brazil it can sometimes be quite overwhelming and so having somebody there who is on a level ability-wise with all those superstars makes a big, big difference. Sparky spent fifteen years as Wales's talisman and is a born leader.

No prizes for guessing who'd be on the left of the three in front – that's right, the 'Old Man' of Old Trafford himself, Mr Ryan Giggs. Let's face it, he would have made it into the 1970 Brazilian team. Genius.

You could probably say pretty much the same thing about the lad who'd be standing next to Giggsy, Gareth Bale; currently the world's most expensive footballer and in my opinion the best player ever in a Wales shirt. I can't say he's the best player ever to *put on* a Wales shirt – that honour would still go to Giggsy – but the way he performs for his country is like nothing I've ever seen before. He's a true game changer.

There has been plenty of talk about Gareth leaving Real Madrid for Manchester United one day, and I'll tell you what, if he did, they would win the Premier League. Seriously, you take my word for it. He's been absolutely immense for Wales recently and just in case you've been swayed by all that negative press coming out of Spain, just take a look at his stats at Real Madrid so far: fifty-four league appearances, twenty-eight goals and fifteen assists. Not too shabby, are they? In my opinion Gareth's being treated appallingly by the Real supporters and the sooner they stop whingeing at every little thing and start getting behind him the better it'll be for everyone.

On the right I've gone for Craig Bellamy, one of the best goal scorers I've ever seen in a football shirt, let alone a Wales shirt. Craig is one of the only players I know whose presence alone can galvanize a dressing room. He had such a huge amount of talent and that had an effect on those around him. He didn't suffer fools, though, and if you didn't pull your weight he'd have no problem taking you to task over it.

I've spent hours and hours mulling over which striker I should choose to play in front of these three and, to be honest, I'm still undecided even now. You see, in my lifetime Wales have often had an embarrassment of riches up front (for a population of three million at least) and many of them list among my all-time favourite players: people like Ian Rush, John Toshack, John Hartson and Dean Saunders – each and every one a top-class player, and in the case of John Hartson one of my best friends.

The fact is, I shouldn't even be talking to Mr Hartson! You see, a few years ago he borrowed a car I owned – a Ferrari no less – so he could go and visit his family in Swansea, and when he brought it back he'd scratched it. You know how I am with cars, for heaven's sake. I was livid! There are two things of mine you don't mess with: one is my hair and the other is my car.

Then there's the advice Harts has given me over the years. He once told me – just as I was trying to forge a career in the media – that I shouldn't talk to the press as much. Maybe there's a hidden message there?

Rooming with Harts, which I did on quite a few occasions while I was on Wales duty, could be very, very dangerous. I was usually an early-to-bed type whereas he used to keep his own hours and if you showed any signs of being awake when he got back he would take a long run-up and dive on you. Now, John Hartson is a big lad so you can imagine the damage that can do to your internal organs.

Pretending to be fast asleep was a much safer bet although your chances of getting back to sleep were less than zero. Harts used to enjoy a light snack when he got back from the pub or wherever, and I remember one night he ordered a whole tray of sandwiches. I was doing my best impression of being out for the count while Harts was stumbling around the room like a bull in a china shop – obviously doing his best not to wake me up – when all of a sudden there was a knock at the door. 'Room service' came the voice from the other side of the door. 'Ooooh, lovely!' said hungry Harts.

I opened the corner of one eye and there in front of me was Harts carrying this huge tray of sandwiches back to his bed. Fair enough, I thought. Perhaps now I can get some sleep. Absolutely no chance! The noise was incredible. In the end I just had to say something.

I rolled back over and sat up. He looked a bit like the Sugar Puffs Honey Monster. 'What on earth are you doing, Harts?'

'I often snack at this time in the morning.'

He answered my question with such a look of seriousness on his face that the only thing I could do was laugh. He's just mad!

In all seriousness John Hartson is not only one of the best strikers I've ever had the pleasure of playing with but he's also one of my best friends. Seeing him win his battle against cancer a few years ago was one of the most inspiring things I've ever witnessed. I love the man to bits. Great player, great bloke.

Right, I've made my decision. At the end of the day how could it be anyone other than Ian Rush – my first ever footballing hero.

When I started getting into football he was the biggest thing in the European game and it didn't matter which team you supported, you couldn't help admiring him. I had mates who supported all kinds of different clubs back then but they all wanted to be Ian Rush, even the Manchester United supporters. In Wales, though, like in Liverpool, he was a god. His Juventus shirt was one of the first I ever had bought for me and so when I eventually got to play with Rushy for Wales back in the mid-1990s it was the archetypal dream come true and a big, big honour.

While he was at Liverpool Rushy earned the nickname 'The Ghost' because of the way he used to sneak up behind defenders, but as any Liverpool or Wales fan will tell you, in addition to being the most prolific goal scorer ever for both club and country, Ian was also a fantastic defender and would track back whenever he was needed. Those who remember him as being a 'poacher' honestly don't know what they're talking about. He was a fantastic all-round player.

There you go then, my all-time Wales XI.

The Savage All-time Wales XI Teamsheet
Southall
Speed
Williams
Radcliffe
Davies
Ramsey
Hughes
Giggs
Bale
Bellamy
Rush

When it comes to the manager I'm going with the current gaffer, Chris Coleman, for the simple reason that he's on the verge of being the first man to take Wales to the finals of a major competition for almost sixty years. A population of three million people, remember – and all rugby mad. That's going to be one heck of an achievement.

Because it's me, and because I can, I'm going to create a new role in my all-time XI, and that role's going to be Chief Motivator. The reason I'm doing this is because when I turned out for Wales there was one player who above any other used to get everyone fired up and who instilled more than a bit of passion into the dressing room. That man was the footballer-turned-actor, Vinnie Jones.

Vinnie Jones really took me under his wing when I first joined the Wales squad and he also shut up a couple of dressing-room critics who, let's just say, weren't too happy about me being called up. He'd probably had the same thing when he got called up, except I'm willing to bet you any money you like that his critics were a bit less vocal than mine. I remember one brilliant night when Vinnie took the entire squad out to a local pub. Nobody was allowed to pay for anything, it was all on him. After we'd all had a few he got up on stage and knocked out an astonishing version of 'Mustang Sally'. The entire place was jumping within seconds. That was the effect he had on people.

What also really impressed me about Vinnie was that even though he was only 'slightly' Welsh, if you see what I mean (in other words he only qualified because he had a Welsh grand-parent or something), he still took the trouble to learn the national anthem, which, to be perfectly honest, is more than I ever did. I once tried learning the words after John Hartson wrote them out for me but I found it almost impossible. Vinnie, though, learned every single word and at each of his nine appearances for Wales he was by far the loudest player on the pitch. I think he was also the only one who could sing in tune. So much for the stereotype of all Welsh people being able to sing.

One of these days I'm going to ask Vinnie if he can give me some tips on how to break into Hollywood – although I don't really see me as a hard-man, do you? Not with my good looks. I see myself more as a romantic lead, someone like Colin Firth or George Clooney. Well, the mobile's always on.

Believe it or not, I made my acting debut recently in a new British film called *Kicking Off*. It's only a cameo role but you never know what it might lead to.

My All-time World XI

This time I'm going for a four–three–three formation as there are obviously no traditions or first-hand experiences to hold me back. In fact, this one's a completely free hand so I'm just going to try and enjoy myself.

If only!

If choosing players for Wales was difficult, this would have to be classed as nigh on impossible. I've been working on this for three days and once again I've swapped and changed more times than John Hartson has ordered room service. I'm surrounded by scraps of paper!

Once again I'm going to go for players I've seen, so apologies to Pelé and many other legends of the game. I can't see them being too bothered, though, can you?

In goal I'm once again going for Peter Schmeichel. I would love to have gone for Neville Southall but as inspirational and as talented as he undoubtedly was I just can't see beyond the Great Dane. Like Ryan Giggs, he could walk into any team from any period. The best ever.

At the back I've got a couple of Italians in the middle and two Brazilians at left and right back.

At right back I've got the great Cafu. Statistics obviously aren't everything in football but his are just ridiculous. He won 142 caps for Brazil. Oh yes, and two World Cups. That's right – TWO! Christophe Dugarry, who I was lucky enough to play alongside while I was at Birmingham, used to go on and on and on because he'd won one World Cup, and why not? Two though? That's just showing off.

In May 2000 I had the pleasure of playing against Cafu and the boys from Brazil in a friendly at a packed Millennium Stadium. We did ourselves proud in the first half and went into the dressing room at half time the proud owners of 0–0 draw.

'Could we actually get one over on the mighty Brazil?' we thought to ourselves as we sat there wondering whose shirt we would try to bag at the end.

Well no, I'm afraid we couldn't, although I did dummy a ball from a John Robinson cross only for Dean Saunders to hook it wide from about ten yards. All that Brazilian skill and flair must have been rubbing off on me. It didn't last, I'm afraid. We managed to hold out for another fifteen minutes but just when we thought we might get something on the counter-attack Elber struck, followed by the aforementioned Cafu, and then, just to round things off, Rivaldo.

Well, we tried.

One Brazilian legend who wasn't playing that night was my choice for left back, Roberto Carlos – thank God!

If it wasn't for Roberto Carlos we would never have had the likes of Ashley Cole playing in the Premier League, so to a certain extent he revolutionized football; definitely at Real Madrid. It was because of his stamina and ability to completely rule that side of the field that Vicente del Bosque could get away with playing Zinédine Zidane on the left in name only, which was quite an effective tactic. Indeed, del Bosque said that there was no need to have anyone on the left side of midfield: 'Roberto can cover the entire left wing on his own.'

Most great players in the world have a trademark or two. Becks had his free kicks, of course, and Andrés Iniesta has his famous La Croqueta move. Roberto Carlos, though, he had more trademarks than an inventors' school, the most famous being his thirty-five-yard bending free kicks.

I can't think of many players who have had such an enormous impact on the game as my mate Roberto. We're as thick as thieves.

I met him last year while I was covering the World Cup and posted a selfie of the two of us on Twitter. Cue the usual barrage of abuse from Lineker, etc. asking if I showed him my League Cup medal. Will it ever stop?! I hope not.

Right, on to my two Italian centre backs.

Whenever I see somebody wearing an Italian football shirt I immediately think of Paolo Maldini, and, because of my Sky interview, football-shirt-in-the bin fiasco, his name produces very mixed emotions for me. In this chapter though we're sticking purely to the football and like Cafu, this is another example where statistics really matter: 647 appearances for AC Milan, 126 caps for Italy, seven Serie A titles and five Champions League titles. FIVE! He never won the League Cup though, did he?

Although 'Il Capitano' never won the World Cup with Italy he did help them secure runners-up and a third place, which, let's face it, is a damn sight more than most of us.

If you asked a hundred pundits and footballers to name their all-time world XI, I guarantee almost all of them would have Maldini on the list. One of the greatest defenders who ever drew breath – fact.

The second centre back on my teamsheet would be yet another World Cup winner, Fabio Cannavaro. He, like Cafu, captained a World Cup-winning team, which, together with scoring the winning goal, has to be the pinnacle of any footballing career. Enough said really. The lad could play.

In midfield, going left to right, I'm starting off with Diego Maradona or, as he's sometimes known, *Barrilete Cósmico*, which means Cosmic Kite. That has to be one of *the* best nicknames in football.

A few years ago the *Daily Telegraph* published a list of football's biggest mouths. I was at number eight, which I have to say was disappointing, and Maradona was at number seven. That's where our talents both meet and end though, unfortunately.

His dribble against England at the 1986 World Cup is still the best international goal I've ever seen and so for that – and the fact that he's widely acknowledged as being one of the greatest footballers of all time – he goes straight on the list and no mistake.

Next to him would be a lad I've just mentioned, Zinédine Zidane. The only link I've got to the French/Algerian midfield genius is that my former teammate Christophe Dugarry is his best mate. Oh yes, and we're about the same height.

What I wouldn't have given to have played alongside him. I have never in my entire life seen anybody as comfortable on the ball as Zidane. Alfredo Di Stéfano once said it was as though he had silk gloves on each boot, and that's a perfect description. From a spectator's point of view I think I would rather watch him than any other player on earth.

On the right I'm going for Andrés Iniesta; a man who many people, including me, believe to be the complete footballer. He's one of the most skilful players on earth, yet he can defend with the best of them. When Frank Rijkaard managed Barcelona he played Iniesta as a false winger, a central midfielder, a deep midfielder and just behind the striker. What's more he was comfortable and unbelievably effective in all four positions.

Thierry Henry played against Iniesta while he was at Arsenal and then alongside him when he played for Barcelona, and he too says he's one of the best players on earth. If he's good enough for Thierry, he's good enough for me.

Up front I'm going for Lionel Messi and both Ronaldos: the Brazilian one in the middle and the even uglier one on the right. Just think about that for a second. Is that a dream team or what?

I've said loads about Messi and 'Ronaldo Jnr', not only in this book but on television, in the newspapers and on radio. We all have, for heaven's sake. After all, they're the two best players in the world at the moment. Here though, I want to talk a little bit about the lad some would say is the *real* Ronaldo. Well he's most certainly the original. For my money Ronaldo Luís

Nazário de Lima, as he's known to his darts team, is the most consistently brilliant striker who has ever walked the earth. More statistics, I'm afraid. These, however, tell an even bigger story than either Cafu or Maldini.

Cruzeiro – 12 goals in 14 appearances
PSV Eindhoven – 42 goals in 46 appearances
Barcelona – 34 goals in 37 appearances
Inter Milan – 49 goals in 68 appearances
Real Madrid – 83 goals in 127 appearances
AC Milan – 9 goals in 20 appearances
Corinthians – 18 goals in 31 appearances
TOTAL – 247 goals in 343 appearances

Have you ever read anything so ridiculous in your life? Then you have the small matter of 62 goals in 98 appearances for Brazil. That's just obscene.

Like his compatriot, Cafu, Ronaldo is also the proud owner of two World Cup winners' medals, but in addition to that he also has a runners-up medal and a World Cup Golden Shoe which he won in 2002. I could go on.

This isn't generally known but Ronaldo is actually a very big fan of mine, as was reported by Gary Lineker at the draw for the football at the 2012 Olympics, which he and Ronaldo attended.

'Brazil's Ronaldo was very excited to meet @RobbieSavage8. Never missed an episode of Strictly apparently!' was what Mr Lineker tweeted afterwards.

Some people suggested that he might have been taking the mickey but I don't think so. Gary would never do that to me.

Funnily enough, when I was over in Brazil covering the 2014 World Cup for William Hill and the BBC I got involved in a very heated debate regarding Ronaldo. It was with Fletch, obviously, and he was saying that Zico was a better player than Ronaldo.

'What? Zico better than Ronaldo? You're having a laugh!'

He wasn't though.

I couldn't believe it. This argument went on for hours and in the end I started getting some of the waiters involved in the conversation thinking that they would back me up.

Would you believe it, some of them actually agreed with Fletch. I was flabbergasted!

It was about a fifty-fifty in the end. I even asked the taxi-driver on the way back to the hotel and when he said Zico I just gave up. I still think I'm right, though.

As manager I'm going for the Special One. I know he's never managed at international level before but for me that would mean nothing to José. You could put that man in a pit full of anacondas and he would still end up climbing out wearing a pair of snakeskin shoes. I have so much respect for that guy. How does he do it? I only wish I knew.

The Savage All-time World XI Teamsheet
Schmeichel
Cafu
Paolo Maldini
Fabio Cannavaro
Roberto Carlos
Diego Maradona

Zinédine Zidane
Andrés Iniesta
Lionel Messi
Ronaldo
Cristiano Ronaldo

My All-time England XI

As a proud Welshman I wondered whether it might be seen as taking a bit of a liberty choosing an all-time England XI, but then again I live in England, I played football in England to a very high standard, my wife's English, my kids support England, I mainly watch English football and I spend well over half my life talking about it, so I thought, why the heck not? Once again I'm going to stick with players I either watched as a kid or played against.

In goal we've got Peter Shilton. Shilts is a good friend of mine and as well as being a fellow Leicester City old boy he was also on *Strictly Come Dancing* – for about a week! Sorry, Shilts.

I spent a few minutes watching a compilation of some of his best saves earlier and you forget just how brilliant he was. In my opinion he had the safest pair of hands England has ever had, which is why he definitely goes down as number one.

At right back I'm going with my old mate Gary Neville. So much is made about the whole Class of '92 thing, and quite rightly, but what about Gary's stint wearing the Three Lions?

Twelve years and eighty-five caps no less, making him England's thirteenth most-capped player. Unlucky for some, you might say. Well, it was for Gary when he got involved in that whole strike-threat debacle when Rio Ferdinand was banned by the Football Association for eight months in 2003 after missing a drugs test. If you read the facts he was absolutely right to act the way he did, yet what did he get for his troubles? He became one of England's most hated footballers and I think that's one of the reasons why his illustrious international career often gets overlooked. It's such a shame because he deserves better than that. A bona fide footballing legend both at club and international level. He's crying out for a make-over though!

At left-back I'm going for another one of my all-time Premier League XI choices, Ashley Cole. I won't embarrass this poor man's Roberto Carlos by going on again about how good he is. Only joking!

My first choice in the middle of the park is going to be Rio Ferdinand, for reasons I've already divulged. It's just impossible to leave him out really. Alongside Rio I'm going for John Terry who, even now, three years after he retired from international football, is still one of the best centre-backs in the country.

That's the back four then. As with my all-time world XI, I'm once again going for a 4–3–3 formation and my first choice in midfield is another player who was born to lead, Bryan Robson – or, as he was better known to those who played alongside him, Captain Marvel.

I almost broke with tradition and went for Sir Bobby Charlton here, for the simple reason that when I decided to get my lion's mane chopped off the *Daily Mirror* ran a feature showing what I would look like wearing various well-known footballing hairstyles and one of those was Sir Bobby Charlton's world famous comb-over. I've just had another quick look at it now and I have to say that it suited him a lot better than it suited me. It wasn't half as bad as the Carlos Valderrama one, though. Honestly, you'd think these newspaper lads would have something better to do!

For me, Bryan Robson is one of the most important players ever to kick a football and when he came out and said that he had cancer a few years ago it was telling just how many players and former players went public with messages of support. Fortunately he's okay now but it reminded me at the time what an enormous impact he's had on the game. He had ninety caps for his country, and, according to Paul Gascoigne, was the best player of his generation. Behind Bobby Moore he has to be one of England's best ever captains.

Standing alongside Captain Marvel would be quite possibly the most written-about British footballer of the twentieth century: the aforementioned Paul John Gascoigne.

It was a massive pleasure for us at BT Sport that Paul decided to make his TV comeback on *Fletch & Sav* in 2015 and what a fantastic time we had. He's a great raconteur. He had us all in stitches from the moment he came on until the moment he went off. Seriously, if his stories and jokes were half as well documented as his troubles he would be top of the bill at *The Royal Variety Performance*.

During the previous year I'd been asked to comment on some photos of Gazza that had been taken some weeks before and showed him looking thin and completely dishevelled. It was a massive shock seeing somebody you admire so much in that kind of state so when he turned up at the *Fletch & Sav* studio looking and feeling so well it was an enormous relief.

I had to man-mark Gazza once while he was at Everton and I was at Leicester, and I never left his side for a minute – partly because I was just doing my job but also because, well, he's Paul Gascoigne. I'd always wanted to meet him and I figured this was probably the best way of spending some time with him. He didn't say much that day and to be honest I just kept on staring at him. He must have thought I was a right weirdo!

Stats mean nothing at all when it comes to Gazza. With him it was all about the experience – about watching it happen. Just like Iniesta he was a complete footballer but at the same time the ultimate playmaker. He could change a game single-hand-edly and at the drop of a hat.

Sorry, Scotland fans, but that wonder goal he scored at Wembley when he flicked the ball over Colin Hendry and stuck it into the left-hand corner – things like that make you glad to be alive.

Last in my three-man midfield would be Steven Gerrard for all the reasons I've mentioned previously. My only regret here is not being able to pick Scholsey but because he played a lot on the left I can't see how I can include him. It's a shame but there we go.

I said earlier in the book that Lord Gary Lineker and Sir Alan Shearer are the two best strikers England has ever had and I stand by that comment 100 per cent, which means, of course, that there's just one more place up for grabs in my all-time England XI.

Once again there are no prizes for guessing who I'm going to pick. It's got to be Wayne Rooney. Could you imagine a three-man attack featuring Lineker, Shearer and Rooney? That's ridiculous.

Wayne Rooney is another one I would describe as being a complete footballer. In fact, for me he's probably *the* complete footballer. I'm not just talking about being able to play in midfield, score goals and then track back. I would have Rooney playing at left back if I needed someone to cover and, do you know what, he would do a job for me. I certainly wouldn't have to worry.

As the manager I'm going to have to go for Sir Bobby Robson. He's one of a very, very rare group of men who succeeded as a player, a domestic manager and an international manager. In fact, offhand the only other one I can think of is Louis van Gaal, although he never represented Holland as a player whereas Sir Bobby won twenty caps for England. Anyway, he's the one I would choose to be leading my all-time England XI out. A real gentleman.

The Savage All-time England XI Teamsheet

Peter Shilton
Gary Neville
Rio Ferdinand
John Terry
Ashley Cole
Bryan Robson
Paul Gascoigne

Steven Gerrard
Wayne Rooney
Gary Lineker
Alan Shearer

The Greatest Players I
Played Alongside and Against

As I've already said, the greatest player I ever played along-side was the Turkish legend Tugay, or Worzel Gummidge as I used to call him. He had already been at Blackburn Rovers a few years when I joined in 2005 and we very quickly became good friends.

Before meeting Tugay the only time I'd ever encountered anyone from Turkey was in 1997 when, while playing for Wales, we travelled to Galatasaray's notorious Ali Sami Yen Stadium in Istanbul for a World Cup qualifying match. Given what happened that night I'm surprised I didn't duck when I was first introduced to Tugay. What a cauldron! The Turkey supporters seemed to enjoy mixing patriotism with extreme violence and from the moment we arrived at the airport we had to be surrounded night and day by security guards.

Dean Saunders had played for Galatasaray just a year or so before and had tried to tell us that things might get tasty.

Nothing could prepare us for what was in store, though. I remember being at a team meeting the night before the match and all the way through you could hear hundreds of fans outside all baying for Welsh blood. How we got out alive I'll never know.

I had played against Tugay a few times while I was at Birmingham and during the last encounter, which Blackburn won 4–1, we'd shared a few words after a tackle. I don't remember the exact details (I tend to forget the ones where I'm at fault) but I think I'd kicked the ball at his head after he'd gone down or something like that. It was nothing really. Anyway, he got up, muttered something complimentary in Turkish, I returned the compliment, and we went on our way.

A year or two later, not long after I'd joined Blackburn, I got a lift with Tugay to training one day. We lived quite close to each other and so later used to take it in turns. His young son was in the car this particular morning and after I got in his son looked at me, turned to his dad and seemed to ask him a question in Turkish. I only recognized one word and that was 'Birmingham'. When he'd finished Tugay started laughing.

'What did he say?' I asked.

'My son has just asked me if you are the horrible man who kicked the ball against my head at Birmingham.'

I looked at his son and said, 'I'm afraid I am. Sorry!'

They say that opposites attract and in footballing terms that was certainly the case with me and Worzel. I was the workhorse who used to run and tackle all day, and he was the maestro who just amazed us all. We actually used to call him the maestro. You could give Tugay the ball in any area and it didn't matter whether he had two, three or even four players around him, he would still do something unbelievable.

I certainly don't mean this in a rude way but he was a complete freak of nature. For a start he was a very heavy smoker. There was always the odd player who used to spark up a cigarette when you were out having a drink but Tugay was a professional chimney. Even on the training field you would look around and he would have one on the go. With him it was all about talent. I suppose he must have been fit to a certain extent but it wasn't the be all and end all. Skill and technique made up 99 per cent of Tugay's game and he tended to let them do the talking. Giggsy had the aura – the star quality – but in terms of sheer skill and genius, Tugay was the one.

My favourite memory of Tugay happened on Boxing Day in 2005. We were away at Liverpool and in between ciggies he produced the best step-over I have ever seen in my entire life. What's more, it was on Steven Gerrard. After that he put in Morten Gamst Pedersen who crossed to Benni McCarthy and bang – one-nil to the Rovers. We won the match, too. I just stood there looking at him thinking, how on earth did you do that you clever so and so? What a day.

I've got so many wonderful memories of playing alongside Tugay and each one is special. He was the perfect combination. Friendly, laidback and disgustingly talented!

A top, top bloke.

Talking of the great Steven Gerrard, he's by far the greatest player I ever played against. For a modern-day midfielder to go box-to-box, create, tackle and lead is pretty special, but to do all four to a genuine world-class standard and maintain it for the best part of two decades is something else.

I loved playing against him in the sense that I used to learn a lot and he would tend to bring out the best in me – great players usually do that. But at the same time I also hated playing against him because, without wanting to put too fine a point on it, he had this habit of making you feel inadequate as a player. He didn't do it on purpose, of course. All he had to do was play football!

Believe me, I've played against some of the absolute greats in midfield, including Frank Lampard. I've got to give this bloke a mention because he was bordering on absolute genius, too. I remember playing against Chelsea while I was at Derby. I was supposed to be man-marking Frank and during those ninety minutes he scored four goals. The lad just left me for dead. I can't believe that I've just reminded myself of that, let alone written it down. It's not one of my proudest moments.

A lot has been made over the years about him and Gerrard not gelling together. It's one of those long-running debates like Messi v. Ronaldo. They first played together for England in 2003 and by the end of the World Cup last year people were still none the wiser. For me the really big puzzle was how you could have David Beckham, Frank Lampard, Steven Gerrard and Paul Scholes in the same team – four of the greatest midfielders in the world at the time – and not come close to winning a thing. Some people say they were almost playing against each other, which I suppose I would have to agree with, but with regards to Gerrard and Lampard I just think they cancelled each other out. They were too similar. Gary

Neville made an interesting point last year when he suggested that a twenty-three year-old Lampard and a thirty-four-year-old Gerrard would have worked a lot better, with Gerrard becoming the sitting midfielder. I think he's probably right but then it's all academic now as both ships have sailed to the United States.

Towards the end of 2014 Steven went through a bit of a bad spell – just a couple of games – and by the way we all reacted you would have thought he'd been sent off in a cup final or scored ten own goals. I was even asked to write a column about what had gone wrong. That's the measure of a truly great player. If you manage to maintain such a ridiculously high standard for so long, the slightest blip is going to be leapt upon. Only players like Gerrard, Messi and Ronaldo receive that kind of scrutiny.

This is one of the things I don't get about Sir Alex Ferguson. He's one of the greatest managers who ever lived and probably has one of the most respected opinions, yet he doesn't think Gerrard should be classed as one of the greats. Either he was just being a reactionary by saying that or he actually meant it. Either way, I think he needs glasses.

Poor old Brendan Rodgers. What a job – losing Luis Suárez one year and then Steven Gerrard the next. You just can't replace players like that, like-for-like, not unless you're very, very lucky, so he's got one hell of a job on his hands. Steven Gerrard's different, though. Even though he's no longer at Anfield he's as important to Liverpool Football Club as Kenny Dalglish or Bill Shankly, which is why it was probably lucky for Brendan that Steven's form dipped a bit in the 2014/15 season.

Had he left Anfield firing on all cylinders I would have feared for Liverpool this coming season even more than I do.

As I write Steven Gerrard is one game in at his new club, LA Galaxy, and not surprisingly scored on his Major League Soccer debut. I honestly hope they get a good three or four years out of him because, for me, the day he retires from football will spell the end of a very, very special era.

The Greatest Manager
I Played For

Before I get on to the greatest manager I ever played for as a professional, and believe me that's been just as difficult as some of the other choices in this book, I would just like to pay a very quick tribute to one of the very first managers I ever played for, my dad, Colin Savage, who we unfortunately lost to Pick's disease, a rare form of Alzheimer's, in March 2012.

I've talked a lot about Dad since he died but mostly about his death. Alzheimer's, as we all know, is destroying more lives now than ever before and so when I was asked by the Alzheimer's Society to help promote all the fantastic work they've been doing I jumped at the chance. Honestly, until you get involved with something like that you have no idea just how many amazing people there are devoting their entire lives to either raising funds or helping find a cure. I should think it's the same with most good causes and those involved are a credit to us all.

Here, I would like to talk about my dad's life, if only briefly. He was quite a shy man and would have been dead embarrassed if I went into any detail. As I said, he was one of the first managers I ever played for, but he was more than that. He was my mentor, and if it hadn't been for his unfailing guidance, love, support and encouragement I would never, ever have become a professional footballer. I've got him to thank for everything.

Like me now, Dad lived, breathed and ate two things: football and family. Nothing else mattered. He even set up a youth team in Bradley, which is where we lived, and he poached me from the team I was playing for! We did well, though, and won all kinds of cups. He was a great motivator, my dad, and the entire team loved him.

Dad was quite a slightly built man and I inherited his slim physique. In his opinion this was no good for a budding professional and so from the age of thirteen he made me drink a can of Guinness every night. He got the stuff free because of his job and had read somewhere that it was supposed to build you up. We had mountains of the stuff in our garage and because he wasn't much of a drinker – and Guinness was never my mum's tipple – it was all mine. Brilliant! Or maybe not.

'It's a meal in itself, Robert,' Dad used to assure me.

If it was a meal it was one of the worst I'd ever tasted. I detested the stuff!

After a while Dad realized that not a lot was happening and so he decided to bump up my carbs instead. What a relief that was. It still didn't work, though. I was just born skinny.

Like thousands of other parents my dad gave up half his life for my footballing career. The moment he got back from work we were off, either to training or to a match, and by the time we got home it was time for bed. He would skip meetings, meals – anything – just so long as I could play football. It's astonishing when you think about it. Pure sacrifice.

One of the reasons I wanted to write about Dad is because I know there'll be stacks of people reading this who had a parent, or parents, just like him. How lucky are we?

These days I'm doing exactly the same thing with my eldest, Charlie – minus the Guinness – and every time we get in the car and set off to training I think about Dad.

I just want to share with you a letter Dad wrote me the day I left home to become a full-time apprentice at Manchester United. I printed it in my autobiography a few years ago but now he's gone it seems even more poignant. People don't often write letters anymore (in fact, I don't think I've ever written one in my life) so it's something I'll always treasure. It sums up everything and was written right at the end of our journey together – a journey that had a pretty happy ending. He was my hero and I feel so lucky to have had him as a dad.

Dear Rob,

Just a note to say what I find difficult to say in words to your face. I have been a lucky man. As well as having been lucky enough to have found a woman like your mum, I have been the luckiest man in the world to have had two boys like you and Jonathan. You now have an opportunity that millions of other young men would give their right arm for. Please don't waste it. You have a God-given gift, so use it, and remember, HARD WORK SUPPLIES ITS OWN

REWARD. Take my advice, and remember to be very wary of the workmates that forever moan about everything under the sun. You usually find that the ones that moan are the ones that don't like hard work. It goes without saying that, no matter what problems you have when you're in Manchester, no matter how big or small, your family – Mum, Jonathan and me – are always here to help. We will all miss you, but most of all Mum. She will miss you like hell, so try to ring home as often as possible. Finally, never stop believing in yourself. We know you are the best, so believe that yourself. There is a great deal of difference between self-confidence and being a bighead. Fortunately, being a bighead has never been a problem with you, so be CONFIDENT. I love you lots, the best of luck, and work hard,

Dad

Fortunately Dad's illness didn't take hold until well after I made it as a Premier League player and that is something I will always be grateful for. Unfortunately, by the time I led him onto the pitch with my two boys at the start of my last ever professional game for Derby County in 2011 he was dying and he was in his own world really, yet he was still the reason I was there. It had all started with his sacrifice and dedication. When the disease got hold of him we were told that sport can often help you to communicate with sufferers as it creates so many memories. With Dad I had a choice of literally thousands of happy memories and as these came to mind I tried reliving them with him. Some registered and some didn't but towards the end they were about the only thing that made him smile.

I remember looking at him that day at Pride Park and feeling so proud, just as he'd looked at me when I signed that contract for Manchester United. It had come full circle in that respect and although the circumstances were far less happy I was still a very, very proud son. Thanks for everything, Dad.

Choosing the best manager I ever played under has been massively difficult. In contention are Martin O'Neill, Peter Taylor, Micky Adams, Steve Bruce, Mark Hughes and Nigel Clough. There are other managers that I've played for but at the end of the day you can't get on with everybody, can you?

I know I'm not usually one for sitting on the fence but if somebody said to me, 'Okay, Sav, on this occasion we'll let you choose the lot', I'd snap off their hand. They're all very different people and have very different strengths, but if you could mould them all together you would probably have the best manager in the world.

Peter Taylor is a fantastic coach and a lovely, lovely man, but I didn't play under him for very long and so for that reason I'll have to move on. Sorry, mate.

Micky Adams too is a really, really nice guy and I got on very well with him at Leicester. That said, he did have cause to tell me off once or twice, not least when he received a complaint about my driving. I tried my best to deny it, but that was pretty futile.

I had a nice, understated bright-yellow Ferrari at the time and one day the club received a complaint from somebody who lived near the training ground – a complaint regarding a bright-yellow Ferrari.

The conversation I had with Micky went something like this.

'Sav, can I have a word please?'

'Sure, boss.'

'In my office.'

'Okay.'

'Right then. We've had a complaint from a member of the public who lives near the training ground about somebody driving a bright-yellow Ferrari. They've been driving a bit fast, apparently.'

'Nothing to do with me, boss.'

The look on Micky's face was a picture.

'I beg your pardon?'

I was indignant.

'Just as I said, boss. It's nothing to do with me.'

'How can you be so sure?' He said starting to laugh.

'I always drive carefully.'

'But they know it was you, Sav.'

'How?' I said, doing my best to look as shocked as possible. 'What proof do they have?'

'Well, by the description they gave.'

'What description?'

Micky picked up the piece of paper that had been handed to him.

'A bright-yellow Ferrari with the letters SAV on the number plate.'

'Sorry, boss. It won't happen again.'

'Thank you, Robbie. See you tomorrow.'

I still to this day have absolutely no idea what possessed me to try and plead my innocence.

Unfortunately, as with Peter, I didn't spend that long working with Micky on a one-to-one basis and so for that reason I'm going to have to move on.

Mark Hughes and Steve Bruce are legends of the game and I've known them both since I was about fourteen years of age. They're also fantastic managers and the fact that they're both still at big clubs is encouraging as it seems more and more foreign coaches are being drafted in. On this occasion, though, it's all about the effect the managers had on my career and for that reason I'm going to have to concentrate on two others.

For me Nigel Clough has the makings of becoming one of the best young managers in the country and I'm still reeling at the way he was treated by Sheffield United. It makes my blood boil.

When he arrived at Derby County in 2009 the place was going through a tough time. Paul Jewell had been the man in charge for about a season-and-a-half and even though he was the man who had brought me in from Blackburn Rovers, we just hadn't seen eye to eye and by the time Nigel got the job in January 2009 I'd been all but frozen out of the first team. In fact, the only playing time I'd had that season was a six-game loan spell at Brighton.

Nigel was only in his early thirties when he became manager and so he had very few pre-conceived ideas about people, which was definitely a positive. Players like me often came with a reputation but to Nigel reputations meant nothing and when he started at Derby everybody was treated the same and given an opportunity to make it into the first team. It was a huge struggle for me because of what had happened under Jewell but gradually, with Nigel's help, I made it back into the first team and finished my career on a high. He also allowed me time to do my media work, which obviously helped me make the transition from player to pundit.

My favourite memory playing under Nigel happened at Elland Road. It was the first game of the 2010/11 season and, given the history of Nigel's dad and his controversial stint as manager at Leeds United, this was always going to be a potentially fiery encounter. The film, *The Damned United*, had recently come out, which certainly wasn't helping matters. No, it's safe to say that it wasn't a good day to be a Clough in Leeds.

We were all aware that things might be a bit tasty, certainly coming to and from the stadium, so you can imagine what we thought when Nigel stopped the coach about 200 metres from the ground.

'Right, lads,' he said. 'Get your stuff and get out. We're walking the rest of the way.'

Nigel may have been young for a manager but he was definitely his father's son and when he told you to jump, you jumped. So, off the coach we got and began walking towards the stadium. There were thousands of Leeds fans everywhere and when they realized who we were they just stood there and stared at us. Nobody said a word, in fact. It was a totally empowering experience from our point of view and by the time we made it onto the pitch we were full of confidence.

Perhaps not surprisingly we totally dominated that game and came away 2–1 winners. We didn't walk 200 metres back to the coach, though. Did we heck! This was Leeds, remember.

The only thing Nigel had missing compared with the man below is a bit of experience; otherwise he'd have been the one. As Bruce Forsyth said to me once or twice on *Strictly*, 'You're my favourite', but on this occasion, gaffer, you're not quite the best. Sorry, mate!

Martin O'Neill is one of the most intelligent people I've ever met; more importantly, though, he's the best man-manager I ever played under and that's why he's number one here.

We didn't always see eye to eye and there were times when I'm sure he would have loved to throttle me, but as the man who both introduced me to the big time and helped me win my one and only medal he had an immeasurable effect on my career.

Remember that conversation I had with him after he had questioned my ability on *Match of the Day*? Well, it was that conversation that really helped me focus on what I *could* do, as opposed to worrying about what I couldn't. He did that with everybody, not just me.

To achieve what he did with the players he had at Leicester City was bordering on what Brian Clough achieved with Nottingham Forest. Now before you all start tweeting me with all kinds of everything, just hear me out. Yes, I know he didn't win two European Cups in succession and the league title, but don't forget that after he got Leicester City promoted to the Premier League, which he did in 1995/96 in his first season, there were probably sixteen or seventeen teams better than them in the league, yet while he was there he took Leicester to the final of the League Cup three times, winning two, and during his four seasons with Leicester in the Premier League they finished ninth, tenth, tenth and eighth. That's fantastic!

For me that's one of the best records in top-flight football, bearing in mind he had me to contend with, and for that reason I'm awarding Martin O'Neill the inaugural 'Best Manager of Robbie Savage's Fantastically Successful Career' award. Congratulations, gaffer!

Me and My Cars

If you were to say to the beautiful Mrs Savage, 'Sarah, tell me about Robbie and his cars', she would probably roll her eyes, say something like, 'Oh my God', and then tell you, over the space of a couple of hours, how much trouble they've been over the years. It wouldn't be a happy conversation, put it that way, but it would certainly be entertaining.

I see it slightly differently, surprise surprise. They're my weakness, you see, the one thing apart from Sarah, my boys, my mum and my dogs that I go soft over.

Footballers and pundits don't often do themselves any favours when it comes to choosing cars; in fact, some people have even accused us of lacking taste. I can't think where they get that from.

The day I signed for Leicester City and became a Premier League player I went out and bought – wait for it – a lovely pink Porsche! A lovely pink Porsche that I was forced to swap for a nice white recovery van after about an hour.

It was the start of my much-admired Don Johnson in *Miami*

Vice phase and in order to complement my blond shoulder-length hair, diamond-white teeth, false tan, white shirt, white shoes and chinos I decided to invest in something equally stylish and tasteful. I was the full package really: high fashion, good looks and now the car to match. Genuine film-star material. How I was never snapped up by Hollywood or even *Emmerdale* is still a complete mystery.

In my defence I was twenty-three years old, had just signed a very lucrative contract after being on about £220 a week, and until then had been driving nothing grander than a white Ford Fiesta. The move from Crewe Alexandra had actually been touch and go as during my medical they discovered I had a split cartilage and I had to wait a full twenty-four hours before I was given the all-clear. It was real squeaky-bum time.

The moment I signed that contract I was down to my local car garage armed with a banker's draft faster than you can say hire purchase. I'd been drooling over this car for months and so it was a very special moment. The garage wanted to prepare the car and asked me to come back the next day but that was no good for me. 'Just give me the keys please,' I asked. 'I've got some serious cruising to do.'

The first person I called was Neil Lennon.

'You've bought what?' he said.

Within about ten minutes he'd called what seemed like every single footballer in the country and I began receiving an absolute barrage of abuse. Nothing new there then. 'Big-time Charlie' was one of the cleaner names they called me. I didn't care, though, I was the closest thing Wrexham had to a genuine 1990s playboy and I was proud.

Next, I called my mate Jamie.

'I've bought a new toy. Fancy going cruising round Chester?'

Now, you don't turn down an offer to ride in the passenger seat of a pink Porsche next to Peter Stringfellow's little brother, do you? Within fifteen minutes I'd picked Jamie up at his house and from that moment on we were the toast of Chester. Talk about turning heads. People were actually stopping in their tracks and staring at us – a mixture of admiration and jealousy in their eyes. At least, I think that's what it looked like. I felt like a king.

After another ten minutes or so, just as we were driving right through the centre of Chester, there was a loud cracking noise and at the same time the car came to an abrupt halt.

'What's happened?' I asked Jamie.

'Search me,' he replied.

By now there was a queue building up behind us.

'Get out and have a look will you?' I asked him.

'Why don't you? I know nothing about cars.'

What a horrible end to an otherwise perfect afternoon.

In the end we both got out of the car, lifted up the bonnet and tried to pretend we knew what we were looking at. By the way, I know absolutely nothing about the workings of a car and, what's more, I'm not interested. This obviously showed as people started shouting at us to move it onto the pavement. Bowing to pressure I slammed down the bonnet and prepared to push, and as I did I caught a glimpse of my reflection in the windscreen. I was black – funeral black. There was oil all down the front of my shirt, trousers and shoes. I even had some on my face.

'Oh God, look at me!' I said to Jamie. 'My car's ruined and so are my clothes.'

'Mm. It's a bit of bad luck this. You'd better call the RAC or whoever.'

After we'd pushed the car onto the pavement I just stood there on the side of the road and went bright red. I must have looked like a matchstick. Every single person who passed us looked over as if to say, 'Ha! Look at you, ★★★★head!'

You would have thought that experience might have put me off cars for a bit, but I was hooked. Once I'd got over the embarrassment of being the most laughed-at man in Chester I was straight out with my cheque book again on the hunt for something new. If I was going to have a hobby I was going to give it 110 per cent.

About four cars later I had a similar piece of luck when I lent a blue Ferrari to a friend of mine.

'Can I just take it out for a quick spin?' he asked. 'I've never driven something like this before.'

'Of course you can,' I said, looking at the car like a proud father.

He sped off but as he did he failed to change out of first gear and had got no further than a hundred yards from the house when smoke began billowing out from underneath the bonnet.

I dropped to my knees. 'Not again!'

Just to add insult to injury I'd only recently agreed to sell the car to somebody and when he turned up to finalize things he just laughed at me.

'What the hell have you been doing to it?' he asked me.

'*I* haven't been doing anything to it,' I said.

That was beyond bad luck really. Once again it didn't put me off. What's that saying? 'If you fall off a horse the best thing to do is get straight back on.'

I spent five years at Leicester City and in that time I became the proud owner of one wife, a Worthington Cup winner's medal, two more Porsches (one red and one blue), a bright-yellow Ferrari, three Mercs and a BMW. Oh yes, and I lost an absolute flaming fortune on each and every single one of them (the cars, that is). That didn't matter, though. Lads I knew used to spend fortunes on gambling and expensive champagne. At least I had something to show for it – apart from recovery vans and mechanic's bills.

When I was at Manchester United, Steve Bruce used to have a Volkswagen Golf GTi and I used to stand looking at it for hours. Steve used to humour me a bit and tell me that if I worked hard I might one day be able to buy one, but at the time I didn't believe him. 'Me, own a Golf?' It seemed impossible at the time.

Eleven years later Steve signed me for Birmingham City and the morning after I joined I pulled into the club car park driving a brand new Ferrari. The gaffer was just getting out of his car when I pulled in and when he saw me he stopped and started laughing.

'You haven't changed, have you, son? Still as flash as ever. Remember my Golf?'

By then I had a bit of a reputation for buying fast and generally useless sports cars. I'm like the opposite of Chris Evans. When he goes out to buy a car he'll visit a private auction somewhere, bid about £20 million, put it in his garage, cherish it, and within a week or so it's worth £25 million, whereas I will go to a dealership, spend a lot less than £20 million but still enough, get the car home, become bored with it within about a month, take it back to the dealership, and end up losing a small fortune! Where am I going wrong? Next time I buy a car I'm going to take Chris Evans with me. I might need to take out a pretty big mortgage first, though. Imagine what Sarah would say. It doesn't bear thinking about. By the way, Chris, how about getting me on as a Star in a Reasonably Priced Car when you start doing *Top Gear*? I'd love to do that.

The car rollcall at Birmingham City was even more impressive than the one at Leicester City. After I got rid of my Ferrari I fell in love with a bright-yellow Lamborghini, as you do, followed by two massive Bentleys, which did about three miles to the gallon, four Range Rovers and an Aston Martin. Not bad, eh?

I blame my chairman at the time, David Gold, for giving me a very bad case of car envy and getting me into Bentleys. He turned up to the training ground in a Bentley one day and I thought, 'Wow, look at that! I've got to have one of those.' Unfortunately for me I didn't tell my teammates about my new-found love of Bentleys. Had I done so, I would have been reminded that, back then at least, they were mainly driven by . . . people of a certain age, shall we say? Within a week I'd bought one. The barrage started on the first second of the first day I drove up to the training ground in it. Think of any rude word you like and I bet you any money I was called it on that first day. I was gutted. When I bought a new car I would usually expect to receive a steady stream of enthusiastic footballers, coaches and managers all smiling and saying things like, 'Flaming heck, Sav, what a car!' This time all I got was 'Oi, Sav! My granddad used to have one of them. You look like a right muppet.' Or words to that effect.

I should have expected it really. The day before, when I'd collected the car, I decided to drive up to north Wales to show it off to the family. When I was about half-way there I was pulled over by a policeman who seemed to think it might have been stolen. When he saw who was driving it he just started laughing.

'Is this really your car, sir?' he said.

'Yes it is!' I replied.

'I have to say I was expecting somebody a little bit older.'

I was mortified.

Bentleys are all the rage now and are driven by all kinds of people, but back then it appeared that was far from the case. Three weeks later I decided to sell the thing and, surprise surprise, I lost a king's ransom.

At Blackburn things became a bit silly as in addition to yet another Range Rover, another Lamborghini, a white Ferrari and a Mercedes 320, I also bought a Hummer so as not to draw too much attention to myself. I daren't tell you how many miles that did to the gallon and it was the worst car in the world to park. It was fun while it lasted, though. At Derby I managed to curb my addiction a bit and stuck with two Lamborghinis – one hard-top and one soft-top – and three Mercs. That was my version of being restrained! Honestly, it was difficult.

Let me just say that since I retired from being a professional footballer I have become a lot more mature about my choice of car and have learned to change them once every year or so as opposed to once every week.

The current family car and the one Sarah drives around in is a Range Rover and the one I drive is a Ghost. Come on, you don't get much more mature than that.

Does it bother me knowing that I might have lost a few quid on cars? Do you know, it doesn't really – in fact, not at all. Most people's lifestyles adjust to what they earn and because I've earned a few quid for quite a few years I've had a few nice cars. Or at least I think they're nice. Seriously, what's wrong with that?

The only real regret I have when it comes to purchasing things that move is the time I decided to buy a boat. Whatever possessed me I'm not entirely sure, but it seemed like a good idea at the time.

Actually, I do know why I bought it: it was because I needed a holiday. Seriously! I'd just joined Derby County at the time and was having a pretty torrid time there. As a team we were awful, the crowd were on my back and a lot of people were saying that my legs had gone. I wasn't used to that kind of treatment, not from my own supporters, at least, and it was probably the first time I realized that my career as a footballer might be coming to an end. That in itself was an awful realization and as a consequence I'd started snapping quite a bit at Sarah and the kids. They were right: I did need to get away.

So, in the summer of 2008, I went out and bought a fifty-foot twin-engine yacht. Had I not been under so much stress and pressure then I doubt I would have bought it (or I might have settled for a dinghy), but at the time it was a very welcome distraction. To be fair, I absolutely loved being Captain Savage and the six weeks we spent on the *Elementary Sarah* were some of the best ever. In fact, I honestly didn't want it to end because of what I thought was waiting for me when I got back home. I was all for growing a beard and sailing quietly off into the sunset, never to kick a ball in anger again. As it was I was only a few months into a two-and-a-half year contract and so I had to pull myself together.

The only mishap I had during my time as a boat owner was when my cousin Matt flew down from Germany for a few days to join us. Once he was on board I was keen to show him all the gadgets and features, not least the six-foot dinghy that was kept at the back of the boat in its very own garage.

'Why don't we use that to get ashore when we go and eat tonight?' Matt asked.

What usually happened when we dropped anchor was that a taxi boat would collect us, take us ashore and then bring us back again.

'We can't all get in that,' I replied.

'No problem,' said Matt. 'Sarah and the boys can go by taxi and we can take the dinghy. Oh, come on. It'll be like something out of James Bond!'

James Bond? It was more like a flipping Carry On film by the time we'd finished.

Getting ashore wasn't a problem and, even though I'd never driven a dinghy with an outboard motor before, I took to it like the proverbial duck to water. In fact Matt was right, I actually did feel a little bit like James Bond as we drove into the harbour, jumped out and tied her up.

'Good suggestion, Matt,' I said. 'That was great!'

After we'd eaten Sarah and the boys got back into the taxi

while Matt and I made like spies again and jumped back into the dinghy.

'Okay, shipmate,' I said. 'Untie the ropes, we'll drift out a bit and then I'll start the motor.'

With that Matt untied the ropes and because there was a bit of a breeze we started moving straight away.

'Start the motor, then,' said Matt.

'I'm trying! It won't start though.'

Now I might not be Mr Mechanical but even I know when something's run out of petrol.

'The tank's empty,' I yelled. 'What are we going to do? We've got no oars.'

'Call Sarah on your mobile. She can get the taxi to come and pick us up.'

'Good idea,' I said.

By this time we were about half a mile from the shore going in the opposite direction to the boat. What's more, the wind was getting stronger and the sea choppier.

'Come on, get your phone out and call Sarah,' shouted Matt. 'We're in trouble here!'

We were about to be in even bigger trouble. As I took my mobile phone out of my pocket and lifted it to my ear a huge wave went underneath us and, in an attempt to prevent myself falling overboard, I dropped my phone into the sea.

Now I was panic stricken. 'Look what you made me do!' I said to my equally panic-stricken cousin. 'What the hell are we going to do now?'

I would rather not repeat the conversation Matt and I had over the ensuing twenty minutes or so, but let's just say there was a lot of finger pointing (when we weren't clinging on for dear life) and a lot of very choice language.

Fortunately for us Sarah realized pretty soon that something was up and so called the taxi back and asked him to come and look for us. We can't have been that difficult to find: two blokes in a six-foot dinghy furiously pointing at each other. Disaster averted then. Just!

Boats are a different world to cars. Even if you take into account some of Chris Evans's classic marques you're still talking about a totally different set of numbers. They're more like aeroplanes cost-wise. We had our boat moored in Antibes, which is in the south of France, and she had a 150-footer on one side of her and a 75-footer on the other. They must have cost some serious dough – many millions, probably.

As with the majority of my beloved cars, I sold the *Elementary Sarah* just a few months later, and although we had fun it must go down as one of the most expensive six-week holidays in history.

Bad Eggs and Bullies

Bad eggs come in all shapes and sizes and over the years I must have experienced just about every one going.

Here are a few examples of what to watch out for.

Fortunately you don't get many of these but the ones who really make me boil are the big-money signings who perform to get a contract and then sit back and just go through the motions. As far as I'm concerned, that's as good as fraud.

I'm obviously not going to make this personal but I've seen and heard of quite a few players who train as if they are on a walking holiday in the Lake District yet when they're not picked for the starting XI they get mardy about sitting on the subs bench. Idiots like that can have an extremely damaging effect on a dressing room, especially in terms of morale. Lads who earn less than them become resentful and before you know it the dressing room's split. You don't have to be a bone-idle idiot to make other players jealous or resentful, although it helps. Just the fact that you earn more can alienate you from the group so you've got to make sure that everyone realizes that you're a team player who really cares about the future of the club.

On the other side of the coin there are one or two examples of players performing out of their skin for selfish reasons, and I'm slightly ashamed to say that I'm actually guilty of being one myself. People often think that when a team suddenly starts performing well after being relegated it's because the pressure is off, but in actual fact it's a mixture of that and also because the players want to attract new clubs. Think about it. If you're at a club that either has suffered or is facing the possibility of relegation you're going to do everything you can to stay in that higher division. You'll have a small window of opportunity and you have to do everything in your power to make it count. No Premier League player wants to play second-tier football and no player in the world wants a drop in wages, so if you play out of your skin while you still have the chance then you're far more likely to be picked up. Yes, it sounds a bit mercenary, but what would you do? Some people might ask why you hadn't been playing like that all season, but it's not as simple as that. Playing in a team fighting against relegation is very different to playing in a team that's been relegated, and I should know.

When I was at Birmingham City we had a few narrow escapes and in my first season there we only managed to miss the drop by seven points. The football wasn't at all pretty at times but it was a case of just doing whatever you had to do. The season before that I'd been at Leicester City and we'd been relegated from the Premier League with plenty of time to spare. I'm satisfied that I put my heart and soul into every single game that season but once we suffered relegation my mind was elsewhere and I was motivated by saving my own skin. I had four or five games where I could send out a message that, despite Leicester City being relegated, I was still a player worthy of a Premier League contract – and it worked. Birmingham came in for me, said they'd been very impressed by my performances for Leicester City and gave me a three-year contract. What's more, I played the best football of my career at St Andrew's so it was a very, very sensible move.

After that I went to Blackburn Rovers in a move that was once again partly engineered by me. What I did at Leicester was okay in my opinion as I never let the club down, but what I did at Birmingham was more to do with manipulation, really, and to this day it's probably the one thing I wish I could go back and change. Without going into too much detail I got it into my head that I had to leave Birmingham City, whatever the club did to try and make me stay, and to be fair they tried just about everything. I just wouldn't listen. It wasn't for financial gain, by the way. There was a lot more to it than that – in fact, I took a pay cut to go to Ewood Park – but at the end of the day it was a situation that could and should have been handled better, especially by me.

Does that make me a bad egg? I hope not. That was the only time in a twenty-year career that I detached myself from the rest of the dressing room but at the time I thought it was what I had to do. If my behaviour ever did affect any of my teammates at Birmingham City then I sincerely apologize.

When it comes to actual bullying I think there's usually a fine line to be drawn between that and banter. While I never experienced any out-and-out bullying in my career I both saw and heard things that would not be tolerated now – in football or any other business. Changing rooms can be harsh environments, where it is often better to be one of the lads, joining in with the banter, initiation ceremonies and practical jokes than a loner sitting in the corner.

I've already told you about some of the rituals I experienced at The Cliff and, as I'm sure you can imagine, that kind of horseplay wasn't unique to United. Whenever I meet up with old pros now, at golf days or charity events, we all agree on two things – firstly, how much we miss playing, and secondly, how much we miss the banter and the craic of the dressing room.

From my point of view, if I wanted to dish it out I had to be able to take it. To make it at professional level, you need a thick skin. Obviously there are certain no-go areas in terms of acceptable banter. But the changing room is still an intimidating place for some kids who can't handle the vulgar, ruthless language and practices of the workplace. If you don't develop a thick skin quickly, or you are not blessed with survival instincts, you are likely to crumble.

So in order for a player to have a successful career as a footballer, not only do they need to have talent and commitment but they also need to be able to handle themselves in a dressing room. Easier said than done.

A lot of fans think players only go through an initiation when they join a new club, and they have to stand on a chair and sing their favourite song in front of the whole squad. But for many players the daily routine involves mind-games where your mettle is tested in the name of improving your character. I never classed it as bullying, but if I carried out some of the stunts outlined above on colleagues at any of my current employers, I would either be sacked on the spot – or knocked spark-out.

Aware that dressing-room humour can be horrible and vindictive, as a senior player and captain at Derby I used to take new signings under my wing to help them integrate with their teammates. And although it was not about their bullying in the school-playground sense of the word, I got into my fair share of scrapes with colleagues over differences of opinion. But there is a fine margin between bravado and bullying and people who work outside sports dressing rooms have no idea how vicious and cutting they can be.

It's not just players, though. I've heard of situations where managers either don't like a certain player or don't rate them and, as opposed to trying to make an effort to either get on with that player or help them find another club, they go down the line of making their life a misery. I've heard of dozens of examples of this happening and, when you think about it, it's the worst kind of bullying. Getting stick from your teammates can be bad enough, but when it's coming from the boss it often gets taken to a different level as more often than not they'll have the support of not only the rest of the dressing room but also the backroom staff, the admin staff and the owners. The manager can turn the people who matter against you and when that happens, especially over a long period of time, it can destroy you.

As with most problems, prevention is always better than a cure and so what I would say to any player at any club who experiences bullying or is affected by disruptive behaviour – just say something. You owe it to your club and to your teammates, but most importantly, you owe it to yourself.

The Future of the FA Cup

I'm a big, big fan of the FA Cup but up until the 2014/15 season I genuinely feared for its future. Ever since the Premier League began to almost dominate not just British football but world football, a lot of the interest, hype and anticipation that used to follow the good old FA Cup – from the preliminary rounds to the final – seemed to just gradually disappear. Until the mid-1990s it had always been *the* event of the domestic footballing calendar and it didn't matter where you were in the world, if football was popular in that country the FA Cup mattered and mattered a lot.

I know I'm biased but I think BT Sport getting involved has helped its cause. Look at their coverage of the 2015 final: it was given the Hollywood treatment for the entire day and presented as something special – something that is as important to the domestic game as Wembley Stadium itself. Wembley will always be there because it will never have a rival, but the FA Cup has been lost in a crowd just recently and in my opinion needs to be pulled out, dusted down and given the respect it deserves.

As a kid, every single football fan I knew used to follow every round of that competition meticulously and as football fans we couldn't rest until we knew which captain of which team was about to hold the Cup aloft at Wembley. It was, and I think still is, the godfather of cup competitions. The oldest and the best.

One of my earliest FA Cup memories was watching the 1981 final featuring Tottenham and Manchester City. It was the 100th anniversary of the competition that year and there were over 100,000 people packed into the old Wembley Stadium. I remember being absolutely blown away by the sense of occasion, not to mention the atmosphere. For a footy-mad lad of just six it was electrifying.

It was a real event, watching the FA Cup final. Family and friends would come from miles around and we would all sit in front of the television and argue about which team was going to win. If your own favourite team wasn't involved you always had to pick one of the two that were and that day I picked Spurs.

The match ended in a draw so it had to go to a replay which Spurs eventually won 3–2. It didn't matter that there wasn't a result, though; it was still the highlight of my footballing year.

That day was memorable for another reason: it was when I had my first taste of an alcoholic drink. My late dad thought it would be a good idea to give me a sip of lager and orange juice, and not surprisingly I was as sick as a dog. I have no idea what on earth he was doing putting orange in lager but ever since then I haven't been able to touch the stuff. Lager, I mean, not orange.

One of my favourite FA Cup memories is when Wrexham knocked out Arsenal back in 1992. Mickey Thomas was the hero of the day and despite having one of the worst mullets ever known to man (he's got no problems in that department now though!) he scored one of the most amazing free kicks I've ever seen in my life and caused exactly the kind of upset that makes the FA Cup such a magical competition. Mickey's a really good mate of mine now, we're both a bit roguish I suppose, but despite playing over 600 games as a professional he'll probably always be known for that one – and it has to be said rather important – free kick.

FA Cup upsets work both ways, of course, and as well as enjoying the spectacle of seeing the mighty Wrexham beat lowly Arsenal I've also been on the receiving end – twice! My God, this is going to be painful.

In 2001 while I was at Leicester City we got drawn against Wycombe Wanderers in the quarter-final of the FA Cup. There were about four of us players watching in the pub at the time of the draw, and when saw that it was Wycombe we all started jumping up and down and cheering. What a massive mistake that was. We thought we were home and dry. After all, we were drawn at Filbert Street. Wycombe who?

You see, had we got through to the semi-final, it transpired that we would have been facing Liverpool at Villa Park. The trouble is, we played as if we thought we were already there. It was the same on the day of the match; Wycombe were just a formality in our eyes and it was all about the semis.

Just the fact that they had reached the quarter-final of the FA Cup, beating Millwall, Grimsby, Wolves and former winners

Wimbledon on the way, should have made us sit up and take notice, but we just didn't take any notice of them.

What happened prior to and during that fateful match has now gone down in FA Cup folklore and is probably one of the great FA Cup stories. Does the name Roy Essandoh ring any bells? It does for me, great big alarm bells!

The Wycombe manager, Lawrie Sanchez, was a bit short on strike power for the fixture and so had put an advert on Ceefax asking for any available strikers to get in touch. Roy's agent spotted the advert, got in touch, and he was hired for the match.

We should have seen it coming. I mean, Lawrie Sanchez? There was FA Cup history here. Apparently just before the game began he told his players that the FA Cup is a competition for heroes – and he should have known, having scored the winning goal for Wimbledon against Liverpool in the 1988 final. Add to that the fact that only eight years previously Wycombe had been playing non-league football and you had all the makings of one massive upset.

To be fair we probably edged the first half and it was me who came closest to scoring via a header from a cross by Andy Impey. To most people, though, it was difficult to tell which team was sixth and which was sixtieth in the pecking order. Wycombe certainly didn't play like underdogs and I fully admit that when we went into the dressing room at half time we were rattled.

When they scored four minutes after the interval we really did start to worry and even when Muzzy Izzet scored the equaliizer we knew that we had a very, very difficult game on our hands. That's the thing about the FA Cup: it takes players to another level. We might not have been playing especially well that day but Wycombe were on fire.

I remember the crowd going mad with us, and rightly so, but from the minute we were drawn against Wycombe Wanderers everybody at the club, fans included, had completely underestimated them and so when Roy Essandoh popped up and headed in the winner from close range in stoppage time we only got what we deserved. To be fair, they should have had a penalty about ten minutes before the end so it could have been even worse!

All credit to Lawrie Sanchez. What he achieved that day with the resources he had at his disposal was nothing short of astonishing.

What a day, though. A few days later one of the newspapers called it our Homer Simpson moment – Essan-doh! Spot on.

Are we finished yet? Can we stop this?

The next one isn't quite as well known as the Wycombe encounter but it's no less embarrassing. I was playing for Derby County at the time and in 2011 we were drawn away at Crawley Town in the third round. We turned up expecting a battle all right, and we certainly hadn't underestimated the opposition like we had at Leicester, but at the end of the day we were simply outplayed by them and in every department. They had more possession than we did, more corners and more attempts on goal, and without doubt were the better team. It all felt like a case of déjà vu to me as in addition to going down 2–1, just as we had against Wycombe, we also got beaten by a goal scored in stoppage time – and by an ex-Wycombe player! How weird is that?

I did feel sorry for Crawley, though, as in the fourth round they would have been hoping for a money-spinning tie against one of the big teams, but instead they got drawn away at Torquay. That's the magic of the FA Cup. You beat Derby County and what do you get? A trip to the seaside. They needn't have worried though, because after beating Torquay 1-0 they were drawn against Manchester United at Old Trafford, where they were eventually knocked out by a goal by Wes Brown.

Unfortunately the FA Cup just wasn't my competition as a player and one of the very few regrets I have from that time was not reaching the final. I got to the semi-finals once while playing for Blackburn, which was still an achievement, but it's not the same. I still dream about scoring the winner in the FA Cup final. I think every player does.

One of the most talked about and celebrated games of football in the whole of last season, and one of the reasons why I'm not quite as worried about the Cup as I used to be, was Bradford City's fourth-round FA Cup victory over Chelsea, widely considered one of the biggest upsets of all time. As far as I'm concerned, that was a much-needed shot in the arm for the FA Cup and had the entire nation sitting on the edge of our seats. It had everything.

The last really big shock I could remember before that game involved that marvellous Mickey Thomas free kick I mentioned; but to be honest even that looked pretty bland compared to this. That earlier match happened at the giant killer's home ground, whereas this miracle happened at Stamford Bridge.

Had Bradford City simply scraped a 1–0 victory (simply!) by defending for ninety minutes and then nicking one on the break then the win would still have been sweet, but it wouldn't have been truly legendary.

Chelsea were still on for the fabled 'Quadruple' at the time and after thirty-eight minutes were 2–0 up, and that's where the match really started for me because three minutes later, when Bradford had got one back, you thought they might, just might, be able to cause an upset – perhaps a draw at best.

When the final whistle went after ninety-eight minutes and Bradford had won the game 4–2 every form of communication known to man went nuclear. Even though I ply my trade as a pundit, I have no direct association with either Bradford City or Chelsea yet my phone did not stop ringing for over a day. Mates and family wanted to talk about the result as did all the companies I work for. It honestly felt like a life-changing moment; one of those 'things will never be the same again' situations.

That's what the FA Cup is all about, I thought, and that's why I'd like to see it return to the glory days.

I'll tell you what else that game reminded me of and that's how much the Cup means to players. It's not just fans and pundits who revel in the magic of the Cup.

Even the great Alan Hansen, who by the time he won his first FA Cup in 1986 had eight First Division titles and three European Cups to his name, admitted that he didn't feel like he'd achieved anything in football until he had secured his first trip to Wembley. That's how much it meant.

★

If the rise of the all-conquering Premier League was responsible for first sticking the knife into the FA Cup it was Manchester United, and ironically enough the FA, who would twist it.

I, like millions of others, was shocked when Manchester United decided to accept the FA's request to skip the FA Cup in 2000 in favour of the inaugural FIFA World Club Cup and I have to admit I wasn't that bothered when they didn't do too well. I don't think anybody was really, even Manchester United fans. Does anyone else remember that game against Vasco da Gama? Poor old Gary Neville had an absolute shocker that day. Romario and Edmundo made mincemeat of him.

To be fair to Sir Alex Ferguson he later said that he regretted making the decision to skip the FA Cup and that he even contacted Tony Blair, whose aide had first suggested they take part in the competition in order to boost England's chances of hosting the 2006 World Cup, to see if there was any way he could keep United in the FA Cup. I'm really glad he came out and said that because when he did it reminded me just how important the FA Cup is to English football. He and Martin Edwards had been put under a ridiculous amount of pressure to comply and so you can't really blame them.

I think the Cup is probably suffering from a similar dilemma to international football. We've all debated the old club versus country argument over the years and I don't think anyone would disagree that it's all down to the rise, strength and influence of the Premier League. Players and clubs have been overwhelmed by its success and the FA Cup, and to a lesser extent international football, have fallen by the wayside somewhat.

Let's not get too negative, though, or else we're liable to forget that although the FA Cup has suffered in recent years both the Premier League and the Champions League have never been stronger. We haven't just lost something here; we've gained. When the FA Cup was king we didn't have anything near as strong as the Premier League in place and so it's just a question of redressing the balance a bit. Making a few tweaks. The big question is how we can make the FA Cup great again without threatening the status of the Premier League. If we can do that – and I believe we can – then English domestic football will rule the world for the foreseeable future. Coming from a proud Welshman that's quite a statement but, seriously, I'm right. Let's have the best of both worlds.

I'm doing my bit to reinvigorate the FA Cup, as in the 2014/15 season I made my debut as a co-commentator in the competition. Warrington Town v. Exeter City was one of my first games and I have to say I enjoyed every single second of it. Being up in that gantry with just a microphone reminded me of watching matches on TV when I was a kid. The presenter always spoke to the commentators just before the game and I always used to wish that I was up there with them.

It was a great night and I even got the result I was hoping for, a shock 1–0 victory to Warrington. My first match and I got an upset. Brilliant!

Naturally I was slated by some of the media for being too passionate but I honestly couldn't give a monkey's. If you're going to have a go at somebody for being too passionate about football then you should switch off the radio or the TV and go and watch a game of snooker or, better still, chess. Seriously, what are these idiots on?

So what can be done to make this competition great again?

Some people have suggested doing away with replays to revive the Cup, but I'm not so sure. Let's look at both arguments shall we? One of the problems you've got is that the Premier League is so lucrative these days – instead of just the top five or six clubs fielding weakened teams for FA Cup games you've got all the Premier League teams at it, but that's completely understandable. At the end of the day the Premier League pays the wages. Lose that through relegation and, as we all know, you could be in serious trouble. Would ditching FA Cup replays change things, then? I don't think so.

The same people argue that out of the two domestic cups in England, it's actually the Capital One Cup that works better and that's because it doesn't have replays. I admit that the Capital One Cup has been gathering pace over the past few years and I think that's excellent for English football, but at the end of the day it's only really a warm-up for the FA Cup. It's like comparing the Europa League with the Champions League.

Personally I have quite a bit of affection for FA Cup replays and for two very good reasons. Firstly, I think they're an important part of the competition. Do you remember watching replays as a kid? When I was young we used to love them because it meant another game of football on TV, but these days they often help generate much needed revenue for smaller clubs. And let's not forget the goals, of course. Some of the best goals I've ever seen have been scored in FA Cup replays. Ricky

Villa's goal in the FA Cup final replay of 1981 springs to mind and that's still one of the best individual efforts I've ever seen.

The second reason I love FA Cup replays is because I was once awarded a new contract on the back of a performance I gave in one of them. It was only my second contract as a Premier League player and was a big, big thing for me.

It was 22 December 1999 and Leicester were playing Hereford United at Filbert Street having been held to a goalless draw at their place about ten days before.

This ended 2–1 and I was on the winning team, and a few days after the match Martin O'Neill got me into his office and told me that he was offering me a new contract because of my performance in that game.

'You're great in the Premier League matches,' he said. 'But to show me the same level of passion and commitment in extra-time of an FA Cup replay against Hereford United as you do against Arsenal or Manchester United in the Premier League is exactly what I want from a player.' Seriously, that was a real game-changer for me.

There you are then, not only are FA Cup replays responsible for one of the best goals I've ever seen but they also helped me win one of the most important contracts of my playing career. How could I come out in favour of ditching them?

The one thing we can't do, of course, is return the FA Cup to being the biggest and most coveted domestic competition – cup or league – in world football, and that's something we have to get our heads around. The days of it being the only big domestic match on television have long gone, thank heaven. What we have to try and do is help the FA Cup find its place within the modern game. The one thing the Cup has to offer over any other competition is glory: your football-playing life is not complete until you've won the FA Cup. It might not have the cash value of the Premier League but that's the point I'm trying to make: although it's had a sponsor for a few years, the commercial aspect has never been the be all and end all. In fact, it always has and I think always will be secondary. The smaller clubs can earn well out of it and that's brilliant, but you know where I'm coming from.

You don't get paid much for taking part but you get a tremendous amount of glory, prestige and respect, and that's what the FA need to push. Olympic football, another competition that doesn't make anyone much money, hasn't worked and in my opinion it never will because, as a result of the way the competition is set up with limited players to choose from, it's not about being the best in the world. The FA Cup's different, though: it is synonymous with the game of football and its history. We're not trying to re-invent the wheel here; we just need to persuade managers, players and chairmen that winning the FA Cup is the footballing equivalent of winning an Olympic Gold medal in a proper event like the 100 metres where the winner is considered the king of the sport. It's all about the glory, not the money. Manage that and you could be on to a winner.

Secret Savage

Here's some stuff you won't necessarily know about me. There's nothing like a bit of light-heartedness to break up the serious footy chat.

I'm a pretty straightforward bloke, really. As you now know, I'm into family, friends, football and cars. I don't like flying, I've got a big nose and I'm one of the most humble yet amusing people on the planet. Oh, and I don't listen to music. Honestly, I never have. Somebody asked me if I was a fan of Primal Scream the other day and just looked at them. Primal what? When journalists ask me what my favourite music is I usually say Hed Kandi. I'm not quite sure what Hed Kandi is but I have a feeling I've listened to some over the years and at the end of the day I've got to say something. Strange, isn't it? Mind you, I don't really watch TV either: just football. It's not that I don't find certain things interesting; it's just I find football more so.

So what else might you not know?

Well, for a start I'm actually more passionate about dogs than I am about cars. If I was to go into detail here it could turn into a right weepy, as like most people I've lost one or two dogs over the years and it's honestly broken my heart. Nobody warned me that they die before you! Seriously, though, I couldn't be without a dog. I don't know where I would be if I didn't have my best friend waiting for me when I got home.

The first dog I ever got was a boxer called Naz. I'd been badgering my mum and dad about getting one ever since I was a little boy but it wasn't until I joined Crewe Alexandra that they eventually relented. I had just spent the last two years living with thirteen other lads at Manchester United and, with my brother Jonathan off to university and my parents leading their own lives, it was a lonely existence being at home. I was quite good at the old 'Please Mum, oh come on, pleeeeease Mum!' and so once she had laid down a few ground rules about walks and cleaning up mess, I was given the go-ahead.

Only people who are really into dogs will get this but the day I got Naz was one of the best days ever. We were a perfect match. Naz was very boisterous, very friendly and never seemed to stop running – exactly like me. The only difference was that I had less saliva round my mouth and usually went to the toilet indoors.

She was around for some of the most important moments of my life. She was there when I got my first Premier League contract, my first sports car and my first house. She even stayed with me when I had to live in a hotel for a while. We were inseparable.

I bought my first house while I was at Leicester, but Sarah was still living at home. When she visited me at weekends she would always recoil in horror when she saw the state of the bedclothes.

'Have you been letting Naz sleep in your bed again? Look at the state of the bedclothes! I'm not sleeping in there.'

After that Sarah would scoop up the bedclothes, put them into the washing machine, and I would leave them there to rot. Not because I expected Sarah to wash them for me; I just didn't know what to do. I just moved us into a different room with fresh linen. Typical man, I suppose. Instead of finding out how to wash the bedclothes, move bedrooms!

After Sarah and I got married we got another boxer, called Tai. We were living in the country by then and because Naz seemed a bit bored we thought we would get her a friend. Tai and Naz got on like an absolute house on fire but because they were both a bit excitable they used to bark – a lot. After a while Sarah and I became quite used to the noise, but when we moved from the country back into a more residential area we began to get one or two complaints. These complaints didn't come from just anybody – they came from the top. They came from Fergie!

Sir Alex Ferguson was our new next-door neighbour for the six months we were in the house and he was obviously used to a quiet life. Perhaps that's why he never said a word to me all the time I was there.

Naz and Tai have both sadly passed away and at the moment we've got a couple French bulldogs called Coco and Gigi. They don't take quite as much walking as boxers do but they're no less mischievous. They don't bark much, which is a relief, but they do make some seriously strange noises! Great fun, though.

Something else you might not know about me is that I'm a world-record holder.

World's most annoying human being?

Possibly, but not officially.

World's best-ever midfielder?

Getting closer, although believe it or not I used my backside to set this world record, as opposed to either my feet or my mouth.

It all came about through 2014's Sport Relief when Alan Shearer and I were asked to participate in something called 'Battle of the Backsides'. Catchy title, don't you think?

Set over three days, it was basically a competition to see which one of us could sit on the most seats at Wembley Stadium – up to 45,000 each!

The word record of seats per minute was set during those three days and I managed to pip Mr Shearer to the post by just one seat – I sat on eighty-six seats and he sat on eighty-five. The other 44,914 still had to be sat on, though, and by the end of the three days we were both in absolute agony. Take my word for it, it's one of the most difficult things you can do. It's not just your bum that kills, your entire body does!

When I broke the record they took a photo of me receiving my certificate and although I'm smiling in it, I was suffering big time. I also still had about 15,000 seats to go. It raised a lot of money for charity but I was sure I was going to get haemorrhoids.

I also won an Oscar, or at least something similar. Believe it or not I didn't win that many awards as a footballer (in fact, Midlands Player of the Year was about the most significant, which, when you think how many teams are involved, is actually quite an accolade). But, as with my world record, when it comes to my most prestigious award it wasn't my feet that made me a winner. This time it was my mouth. Seriously. In May 2011, I was presented with the Sony Radio Academy Rising Star award in recognition for my appearances on *606*. The Sony Awards are basically the radio equivalent of the Oscars (all right, perhaps the BAFTAs) and within a few months of me co-presenting the show with Fletch I was told I'd been nominated. I couldn't believe it! The Rising Star award is for the best newcomer, and I was pitched against, among others, Ronnie Wood from the Rolling Stones. I think Ronnie was quite surprised that I'd been nominated, but I was just as surprised about him. Rising star? He'd been on the radio since the 1960s!

According to Sony the reasons I was nominated was because I was 'opinionated, passionate and provocative' and had 'reinvigorated the style of a football phone-in in a short space of time in which even non-football fans can enjoy'.

Perfect! That last part of the sentence, 'in which even non-football fans can enjoy', was the bit that did it for me. You see, as a pundit and as a presenter I've always set out to make my comments as inclusive and as entertaining as possible. Is it such a bad thing? The purists might not like it but that's just one of those things. They'll get over it.

If that quote wasn't praise enough, the winner was decided not by members of the radio industry, but by the public. What a way to start a new career.

Even though I always try and make out that being slagged off doesn't get to me, it does from time to time. Honestly, I defy anyone to take as much stick as I do and not get down occasionally. So, getting a vote of confidence like that so early on in my broadcasting career was a massive boost and it's easily one of my proudest achievements. I didn't ask to get nominated, just like I didn't ask to win the award in the Midlands. I just turned up and tried my best.

One thing Fletch reminded me of when we were talking about this chapter was that I must make at least 200 telephone calls every day. I'm hyperactive, you see, and I'm also a big worrier, but as I keep on saying I also take what I do very, very seriously. This means that if I'm not on the phone checking a stat with somebody or trying to prove to Fletch that I'm right about a debate we've been having, I'll be either talking to Grant at BT about the next *Fletch & Sav*, to the boys at the *Mirror* about my column, or to Lee at William Hill about my next podcast. Once I've exhausted those avenues I'll start bothering my mum, my wife, my kids and my mates. Honestly, if I have a phone in my hand nobody is safe!

Did you know that as well as being able to score penalties with round balls I can score them with egg-shaped ones too? I didn't realize this myself until a few days before this book went to priess, when I was lucky enough to be asked to take part in the inaugural Rugby Aid game featuring England v. The Rest of the World. We had a great day down at the Stoop and Mike Tindall and his colleagues at the Rugby for Heroes charity managed to get some really big names involved – and me. We ended up beating England 36–29 and I scored three conversions. Count them – THREE! My six points made all the difference. It made me wonder for a minute whether I could have made it as a rugby player, and then I remembered. With my hair? No chance!

That reminds me. I won a tennis tournament at the Queen's Club a few years ago. It was a charity event that took place just before the main grass-court championship and my doubles partner, Paul Hogarth, and I beat a couple of club players in the final. Not bad, eh? Just before the final I posted a photo of myself on Twitter wearing all my tennis gear and one of the first replies I got – from a certain Mr Darren Fletcher – read: 'Chris Evert hasn't aged well, has she?' Do you see what I have to put up with? Honestly, it's relentless!

There's one last thing you won't know about me, and to tell you the truth neither did I until I was told. Sometimes I do strange things in my sleep. Nothing rude. No, this is just weird. Apparently if I'm lying on my back I sometimes lift an arm straight out in front of me. I suppose this could be my wife winding me up but, if it isn't, the only explanation I have to offer is that I might be reliving the build-up to the penalty I scored in the dying moments of my 600th appearance, which was against Preston North End, and I'm pointing to the penalty spot in my sleep. Either that or Graham Poll's showing me where the toilets are.

Afterword

So that's it then, the world of Robbie Savage – or at least the first volume. Seriously, I've only just scratched the surface here! As long as I'm drawing breath I'll always be passionate about football and as long as people want to listen to me, interact with me or read what I've got to say I'll keep on talking, tweeting and writing. I'm a bit excitable sometimes, and ever so slightly opinionated, but apart from the odd attack of foot-in-mouth disease and saying things like 'I'll tell you what . . .' and 'That's diabolical!' quite a lot, I'm harmless really.

As you all know my secret weapons as a footballer were playing to the crowd, entertaining them and, just occasionally, winding them up. Sometimes it worked and sometimes it went a bit wrong, but it was an important part of my game and it's something about which I'm quite proud. Not everyone can do it, you see. It's a skill. These days those secret weapons have become my bread and butter and I hope that through reading this book I have managed to entertain you more than I have wound you up. At the end of the day, it doesn't matter who you are or what you do, if you've bought this book the chances are we'll have one thing in common and that's a love of football. There's a reason why it's the most popular sport on earth. Actually, there's probably more like a million reasons. Football is something that has consumed me for well over thirty years now and, I'll tell you what (sorry), I cannot wait for the next thirty.

Author's Note

Robbie is donating 25 per cent of the royalties from the sales of this book to the Alzheimer's Society.

The Alzheimer's Society is the UK's leading dementia support and research charity, providing support for anyone affected by any form of dementia in England, Wales and Northern Ireland.

Dementia can happen to anyone and there's currently no cure. There are 850,000 people with dementia in the UK and the number is set to rise to one million by 2021.

Robbie's father, Colin, had Pick's disease, a type of dementia that gradually robs people of the ability to perform tasks such as walking, talking and eating. Robbie became an ambassador for the Society in 2011.

'My Dad had Pick's disease, a degenerative brain condition with similar symptoms to Alzheimer's. As a proud ambassador of the Alzheimer's Society, I can't speak highly enough of the work they do to support people living with dementia, their carers and their families.'